LAW
&
MENTAL
HEALTH
PROFESSIONALS

OHIO

Law & Mental Health Professionals Series

Bruce D. Sales and Michael Owen Miller, Series Editors

ALABAMA: Bentley, Reaves, and Pippin
ARIZONA, 2ND ED.: Miller, Sales, and Delgado
CALIFORNIA: Caudill and Pope
CONNECTICUT: Taub
DELAWARE: Britton and Rohs
FLORIDA, 2ND ED.: Petrila and Otto
GEORGIA: Remar and Hubert
KENTUCKY: Drogin
MASSACHUSETTS, 2ND ED.: Brant
MICHIGAN: Clark and Clark
MINNESOTA: Janus, Mickelsen, and Sanders
NEVADA: Johns and Dillehay
NEW JERSEY, 2ND ED.: Wulach
NEW YORK: Wulach
NORTH DAKOTA: O'Neill and Lochow
OHIO: VandeCreek and Kapp
PENNSYLVANIA: Bersoff, Field, Anderer, and Zaplac
SOUTH CAROLINA: Follingstad and McCormick
SOUTH DAKOTA: Cichon
TEXAS, 3RD ED.: Shuman
VIRGINIA: Porfiri and Resnick
WASHINGTON: Benjamin, Rosenwald, Overcast, and Feldman
WISCONSIN: Kaplan and Miller
WYOMING: Blau

LAW & MENTAL HEALTH PROFESSIONALS

OHIO

Leon VandeCreek, PhD

Marshall Kapp, JD, MHP

American Psychological Association
Washington, DC

Published by
American Psychological Association
750 First Street, NE
Washington, DC 20002

Copies may be ordered from
APA Order Department
P.O. Box 92984
Washington, DC 20090-2984

Typeset in Palatino by World Composition Services, Inc., Sterling, VA

Printer: Edwards Brothers, Inc., Ann Arbor, MI
Cover designer: Rubin Krassner, Silver Spring, MD
Project Manager: Debbie Hardin, Carlsbad, CA

The opinions and statements published are the responsibility of the authors, and such opinions and statements do not necessarily represent the policies of the American Psychological Association.

The information in this publication is intended for general guidance and is not meant to be a substitute for legal advice. The publisher, editors, and authors accept no responsibility for loss occasioned to any person or organization acting or refraining from action as a result of using any material in this publication. Readers are advised to seek the advice of a competent lawyer before making decisions based on their reading of this publication.

Library of Congress Cataloging-in-Publication Data
VandeCreek, Leon.
  Law and mental health professionals. Ohio / Leon VandeCreek and Marshall Kapp.—1st ed.
    p. cm—(Law & mental health professionals series)
Includes bibliographical references and index.
  ISBN 1-59147-205-9
1. Mental health personnel—Legal status, laws, etc.—Ohio. 2. Mental health laws—Ohio. 3. Forensic psychiatry—Ohio. I. Kapp, Marshall B.
II. Title. III. Series.
  KFO326.5.P73.V36 2005
  344.77104'4—dc22   2004021065

Printed in the United States of America
First Edition

Contents

Editors' Preface

The Need to Know the Law

For years, providers of mental health services (hereinafter mental health professionals or MHPs) have been directly affected by the law. At one end of the continuum, their practice has been controlled by laws covering such matters as licensure and certification, third-party reimbursement, and professional incorporation. At the other end, they have been courted by the legal system to aid in its administration, providing such services as evaluating the mental status of litigants, providing expert testimony in court, and engaging in therapy with court-referred juveniles and adults. Even when not directly affected, MHPs find themselves indirectly affected by the law because their clients sometimes become enmeshed in legal entanglements that involve mental status issues (e.g., divorce proceedings or termination of parental rights hearings).

Despite this pervasive influence, most professionals do not know about, much less understand, most of the laws that affect their practice, the services they render, and the clients they serve. This state of affairs is particularly troubling for several reasons. First, not knowing about the laws that affect one's practice typically results in the MHPs not gaining the benefits that the law may provide. Consider the law relating to the incorporation of professionals. It confers significant benefit, but only if it is known about and applied. The fact that it has been enacted by the state legislature does not help the MHP any more than an MHP will be of help to a distressed person who refuses to contact the MHP.

Second, not knowing about the laws that affect the services they render may result in incompetent performance of, and liability for, the MHP either through the civil law (e.g., malpractice law) or through criminal sanctions. A brief example may help underscore this point. When an MHP is asked to evaluate a party to a lawsuit and testify in court, the court (the law's term for the judge) is asking the professional to assess and testify about whether that litigant meets some legal standard. The court is often not concerned with the defendant's mental health per se, although this may be relevant to the MHP's evaluation of the person. Rather, the court wants to know whether the person meets the legal standard as it is set down by the law. Not knowing the legal standard means that the MHP is most likely evaluating the person for the wrong goal and providing the court with irrelevant information, at least from the court's point of view. Regretfully, there are too many cases in which this has occurred.

Third, not knowing the law that affects the clients that MHPs serve may significantly diminish their capability for handling their clients' distress. For example, a client who is undergoing a divorce and a child custody dispute may have distorted beliefs about what may happen during the legal proceedings. A basic understanding of the controlling law in this area will allow the therapist to be more sensitive in rendering therapy.

The Problem in Accessing Legal Information

Given the need for this information, why have MHPs not systematically sought it out? Part of the reason lies in the concern over their ability to understand legal doctrines. Indeed, this is a legitimate worry, especially if they had to read original legal materials that were not collected, organized, and described with an MHP audience in mind. This is of particular concern because laws are written in terms and phrases of "art" that do not always share the common law definition or usage, whereas some terms and phrases are left ambiguous and undefined or are used differently for different legal topics. Another part of the reason is that the law affecting MHPs and their clients is not readily available— even to lawyers. There are no compendiums that identify the topics that these laws cover or present an analysis of each topic for easy reference.

To compound the difficulty, the law does not treat the different mental health professional disciplines uniformly or always specify the particular disciplines as being covered by it. Nor does the law emanate from a single legal forum. Each state enacts its own rules and regulations, often resulting in wide variations in the way a topic is handled across the United States. Multiply this confusion by the one hundred or so topics that relate to mental health practice. In addition, the law within a state does not come from one legal source. Rather, there are five primary ones: the state constitution; state legislative enactments (statutes); state agency administrative rules and regulations; rules of court promulgated by the state supreme court; and state and federal court cases that apply, interpret, and construe this existing state law. To know about one of these sources without knowing how its pronouncements on a given topic have been modified by these other sources may result in one's making erroneous conclusions about the operation of the law. Finally, mental health practice also comes under the purview of federal law (constitutional and statutory law, administrative rules and regulations, and case law). Federal law authorizes direct payments to MHPs for their services to some clients, sets standards for delivery of services in federal facilities (e.g., Veterans Administration hospitals), and articulates the law that guides cases that are tried in federal courts under federal law.

Purposes of This Series

What is needed, therefore, is a book for each state, the District of Columbia, and the federal jurisdictions that comprehensively and accurately reviews and integrates all of the law that affects MHPs in that jurisdiction (hereinafter *state*). These materials should be written so that they are completely understandable to MHPs as well as to lawyers. To accomplish these goals, the editors have tried to identify every legal topic that affects mental health practice, making each one the subject of a chapter. Each chapter, in turn, describes the legal standards that the MHP will be operating under and the relevant legal process that the MHP will be operating within. If a state does not have relevant law on an issue, then a brief explanation of how this law works in other states will be presented while noting the lack of regulation in this area within the state under consideration.

This type of coverage facilitates other purposes of the series. Although each chapter is written in order to state exactly what is the present state of the law and not argue for or against any particular approach, it is hoped that the comprehensiveness of the coverage will encourage MHPs to question the desirability of their states' approach to each topic. Such information and concern should provide the impetus for initiating legislation and litigation on the part of state mental health associations to ensure that the law reflects the scientific knowledge and professional values to the greatest extent possible.

In some measure, states will initially be hampered in this proactivity because they will not know what legal alternatives are available and how desirable each alternative actually is. When a significant number of books in this series is available, however, it will allow for nationally oriented policy studies to identify the variety of legal approaches that are currently in use and to assess the validity of the behavioral assumptions underlying each variant and, ultimately, lead to a conclusion as to the relative desirability of alternate approaches.[1] Thus, two other purposes of this book are to foster comprehensive analyses of the laws affecting MHPs across all states and of the validity of the behavioral assumptions

---

1. Sales, B. D. (1983). The legal regulation of psychology: Professional and scientific interactions. In C. J. Scheirer & B. L. Hammonds (Eds.), *The master lecture series: Vol. 2. Psychology and law* (pp. 5–36). Washington, DC: American Psychological Association.

underlying these laws, and to promote political, legislative, and legal action to change laws that are inappropriate and impede the effective delivery of services. Legal change may be required because of gaps in legal regulation, overregulation, and regulation based on invalid behavioral and social assumptions. We hope that this process will increase the rationality of future laws in this area and improve the effectiveness and quality of mental health service delivery nationally.

There are three remaining purposes for this series. First, although it will not replace the need for legal counsel, this series will make the MHP an intelligent consumer of legal services. This ability is gaining importance in an era of increasing professionalization and litigiousness. Second, it will ensure that MHPs are aware of the law's mandates when providing expert services (e.g., evaluation and testimony) within the legal system. Although chapters will not address how to assess clinically for the legal standard, provider competency will increase because providers now will be sure of the goals of their service (e.g., the legal standard that they are to assess for) as well as their roles and responsibilities within the legal system as to the particular topic in issue. Third and finally, each book will make clear that the legal standards that MHPs are asked to assess for by the law have typically not been translated into behavioral correlates. Nor are there discussions of tests, scales, and procedures for MHPs to use in assessing for the behavioral correlates of the legal standards in most cases. This series will provide the impetus for such research and writing.

Content and Organization of Volumes

Each book in this series is organized into eight sections. Section 1 addresses the legal credentialing of MHPs. Section 2 deals with the different business forms for conducting one's practice, insurance reimbursement, and tax deductions that clients may receive for using mental health services. With the business matters covered, the book then turns to the law directly affecting service delivery. Section 3 covers the law that affects the maintenance and privacy of professional information and discusses the law that limits service delivery and sets liability for unethical and illegal behavior as a service provider. Sections 4 through 8 consider each area of law that may require the services of MHPs: adults, minors, and families; other civil matters; topics that apply similarly in both civil and criminal cases; criminal matters; and voluntary and involuntary receipt of state services by the clients of mental health services.

Collectively, the chapters in these sections represent all topics pertaining to the law as it affects MHPs in their practices. Two caveats are in order, however. First, the law changes slowly over time. Thus, this volume will be updated on a regular basis. As MHPs become more involved in the legal system, new opportunities for involvement are likely to arise. To be responsive to these developments, revisions will also contain additional chapters reflecting these new roles and responsibilities.

Some final points about the content of this book are in order. The exact terms that the law chooses are used in the book even if they are a poor choice from an MHP's point of view. Where terms are defined by the law, that information is presented. The reader will often be frustrated, however, because as has already been noted, the law does not always define terms or provide detailed guidance. This does not mean that legal words and phrases can be taken lightly. The law sets the rules by which MHPs and their clients must operate; thus, the chapters must be read carefully. This should not be too arduous a task because chapters are relatively short. However, such brevity will leave some readers frustrated because chapters may appear not to go far enough in answering their questions. Note that all of the law is covered. If there is no law, however, there is no coverage. If a question is not answered in the text, it is because Ohio law has not addressed the issue. Relatedly, if an obligation or benefit is created by a professional regulation (i.e., a rule of a professional organization) but is not directly recognized by the law, it is not covered. Thus, for example, professional credentials are not addressed in these volumes.

Finally, we want to point out that in some instances, the pronoun "he" is used generically to refer to both genders. Most notably, the pronoun is used when quoting directly from the law. Legal language is generally consistent in its preference for using the masculine form of the pronoun; it is not always feasible to attempt a rewording.

Bruce D. Sales
Michael Owen Miller
Series Editors

Authors' Preface

This book is principally a treatment of state law applicable to mental health professionals (MHPs). The sources of state law treated in this work include the state constitution, state statutes, state administrative rules, state judicial decisions, and state judicial rules. The Ohio constitution establishes the framework for state government and describes various individual rights that occupy a high degree of importance in Ohio. Citations to the Ohio constitution appear in the following form: OHIO CONST. art. I, § 1. This reference indicates that the citation is to the first article, first section, in the Ohio constitution.

Citations to state statutes, which result from legislation passed by the Ohio General Assembly, appear in the following form: OHIO REV. CODE § 4732. This particular citation is a reference to the bound volumes of statutes published by the Anderson Publishing Company.

This compilation of statutes and the Ohio constitution contains additional useful material. The compilers attempt to include a citation and, where needed, a brief summary of the most significant reported cases that have discussed the statute or constitutional provision in question. A researcher may use these case annotations to begin research on how the statute or constitutional provision has been interpreted by the courts.

State administrative rules are created by the state agencies operating under the authority delegated to them by the legislature to carry out specific agency functions. For example, the legislation creating the Board of Psychology does not list all types of professional misconduct but rather gives the Board the authority to make administrative rules delineating specific types of misconduct that can result in the suspension or revocation of a license. These rules do not appear in the statutes but instead are kept in a series titled *Ohio Administrative Code* published by the Anderson Publishing Company. References to the administrative code appear in the following form: OHIO ADMIN. CODE § 4732-1.01.

State judicial decisions are the product of judge-made law. Reported decisions are typically those of appellate courts. They consist of decisions of the Ohio supreme court, which is the highest state court, and of the Ohio courts of appeals. Citations to these decisions appear in the following format: *Doe v. Doe*, 70 Ohio St. 3d 376 (1999). This particular citation refers to a 1999 decision by the Ohio supreme court that is found in the *Ohio State Reports*. A reference to an appeals court decision would appear in the following manner: *Able v. Able*, 75 Ohio App.2d 295, 433 N.E.2d 624 (1995). Ohio supreme court and appellate court decisions are reported in bound volumes published by the West Publishing Company and others. The decisions also appear in a reporter of cases in the geographic region titled *North Eastern Reporter*. The court of appeals case cited here is located in the second series of that compilation. The number 433 represents the volume in which the case appears, and 624 is the page of the volume on which the case begins. The parties to the case are Able and Able.

Ohio is divided into 12 appellate districts. Although a court decision by one district court of appeals is binding only in the counties covered in that appeals court area, such decisions carry considerable precedential weight in other districts in Ohio. Appellate districts may reach conflicting legal rulings. Such conflicts can be resolved if and when the Ohio supreme court rules on a case that enforces a uniform state standard of judicial interpretation in that particular area of law.

State judicial rules, as contrasted with judicial decisions, are the product of judges acting in a rule-making rather than a judicial capacity. That is, they promulgate rules governing the nature and form of legal proceedings. In this role, judges make rules of general application in the courts, not usually in the context of deciding cases. The *Rules of Superintendence for the Courts of Ohio* are applicable to all courts of appeal, courts of common pleas, municipal courts, and the county juvenile courts. These rules are promulgated pursuant to OHIO CONST. art. IV, § 5(A)(1). The rules appear in *Baldwin's Ohio Revised Code Annotated* and are cited as follows: SUP. R. 1.

Although the focus of this work is on state rather than federal law applicable to MHPs, occasional reference is of necessity made to federal decisions interpreting or limiting state law. The citations to these decisions are from the U.S. district court (F. Supp.), the U.S. court of appeals (F., F.2d, or F.3d), and the U.S. Supreme Court (U.S., S. Ct., or L.Ed.). As is the case with the reports of state decisions, the number preceding the reporter is the volume number and the number following is the page on which the case begins. References to federal legislation appear in the form 26 U.S.C. § 213(a) (1987). This particular citation to the United States Code, the repository of federal legislation, is from title 26, section 213(a), in the 1987 volume.

Although we continually have updated the manuscript, the laws are changing even as we go to press. We suggest that this text be used as a foundation from which to identify current issues and find the relevant law that sometimes may need to be updated.

Before taking any action that might result in legal consequences, you are urged to consult with an attorney.

Finally, although some chapters were updated until the manuscript went to press, the reader should consider the entire volume current as of June 2002.

Acknowledgments

The writing of this work benefited from the review of several mental health and legal professionals in Ohio. Howard H. Sokolov, from the Office of Forensic Services in the Ohio Department of Mental Health, Paul Nidich, an attorney with University of Cincinnati's Law and Psychiatry program, and Glennon Karr, an attorney in private practice and legal counsel for the Ohio Psychological Association read the entire draft of the book and gave helpful comments.

Ron Ross, executive director of the Ohio State Board of Psychology reviewed the chapter on licensure for psychologists, and Carol Holdcraft reviewed the chapter on licensure for nurses. Their efforts are sincerely appreciated.

Legal Credentialing

1.1

Licensure and Regulation of Mental Health Professionals

Ohio law provides for the general licensing and regulation of professionals. The licensing and regulation of all professionals, including MHPs, is administered by separate licensing boards for each profession. This chapter reviews the laws and administrative regulations that govern the health professions generally and thus are relevant to mental health professionals (MHPs). Specific licensing laws for each mental health profession and the regulations established by the corresponding boards are covered in the remainder of this section of the book.

(A) Licensing

The individual state licensing boards are responsible for promulgating the licensure requirements for members of that profession (see later in this chapter). The individual boards do not report to a superior or broader board or bureau. The state boards have the power to revoke, suspend, and refuse to grant or renew a professional license for certain conduct.

(B) Supervision of Professions

All licensing boards are subject to some common guidelines and due process procedures provided by state law. For example, whenever a licensure board adopts, amends, or rescinds a rule, the board must provide reasonable public notice in the *Register of Ohio* in a form the agency determines, at least 30 days before the date set for a hearing on the rule.[1] Licensure laws are subject to sunset provisions and, therefore, whenever a board adopts or amends a rule, the board assigns a review date to the rule that is not more than five years after its effective date (see chapter 1.14, Sunset of Credentialing Agencies).[2] Boards may not make rules that limit or restrict the right of any licensee to advertise in compliance with the law.[3] All boards must permit and develop procedures for holding hearings for any licensee who requests a hearing as a result of allegations of misconduct.

Each board makes an annual report to the Legislative Service Commission of its receipts and disbursements and of its official acts of the preceding year.[4] All licensing boards are required to notify each licensee of renewal procedures and fees, with renewal notices granting at least a 30-day response time. On receipt of the correct fee by the treasurer of the state and acceptance of the renewal application by the board, the applicant is listed as a licensed professional and must be notified of acceptance within 30 days.[5] A licensee who has filed an application for renewal of a license in a timely manner may not be required to discontinue practicing because of the failure of a board to act on the application.[6]

No licensing board may restrict entry into the profession by unreasonably restricting the number of educational institutions it certifies or accredits as providing appropriate training for the profession. On the other hand, boards are not prohibited from prescribing and enforcing educational and training requirements and standards.[7]

(C) State Professional Boards

The state licensing boards that relate to MHPs are the Medical Board, the Board of Nursing, the Counselor and Social Worker Board, and the Board of Psychology. These regulatory boards establish licensure qualifications and administer licensure examinations. The boards also have the power to revoke, suspend, restrict, refuse to issue or renew a license, or take other disciplinary

---

1. OHIO REV. CODE § 119.03(A).
2. OHIO REV. CODE § 119.04(A).
3. OHIO REV. CODE § 119.061.
4. OHIO REV. CODE § 4743.01.
5. OHIO REV. CODE § 4745.02.
6. OHIO REV. CODE § 119.06(C).
7. OHIO REV. CODE § 4745.02.

action against an MHP for cause. (See later chapters in this section for additional discussion of these boards.)

(D) Professional Misconduct

Each licensing board has established its own code of ethical practice, defined professional misconduct, and specified penalties (see later chapters in this section.)

(E) Proceedings in Cases of Professional Misconduct

Each board has established its own proceedings in cases of professional misconduct. In addition, any person who is adversely affected by an order of a board to deny the issuance or renewal of a license or revoke or suspend a license may appeal that order to the court of common pleas of the county in which the person is a resident or where the person's business is located, except that appeals from orders of the Medical Board and the Board of Nursing are made to the court of common pleas of Franklin County where the state capitol and board offices are located.[8]

(F) Penalties for Professional Misconduct

The relevant board has the authority to revoke, suspend, restrict, refuse to issue, or refuse to renew a license for causes enumerated in applicable law and regulation. Boards may also require that a licensee engage in remedial training and education and supervision as a condition of continued licensure or reinstatement of a license.

(G) Unauthorized Practice of a Profession

Unauthorized practice includes such acts as (a) practicing a profession without a license that is required by statute; (b) using a title

---

8. Ohio Rev. Code § 119.12.

that may be confused with a designation provided in a statute without being duly licensed; (c) performing an act that is restricted by statute or regulation to individuals holding a license without being licensed; and (d) failing to register as a practitioner as required by statute.

1.2

Licensure and Regulation of Psychiatrists

The licensure and regulation of physicians, including psychiatrists, is governed by statutory law that establishes the State Medical Board.[1] The Medical Board establishes qualifications and procedures for the licensure of physicians, defines the practice of medicine, regulates the conduct of physicians, establishes exceptions to licensure, and recommends sanctions for violations of the statute. There is no separate licensure provision pertaining to the practice of psychiatry; the law is a generic one that regulates the practice of medicine without regard to specialty. Specialties within medicine are distinguished by the nature of specialized internship and residency training and by specialty board certification.[2]

(A) State Medical Board

The governor, with the advice and consent of the senate, appoints the State Medical Board, which comprises 12 members, eight of whom are physicians licensed to practice in Ohio. Seven members of the Board must hold the degree of Doctor of Medicine; one member represents podiatric medicine; one represents osteopathy; one represents consumers; and two additional members represent the interests of consumers and are not members of, or associated with, a health care provider or profession. At least one

---

1. OHIO REV. CODE § 4731.
2. See website for American Association of Physician Specialists, Inc. (AAPS) at http://www.aapsga.org/certification/psychiatry

consumer member must be at least 60 years of age. All board members serve five-year terms.[3]

(B) Licensure

The State Medical Board conducts a written examination for all physicians, including those who intend to practice psychiatry.[4] For students trained in the United States and who are U.S. citizens, to be eligible for admission to the examination applicants must hold a diploma from an allopathic (Doctor of Medicine: MD) or osteopathic (Doctor of Osteopathy: DO) medical school accredited by the Liaison Committee on Medical Education or by the American Osteopathic Association and have successfully completed at least 12 months of graduate medical education (internship) or its equivalent.[5]

Two avenues are available for graduates of foreign medical schools to qualify for the examination. First, applicants may gain access if they hold a certificate from the Educational Commission for Foreign Medical Graduates and have successfully completed at least 12 months of graduate medical education.[6] If an applicant holding this certification received the core clinical instruction of medical education at an institution in the United States, the Board may require that the applicant have received the instruction either at an institution that maintained an affiliation with a medical school accredited by the Liaison Committee on Medical Education or by the American Osteopathic Association or at an institution with a graduate medical education program accredited by either the Accreditation Council for Graduate Medical Education or the American Osteopathic Association.[7]

The second avenue for a graduate of a foreign medical school to qualify for the examination is to be a qualified graduate of a fifth pathway training program[8] as recognized by the Board.[9] Applicants who follow the fifth pathway training program must complete supervised clinical training obtained in the United States as a substitute for the internship or social service requirements of a foreign medical school.[10]

---

3. Ohio Rev. Code § 4731.01.
4. Ohio Admin. Code §§ 4731-6-03, 4732-6-05, and 4732-6-07.
5. Ohio Rev. Code § 4731.091(B)(1).
6. Ohio Rev. Code § 4731.091(B)(2).
7. Ohio Rev. Code § 4731.091(C)(1)–(2).
8. Ohio Rev. Code § 4731.092.
9. Ohio Rev. Code § 4731.091(B)(3).
10. Ohio Rev. Code § 4731.091(2).

Applicants whose eligibility for examination is based in part on certification from the Educational Commission for Foreign Medical Graduates must pass a proficiency examination in spoken English.[11]

All applicants for the examination after December 1999 must successfully complete the written exams of steps 1 and 2 of the United States Medical Licensing Examination (USMLE). Before December 1999, applicants could meet this requirement by passing part I of the National Board of Medical Examiners (NBME) examination or step 1 of the USMLE and part II of the NBME or step 2 of the USMLE or by successfully completing component 1 of the Federation Licensing Examination.[12]

Diplomates of the National Board of Medical Examiners or the National Board of Osteopathic Medical Examiners and physicians licensed by the Medical Council of Canada are eligible for consideration for licensure in Ohio without examination if they meet all the other eligibility standards for Ohio applicants.[13]

An applicant who holds a license in another state to practice allopathic or osteopathic medicine is eligible for consideration for the examination by endorsement.[14]

Physicians must renew their licenses every two years, in even-numbered years. The Board mails to each registrant an application for renewal and requests the registrant report any criminal offense that constitutes grounds for refusal of registration.[15] In addition, registrants must certify that in the preceding two years they have completed 100 hours of continuing medical education.[16] Failure to renew the license results in suspension of the right to practice.

(B)(1) Exceptions to Licensing

Individuals seeking to pursue an internship, residency, or clinical fellowship who are not licensed must apply to the Board for a training certificate. The certificate is valid for up to one year, but may be renewed for a maximum of five years. Practice is limited to the duties of the training program.[17]

The Board may issue, without examination, a special activity certificate to any person seeking to practice medicine in conjunction with a special activity, program, or event that is scheduled to take place in Ohio. To be eligible, the person must hold a telemedicine certificate (which permits the person to practice

---

11. OHIO REV. CODE § 4731.142.
12. OHIO ADMIN. CODE § 4731-6-03(3).
13. OHIO ADMIN. CODE § 4731-6-15.
14. OHIO ADMIN. CODE § 4731-6-16.
15. OHIO REV. CODE § 4731.22.
16. OHIO REV. CODE § 4731.281; OHIO ADMIN. CODE § 4731-10-02.
17. OHIO REV. CODE § 4731.291.

medicine in Ohio through the use of any communication, including oral, written, or electronic communication from another state)[18] issued by the Board or be licensed to practice medicine in another state or country that has essentially the same requirements as Ohio. The special activity certificate is valid for up to 30 days or the duration of the special event, whichever is shorter.[19]

A visiting medical faculty certificate is available, without examination, to a physician who holds a current, unrestricted license in another state or country and has been appointed to serve in Ohio on the academic staff of a medical school. The person may practice medicine only as is incidental to his or her teaching duties. The certificate is valid for up to one year or the duration of the academic appointment, whichever is shorter.[20]

A limited certificate to practice may be granted, without examination, to individuals who are not citizens of the United States but who hold medical degrees, for the purpose of permitting practice in a state-operated institution under the supervision of the medical staff until the next scheduled licensure examination. Practice is limited to work under the supervision of a member of the medical staff and only within the confines of the institution. The certificate is valid for up to one year but may be renewed with the permission of the medical staff up to four times.[21]

The Board may issue, without examination, a volunteer's certificate to a person who is retired from practice, so that the person may provide medical services to indigent and uninsured persons at nonprofit shelters or health care facilities. To qualify for a volunteer's certificate, the person must present evidence that he or she maintained a full license in good standing before retirement for at least 10 years or practiced for at least 10 years in one or more of the branches of the U.S. armed services. The holder of a volunteer's certificate may not accept any form of remuneration for medical services that he or she provides.[22]

(C) Regulation

The State Medical Board is empowered to revoke, or may refuse to grant a license to, a person found to have committed fraud,

---

18. Ohio Rev. Code § 4731.296.
19. Ohio Rev. Code § 4731.294.
20. Ohio Rev. Code § 4731.293.
21. Ohio Rev. Code § 4731.292.
22. Ohio Rev. Code § 4731.295.

misrepresentation, or deception in applying for a license. In addition, the Board may reprimand or place on probation, limit, revoke, or suspend the license of a physician for just cause.[23]

(C)(1) Disciplinary Actions

The Board has the power to take disciplinary action against a physician who

1. permits his or her name to be used when the person is not actually directing the treatment plan;
2. is careless in selecting and using drugs;
3. illegally or illegitimately sells, prescribes, gives away, or administers drugs;
4. breaches confidentiality;
5. accepts referral fees;
6. solicits patients or engages in fraudulent advertising;
7. fails to meet minimal standards of care;
8. misrepresents that an incurable disease or illness is curable for financial advantage;
9. misrepresents practice for financial advantage;
10. is convicted of, or pleads guilty to, a felony;
11. commits an act that constitutes a felony in Ohio regardless of the jurisdiction in which the behavior occurred;
12. is convicted of, or pleads guilty to, a misdemeanor committed in the course of practice;
13. commits an act that constitutes a misdemeanor in Ohio regardless of the jurisdiction in which the behavior occurred, if the behavior was committed in the course of practice;
14. is convicted of, or pleads guilty to, a misdemeanor involving moral turpitude (acts of moral turpitude are characterized by baseness, vileness, or depravity, and as behavior that gravely violates moral sentiment or accepted moral standards of the community);[24]
15. commits an act that constitutes a misdemeanor in Ohio regardless of the jurisdiction in which the behavior occurred, if the behavior involved moral turpitude;
16. violates conditions placed on his or her practice by the Board;

---

23. Ohio Rev. Code § 4731.22(A).
24. Rossiter v. Ohio State Medical Board, 155 Ohio App.3d 689, 802 N.E.2d 1149 (2002).

17. fails to pay license renewal fees as specified;

18. pays referral fees or creates any arrangement for paying referral fees with another medical professional;

19. violates a code of ethics of a national professional organization;

20. is unable to practice in accordance with acceptable standards of care;

21. violates or attemptes to violate any provisions of the medical licensing law;

22. violates any abortion rule adopted by the Public Health Council;

23. has his or her license to practice medicine by another state limited, revoked, or suspended;

24. has his or her clinical privileges revoked, suspended, restricted, or terminated by the Department of Defense or the Veterans Administration;

25. has his or her status as a provider of services under Medicare or Medicaid terminated or suspended;

26. is impaired in his or her ability to practice according to acceptable standards of care because of excessive use of drugs, alcohol, or other substances;

27. has a second or subsequent violation of conflict of interest limitations on patient referrals;

28. inappropriately waives, or advertises that he or she will waive, all or part of a deductible or copayment that a patient is obligated by contract to pay;

29. fails to follow universal blood and body fluid precautions established by Ohio;

30. fails to fulfill responsibilities established between the physician and advanced practice nurses;[25]

31. fails to follow state guidelines regarding notice of lack of malpractice insurance;

32. fails to provide appropriate supervision of a physician's assistant; or

33. fails to maintain a standard of care arrangement with various nurse specialists and nurse practitioners.[26]

---

25. Ohio Rev. Code § 4723.56.
26. Ohio Rev. Code § 4731.22(B).

(C)(2) Investigations by the Board

In all investigations and proceedings, the Board protects patient confidentiality. It does not release names or identifying information about patients without proper consent or unless a waiver of privilege exists (see chapter 3.4, Privileged Communications).[27]

Ohio law specifies that if a person who is convicted of or pleads guilty to one or more specified drug offenses[28] is a professionally licensed person, in addition to any other sanctions imposed for the violation, the court must transmit a certified copy of the judgment entry of conviction to the licensing board in question.[29]

If the Board determines that there is clear and convincing evidence that a physician has violated the Medical Practice Act and that the physician's continued practice presents a danger to the public, it may suspend the physician's license without a hearing.[30] If the physician requests a hearing, the Board must schedule the hearing within 15 days. The Board may issue subpoenas to compel the attendance and testimony of witnesses and production of books, records, and papers.[31] Within 30 days of the hearing, the hearing officer must submit a written report to the Board describing findings and recommendations. The Board then considers the report and any objections to it and makes its decision regarding the physician's license and ability to practice.

Any matter that is the subject of a hearing may be settled through mutual consent of all involved parties at any time before the close of the hearing. Such settlements are called *consent agreements*. Consent agreements must be ratified by the Board.[32]

(C)(3) Penalties for Violations

The Board has the power to limit, reprimand or place on probation, suspend, and revoke a physician's license.[33]

If the Board suspends the physician from practice, it may order conditions that must be met under which the license may be reinstated. Such conditions may include a mental or physical examination, additional training, practice limitations, participation in counseling programs, and demonstration that he or she can

---

27. OHIO REV. CODE § 4731.22(C)(1).
28. OHIO REV. CODE §§ 2925.02–2925.37.
29. OHIO REV. CODE § 2925.38.
30. OHIO REV. CODE § 4731.22(D).
31. OHIO ADMIN. CODE § 4731-13-13.
32. OHIO ADMIN. CODE § 4731-13-17.
33. OHIO REV. CODE § 4731.22(B).

resume practice.[34] The Board also oversees a system of treatment programs for impaired practitioners.[35]

The Board may summarily suspend from practice a physician who is addicted to controlled substances, until the physician offers proof to the Board that he or she is no longer addicted.[36]

---

34. OHIO ADMIN. CODE § 4731-13-16.
35. OHIO ADMIN. CODE § 4731-16.
36. OHIO REV. CODE § 3719.121.

Licensure and Regulation of Psychiatric Nurses

The licensure and regulation of nurses, including psychiatric nurses, is governed by statutory law that establishes a Board of Nursing, defines the practice of nursing, establishes qualifications and procedures for the licensure of practical nurses and registered nurses, and certifications for nurse anesthetist, clinical nurse specialist, nurse-midwife, and nurse practitioner. In Ohio, licensed registered nurses differ from licensed practical nurses in that the latter nurses are permitted to engage in a more restricted set of activities and must work under the supervision of a physician, dentist, podiatrist, optometrist, chiropractor, or a registered nurse.[1] The Board also establishes exceptions to licensure and regulates the conduct of licensed and certified nurses. In addition, the Board promulgates rules and regulations to carry out the provisions of the statute. There is no separate licensure pertaining to the practice of psychiatric nursing; the law is a generic one that regulates the practice of nursing without regard to specialty. Psychiatric nurses are distinguished from other nurses in that they are registered nurses with a master's degree or doctorate in nursing with a specialization in psychiatric nursing.

(A) Board of Nursing

The governor, with the advice and consent of the state senate, appoints members to the Board of Nursing, which consists of 13 members who are citizens of the United States and residents of Ohio. Eight of the members are registered nurses, each of whom is

---

1. OHIO REV. CODE § 4723.01(B), (F).

a graduate of a program approved by the Board, holds a currently active license to practice as a registered nurse, and has been actively engaged in the practice of nursing as a registered nurse for the five years immediately preceding appointment to the Board. One of the eight registered nurse members must hold a valid certificate of authority to practice as a certified registered nurse anesthetist, clinical nurse specialist, certified nurse-midwife, or certified nurse practitioner. Four members are licensed practical nurses, each of whom is a graduate of a program approved by the Board, holds an active license to practice as a licensed practical nurse, and has been actively engaged in the practice of nursing as a licensed practical nurse for the five years preceding appointment. One member of the Board represents the interests of consumers. Neither this member nor any person in this member's immediate family may be a member of or associated with a health care provider or profession or have a financial interest in health care delivery or finance.[2]

Terms of office are for four years, and the governor may reappoint members to one additional term. The governor may remove any member of the Board for neglect of any duty required by law or for incompetency or unprofessional or dishonorable conduct.[3]

The Board of Nursing has specific powers and duties. Specifically, the Board is responsible for (a) governing the administration and conduct of examinations for licensure to practice nursing as a registered nurse or as a licensed practical nurse; (b) establishing standards for continuing education; (c) establishing standards for approval of peer support programs for nurses who misuse drugs or alcohol or who have an illness; (d) establishing requirements for courses in medication administration by licensed practical nurses; (e) establishing criteria for specialty certification; (f) establishing universal blood and body fluid precautions; and (g) establishing criteria for nurses to practice as certified nurse anesthetists, clinical nurse specialists, certified nurse-midwifes, certified nurse practitioners,[4] and advanced nurse practitioners.[5]

(B) Licensure

To apply for licensure as a registered nurse or a practical nurse, an applicant must have completed the requirements of a nursing

---

2. Оню Rev. Code § 4723.02.
3. *Id.*
4. Оню Rev. Code § 4723.06.
5. Оню Rev. Code § 4723.52.

education program approved by the Board.[6] Graduates from a nursing education program approved by a jurisdiction other than Ohio must submit to the Board official documents from the program for the Board's review. If the Board determines that the applicant's training was substantially similar, the Board will approve the applicant to sit for the licensure examination. If the Board determines that the applicant's training was not substantially similar to that obtained in an approved program in Ohio, the Board may deny admission to the exam or condition the applicant's admission to the examination on the applicant's successful completion of additional training.[7]

Foreign educated applicants also must submit documentation of their training. In addition, foreign applicants must submit their credentials for a full education course-by-course report performed by the Commission of Graduates of Foreign Nursing Schools, and they must present evidence of having a working knowledge of English. The Board evaluates all of these documents and determines whether the applicant's training was substantially similar to that required in Ohio. The Board may deny admission to the examination or condition the foreign applicant's admission to the examination on the applicant's successful completion of additional training.[8]

The National Council Licensure Examination—RN is the approved examination for licensure as a registered nurse[9] and the National Council Licensure Examination—PN is the approved examination for licensure as a practical nurse[10] in Ohio. The Board grants a license if the applicant passes the examination and the Board determines that the applicant has not committed any acts that would be grounds for disciplinary action, or, if so, that the applicant has made restitution or been rehabilitated.[11]

Applicants licensed in another jurisdiction, who were granted licensure after passing an examination approved by the board of that jurisdiction that is equivalent to that required in Ohio, and who meet all other Ohio standards may be licensed by this Board by endorsement.[12]

Once licensed, nurses must renew their license every two years.[13] Licensees must report any criminal offenses that would constitute grounds for denial of renewal.[14]

---

6. OHIO ADMIN. CODE § 4723-5.
7. OHIO ADMIN. CODE § 4723-7-02(C).
8. OHIO ADMIN. CODE § 4723-7-03.
9. OHIO ADMIN. CODE § 4723-7-01(A).
10. OHIO ADMIN. CODE § 4723-7-01(B).
11. OHIO REV. CODE § 4723.09.
12. Id.
13. OHIO REV. CODE § 4723.24.
14. Id.

Except in the case of a first renewal after licensure by examination, each licensed registered and practical nurse must, in each two-year period, complete a minimum of 24 hours of approved continuing nursing education. At least one hour of the continuing education must be directly related to the statutes and rules regarding the practice of nursing in Ohio.[15] Nurses who are certified as advanced practice nurses must in addition complete a minimum of 12 hours of continuing education in pharmacology.[16] Clinical nurse specialists and nurse practitioners who hold national certification may have specific continuing education requirements imposed by the national certifying body.[17]

The Board of Nursing may grant specialty certifications to nurses who complete specific advanced training, including clinical nurse specialists, certified nurse-midwives, and certified nurse practitioners.[18] The Board may also authorize these specialists to prescribe drugs and therapeutic devices if the nurse meets the educational and training requirements established by the law that includes an instructional program in advanced pharmacology.[19]

(B)(1) Exceptions to Licensing

Provisions are made for the practice of nursing for individuals who are not licensed, including

1. students who practice as part of their professional training;
2. persons licensed in another jurisdiction and employed by the federal government;
3. persons who assist other licensed health care professionals and are under their supervision;
4. persons employed as nursing aides, attendants, orderlies, and other auxiliary workers;
5. persons licensed in other jurisdictions and whose employment entails the transportation of patients in Ohio for no longer than 48 hours;
6. persons who provide nursing services to family members or in emergencies;
7. persons who care for the sick within religious tenets of any church; and
8. persons who provide care during a disaster.[20]

---

15. OHIO REV. CODE § 4723.24(A).
16. OHIO REV. CODE § 4723.56(F).
17. OHIO ADMIN. CODE § 4723-8-10.
18. OHIO ADMIN. CODE § 4723-8-07.
19. OHIO REV. CODE §§ 4723.48; OHIO ADMIN. CODE § 4723-9-02.
20. OHIO REV. CODE § 4723.32.

The Board may grant a nonrenewable temporary permit for up to 180 days to practice nursing to an applicant for licensure by endorsement if the Board is satisfied that the applicant holds a current, active license in good standing in another jurisdiction.[21]

(C) Regulation

(C)(1) Disciplinary Actions

The Board of Nursing is empowered to take disciplinary actions against applicants and licensees who[22]

1. have action taken by another jurisdiction against a nurse's license other than for failure to renew;
2. practice without a license or while a license is suspended;
3. are convicted of or admit guilt of a misdemeanor committed in the course of practice;
4. are convicted of or admit guilt of any felony or of a crime of gross immorality or moral turpitude;
5. sell, give away, or administer drugs for illegal purposes;
6. are convicted of or admit guilt of an act in another jurisdiction that would constitute a misdemeanor, felony, or a crime of moral turpitude in Ohio;
7. self-administer any drug not in accordance with a prescription;
8. are impaired as a result of misuse of controlled substances;
9. are impaired as a result of a physical or mental disability;
10. assault or harm a patient or deprive a patient of the means to summon assistance;
11. obtain money or anything of value by intentional misrepresentation;
12. are adjudicated as mentally ill or mentally incompetent;
13. are suspended or terminated by the Department of Defense or Veterans Administration for an act that would violate Ohio's licensing law for nurses;
14. violate any restrictions placed on a licensee by the Board;
15. fail to use universal blood and body fluid precautions prescribed by the Board;
16. fail to follow accepted standards of care;

---

21. OHIO REV. CODE § 4723.09.
22. OHIO REV. CODE § 4723.28.

17. engage in practice that exceeds the scope of practice permitted under the law;

18. assist someone in the unlicensed practice of nursing;

19. in the case of a certified registered nurse anesthetist, clinical nurse specialist, certified nurse-midwife, or certified nurse practitioner, waive the deductible or copayment of a patient when such a practice is not permitted by the patient's contract;

20. engage in nursing activities that fall outside of the scope of practice and fail to meet quality assurance standards;

21. fail to maintain a standard care arrangement that is a written treatment plan developed by a collaborating physician or podiatrist;[23]

22. fail to comply with requirements of participation in a treatment program for chemically dependent nurses or a practice intervention and improvement program;[24]

23. fail to prescribe drugs and therapeutic devices in accordance with professional standards;

24. perform or induce an abortion; or

25. fail to maintain professional boundaries with a patient or engaging in sexual contact or sexually demeaning verbal behavior with a patient.[25]

In addition, the Board has the power to discipline nurses who, without proper certification, engage in activities reserved for those with special certifications to practice as a certified registered nurse anesthetist, certified nurse specialist, certified nurse-midwife, or certified nurse practitioner or who use these titles inappropriately.[26]

(C)(2) Investigations by the Board

The Board of Nursing has the power to conduct investigations regarding any nursing practices that appear to violate the licensure statute or Board rules.[27] Employers of nurses and nursing associations are required to report to the Board the names of nurses whose employment has been terminated because of misconduct or whose practices were found to present a danger to the public.[28] Persons and agencies that report suspicions of misconduct in good faith to the Board are immune from civil action.[29]

---

23. OHIO REV. CODE § 4723.01(N).
24. OHIO REV. CODE § 4723.35.
25. OHIO REV. CODE § 4723.28(B).
26. OHIO REV. CODE § 4723.44.
27. OHIO REV. CODE § 4723.28.
28. OHIO REV. CODE § 4723.34.
29. OHIO REV. CODE § 4723.341.

The Board may apply to a court for an order to stop the practice of a nurse for violating any provisions of the law.[30] In such an instance, the nurse will be provided with a hearing and information about the violation will be considered. Information received by the Board in its investigations is considered confidential and is not subject to subsequent civil action, except that the Board may disclose the information to law enforcement officers and government agencies investigating the person licensed by the Board.[31]

If a nurse is convicted of or pleads guilty to one or more drug offenses specified in the law,[32] the court must transmit a certified copy of the judgment entry of conviction to the licensing board.[33]

The Board may hold hearings to determine whether the practice of a nurse violated any provisions of the licensure law or rules. The Board has the power to subpoena witnesses and require the production by witnesses of documentary evidence.[34] The Board may also compel a licensee, or an applicant for a license, to submit to a mental or physical examination. Failure of the person to submit to the examination constitutes an admission of the allegations.[35]

Any action taken by the Board resulting in a suspension from practice must be accompanied by a written statement of the conditions under which the person may be reinstated.[36]

(C)(3) Penalties for Violations

The Board of Nursing may refuse to grant a license to an applicant and may reprimand or otherwise discipline a licensee, revoke permanently, suspend, or place restrictions on any licensee for cause. Individuals who practice nursing without a license are guilty of a felony of the fifth degree on a first offense (maximum penalty of 12 months in prison and/or a fine of up to $2,500)[37] and a felony of the fourth degree for each subsequent offense (maximum penalty of 18 months in jail and/or a fine of up to $5,000). Nurses who continue to practice when their license has lapsed for failure to renew or has been classified as inactive are guilty of a minor misdemeanor[38] (punishable with a maximum fine of $100).[39]

---

30. OHIO REV. CODE § 4723.40.
31. OHIO REV. CODE § 4723.28.
32. OHIO REV. CODE §§ 2925.02–2925.37.
33. OHIO REV. CODE § 2925.38.
34. OHIO REV. CODE § 4723.29.
35. OHIO REV. CODE § 4723.28(D).
36. OHIO REV. CODE § 4723.28(J).
37. OHIO REV. CODE § 29.29.13.
38. OHIO REV. CODE § 4723.99.
39. OHIO REV. CODE § 2929.21.

The Board has developed an alternative program for treating chemically dependent nurses who voluntarily enter treatment. The Board may abstain from disciplinary action against a nurse who enters the program if it finds that the nurse can be treated effectively and there is no impairment of ability to practice effectively. As a condition of being admitted to the monitoring program, the nurse must surrender her or his license until such time as the program coordinator determines that the nurse is capable of resuming practice.[40]

---

40. OHIO REV. CODE § 4723.35.

1.4

Licensure and Regulation of Psychologists

The licensure and regulation of psychologists and school psychologists are governed by statutory law that establishes a state Board of Psychology, defines the practice of psychology and school psychology, establishes qualifications and procedures for the licensure of psychologists and school psychologists, establishes exceptions to licensure, regulates the conduct of licensed psychologists and school psychologists, and provides for administrative hearings. In addition, the Board promulgates rules and regulations to carry out the provisions of the statute.

As noted in chapter 1.1 (Licensure and Regulation of Mental Health Professionals), several amendments to the licensure law for psychology went into effect on May 12, 2002, as part of the legislature's effort to strengthen sanctions against psychologists and other mental health professionals who engage in sexual contact or sexual conduct with patients. Specific to this chapter, as noted later, the amendments change the composition of the Board, allow the Board to suspend a license without a hearing for certain offenses, and specify how the Board must respond to offenses involving sexual contact or sexual conduct.

(A) Board of Psychology

One of the recent amendments to the licensure law for psychology increased the number of public members of the Board from one to three. Allowing for a period of transition, the Board of Psychology now consists of nine individuals who must be citizens of the United States and residents of Ohio. Three members must be patient advocates who are not mental health professionals and who either are parents or other relatives of a person who has received mental health services or are representatives of patient advocate organizations. Each of the other members must be licensed psychologists or licensed school psychologists. Terms of office are for five years. Members may not serve more than two consecutive five-year terms. The psychologist members of the Board are selected to represent the diverse fields of specialization and practice in the fields of psychology and school psychology.[1]

The governor, with the advice and consent of the senate, appoints members to the Board. The governor also may remove any member for malfeasance, misfeasance, or nonfeasance after a hearing.[2]

(B) Licensure

All psychologists and school psychologists are licensed by examination administered by the Board of Psychology. The education and experience requirements to sit for the examination, however, are different for psychologists and school psychologists.

For admission to the licensure exam as a psychologist, the applicant must have graduated from a doctorate program in psychology or from a doctoral degree program deemed equivalent by the Board,[3] from an educational institution accredited, or recognized by national or regional accrediting agencies.[4] In addition, the applicant must have completed at least two years of supervised professional experience in psychological work, at least one year of which must be postdoctoral.[5] The Board maintains a record of each specific degree program that it recognizes as acceptable, and it has adopted guidelines for the types of supervised professional experiences that are acceptable.[6]

For admission to the licensure exam as a school psychologist, the applicant must have graduated with a master's degree in school psychology, or a degree considered equivalent by the Board, from an educational institution accredited or recognized by national or regional accrediting agencies, including those approved by the state board of education for the training of school psychologists.[7] In addition, the applicant must have completed at least 60 quarter hours of course credit, or the semester-hour

---

1. Ohio Rev. Code § 4732.02.
2. Id.
3. Ohio Admin. Code § 4732-9-01(A)–(G).
4. Ohio Rev. Code § 4732.10(B)(4).
5. Ohio Rev. Code § 4732.10(B)(5).
6. Id.
7. Ohio Rev. Code § 4732.10(C)(1).

equivalent, at the graduate level, of accredited study in course work relevant to the study of school psychology.[8] Applicants also must have completed an internship of supervised experience in an educational institution approved by the Ohio Department of Education for school psychology or one year of other training acceptable to the Board.[9] Finally, applicants must furnish proof of at least 27 months, exclusive of internship, of full-time experience as a certificated school psychologist (see chapter 1.7, Certification and Regulation of School Psychologists) of employment by a board of education or a private school meeting the standards set by the state Board of Education, or of experience that the Board considers equivalent.[10]

Applicants for licensure for psychology and school psychology must complete a two-step examination. The first examination for the psychology license is the Examination for Practice in Professional Psychology (EPPP), which is a national examination. The second step is an examination by the Board conducted under rules established by the Board.[11] The first examination for the school psychology license is the School Psychology Specialty Area examination. After a passing score is earned and the candidate has accumulated three years of school psychology work experience in a school setting, the applicant may apply for the Board's exam. The state examination for school psychologists is prepared and conducted by a school psychology licensing committee responsible to the Board. The committee consists of five licensed school psychologists or licensed psychologists who are certified school psychologists appointed by the Board. The Board may examine applicants on any areas of psychology that it deems appropriate, but the major focus of the state examination is on the Ohio licensure law and its rules of professional conduct.[12]

Once licensed, each psychologist and school psychologist must renew his or her license every two years. Registration for renewal of a license must be made on a form provided by the Board and must include information about the licensee's area(s) of psychological competence and compliance with legal and ethical regulations, among other things. Licensees are also asked to give evidence of having completed during the biennium the continuing education requirements that were in effect for the previous two-year period.

Until the end of the 2000 to 2002 biennium, each psychologist and school psychologist had to complete in the preceding two-

---

8. OHIO REV. CODE § 4732.10(C)(5).
9. OHIO REV. CODE § 4732.10(C)(6).
10. OHIO REV. CODE § 4732.10(C)(7).
11. OHIO REV. CODE § 4732.11.
12. Id.

year period not fewer than 20 hours of continuing education in psychology.[13] Beginning with the 2002 to 2004 biennium, each psychologist and school psychologist must complete 23 hours of continuing education, at least three hours of which must be in professional conduct and ethics.[14] Continuing education requirements are prorated for individuals who obtain licensure midway through the biennium.[15]

A license is automatically suspended if the biennial registration is not completed within the specified time. Within five years, the Board may reinstate any such suspended license on payment of the fee and a penalty fee.[16]

(B)(1) Exceptions to Licensing

A license is not required for:

1. a certified school psychologist, while practicing school psychology within the scope of his or her employment by a board of education or by a private school;

2. a nonresident psychologist temporarily employed in Ohio to provide psychological services for not more than 30 days, who, in the opinion of the Board, is equivalent to an Ohio licensed psychologist or school psychologist and is licensed or certified in his or her home state or country;

3. a person who is employed by a licensed psychologist or school psychologist;

4. a person who holds a master's degree or doctoral degree in psychology while working under the supervision of a licensed psychologist;

5. any properly supervised student studying psychology;

6. duly ordained ministers while functioning in their ministerial capacity;

7. qualified social workers while functioning in their capacity as social workers;[17]

8. federal employees when their activities are part of their duties;

9. Any persons who are licensed, certified, or registered under other provisions of the *Ohio Revised Code* when they are using procedures that are allowed and within the standards and ethics of their profession, provided they do not use the title of psychologist; or

---

13. OHIO REV. CODE § 4732.141(A).
14. OHIO REV. CODE §§ 4732.141(A)(2), 4732-1-06.
15. OHIO REV. CODE § 4732.141(D).
16. OHIO REV. CODE § 4732.14.
17. OHIO REV. CODE § 4732.22.

10. persons who offer services of a psychological nature, provided they do not use the title of psychologist and do not engage in psychological procedures that the Board judges to be a serious hazard to mental health.[18]

The Board has judged the following psychological procedures to be a serious hazard to mental health and require professional expertise in psychology:

1. psychological and school psychological diagnosis;
2. psychological and school psychological prescription;
3. psychological and school psychological client supervision;
4. sensitivity training;
5. confrontation groups;
6. hypnotic techniques for diagnostic, treatment, or other psychotherapeutic purposes;
7. individual intelligence testing, assessment of cognitive processing, or determination of individual intelligence;
8. personality evaluation;
9. individual and group psychological psychotherapy;
10. psychological behavior psychotherapy such as, but not limited to, implosive therapy, aversive therapy, and desensitization;
11. couples and family psychological psychotherapy; and
12. psychological psychotherapy for sexual dysfunctions or disorders.[19]

(C) Regulation

The Board of Psychology regulates psychologists and school psychologists and has the power to discipline them.

(C)(1) Disciplinary Actions

If the Board of Psychology believes that a licensee's practice places members of the public in serious danger, it may request that the person's practice be enjoined by the court of common pleas of the county in which the practice is occurring.[20]

After considering charges and providing a hearing, the Board may refuse to issue a license to an applicant and may issue a reprimand or suspend or revoke the license of a psychologist

---

18. OHIO REV. CODE § 4732.23.
19. OHIO ADMIN. CODE § 4732-5-01.
20. OHIO REV. CODE § 4732.24.

or school psychologist.[21] Disciplinary actions may be initiated if a psychologist:

1. is convicted of a felony or any offense involving extreme immorality or moral turpitude;
2. uses fraud or deceit in procuring the license or assisting another person in fraudulently obtaining a license;
3. accepts referral fees without full disclosure in advance to the consumer of the terms of the agreement;
4. breaches confidentiality;
5. is negligent in practice;
6. uses controlled substances or alcohol to the extent that it impairs the ability to perform professional duties;
7. violates any rule of professional conduct promulgated by the Board;
8. practices in an area for which one is clearly untrained or incompetent;
9. is adjudicated as incompetent by a court for the purpose of holding the license;
10. waives the deductible payment or copayment that a patient is required to pay by contract, if the waiver is used as an enticement to receive services from the provider;
11. advertises that he or she will waive the deductible payment or copayment.[22]

(C)(2) Investigations by the Board

Some of the recent amendments to the law affect how the Board responds to complaints. Specifically, on receiving a complaint on any of the grounds listed in the previous section, the Board may suspend the license of a psychologist or school psychologist before holding a hearing if it determines that there is an immediate threat to the public. If it suspends a license, the Board must notify the licensee and the licensee may then request a hearing. If the person does not request a hearing in a timely manner, the Board will permanently revoke the license.[23]

If a licensed psychologist or school psychologist is convicted of or pleads guilty to one or more drug offenses specified in the law,[24] the court must transmit a certified copy of the judgment

---

21. OHIO REV. CODE § 4732.17.
22. OHIO ADMIN. CODE § 4732-17-03(A).
23. OHIO REV. CODE § 4732.171.
24. OHIO REV. CODE §§ 2925.02–2925.37.

entry of conviction to the Board so it can determine whether the licensee has violated the licensing law.[25]

When the Board considers revoking, suspending, or refusing to issue or reissue a license, it must follow specific notice and hearing steps, including: (a) giving notice by certified mail of the right to a hearing; (b) including in the notice the charges or other reasons for proposed action; (c) informing the recipient via the notice that at the hearing he or she may appear in person, be represented by an attorney, or present arguments in writing, and that at the hearing he or she may present evidence and examine witnesses; (d) setting a hearing date between 7 and 15 days from the time the licensee requests a hearing; and (e) empowering one or more of its members to conduct the hearing.[26]

The person has a right to appeal any adverse decision by the Board. Appeal is made to the court of common pleas of the county in which the psychologist or school psychologist practices. If the psychologist or school psychologist is not a resident of and has no place of business in Ohio, he or she may appeal to the court of common pleas of Franklin County, Ohio.[27]

(C)(3) Penalties for Violations

The Board may issue a reprimand, suspend, or revoke the license of a licensed psychologist or school psychologist. In addition, the Board's disciplinary actions are carried out in accordance with approved administrative procedures.[28] At any time, the Board may restore a person's license as circumstances warrant.[29]

The recent amendments to the licensure law for psychologists also added specific penalties for licensees who engage in sexual contact or sexual conduct with patients. If the Board determines at the conclusion of a hearing that a psychologist or school psychologist has engaged in sexual conduct or had sexual contact with a patient, the Board must suspend the license or permanently revoke the license. If the Board concludes that neither of these options is appropriate, it may impose another sanction, but it then must issue a written finding that explains its rationale for not suspending or revoking the license and post such written explanations on its website.[30]

The Board must refuse to issue or renew a license or suspend a license for an individual who is in default under a child support

---

25. OHIO REV. CODE § 2925.38.
26. OHIO ADMIN. CODE § 4732-17-03(B).
27. OHIO ADMIN. CODE § 4732-17-03(B)(6).
28. OHIO REV. CODE chap. 119.
29. OHIO REV. CODE § 4732.18.
30. OHIO REV. CODE § 4732.172; http://Psychology.Ohio.gov/pdfs/disciplinaryactions.pdf

order.[31] Individuals who engage in unlicensed practice of psychology or school psychology may be fined by the Board between $100 and $500 or imprisoned for not less than six months nor more than one year, or both.[32]

Any findings made, and the records of sanctions imposed by the Board, are public records (see chapter 3.6, State Freedom of Information Act).[33] In addition, recent amendments require the Board to make available on the Internet[34] the names of licensed psychologists and school psychologists and the names of all licensed psychologists and school psychologists who have been reprimanded by the Board for misconduct, whose licenses are under active suspension, and whose licenses have been suspended or revoked for misconduct, and the reason for each reprimand, suspension, or revocation.[35]

---

31. Ohio Admin. Code § 4732-17-03(C).
32. Ohio Rev. Code § 4732.99.
33. Ohio Rev. Code § 149.43.
34. http://psychology.Ohio.gov/pdfs/disciplinaryactions.pdf
35. Ohio Rev. Code § 4732.31(A).

Subdoctoral and Unlicensed Psychologists

The status of subdoctoral-level psychological personnel is an important issue, because it pertains both to the law and to the practice of psychology. For example, in a few states, master's-level psychologists have the right to practice independently. In other states, master's-level psychologists are recognized by the law as valuable aides to doctoral-level mental health professionals but cannot practice independently. In Ohio, a doctoral degree is required for the practice of psychology, and a master's degree is required for the practice of school psychology, as noted in chapter 1.4 (Licensure and Regulation of Psychologists).

(A) Psychologists Exempted From Licensure

As noted in the previous chapter, licensure is not required for certain individuals by statute. In addition, the licensing law does not restrict the use of the term *social psychologist* by a person who has earned a doctoral degree in social psychology or in sociology with a social psychology major.[1]

Provisions are made for unlicensed employees of psychologists and school psychologists to use an appropriate title that implies supervised or training status,[2] although such individuals may not use the title of *psychologist, psychology associate,* or *school psychology associate.*[3] Graduate students in training to become

---

1. OHIO REV. CODE § 4732.23(D).
2. OHIO ADMIN. CODE § 4732-15-01(A) and (B).
3. OHIO ADMIN. CODE § 4732-15-01(D).

psychologists and school psychologists may carry out appropriate tasks while under the supervision of a licensed psychologist or school psychologist and they must use titles that clearly indicate student status in the profession.[4]

Individuals who teach or conduct research in psychology are exempted from licensure requirements, provided the teaching and research does not otherwise involve the professional practice of psychology in which student or client welfare are affected.[5]

(B) Rights and Responsibilities of Subdoctoral and Unlicensed Psychologists

Subdoctoral and unlicensed psychological personnel must operate under the supervision of a licensed psychologist or school psychologist, and they must be registered by the supervising psychologist or school psychologist with the Board of Psychology.[6]

---

4. OHIO REV. CODE § 4732.22(E).
5. OHIO ADMIN. CODE § 4732-5-02(11) and (12).
6. OHIO ADMIN. CODE § 4732-13-04(B)(24).

Licensure and Regulation of Counselors, Social Workers, and Marriage and Family Therapists

The licensure and regulation of counselors, social workers, and marriage and family therapists is governed by statutory law that establishes a Counselor, Social Worker, and Marriage and Family Therapist Board, defines terms contained within the act, and establishes qualifications and procedures for licensure. In addition, the Board is authorized to promulgate rules and regulations to carry out the provisions of the statute. The authority to regulate and license marriage and family therapists was granted to this Board, earlier called the Counselor and Social Worker Board, in April 2003.

(A) Counselor, Social Worker, and Marriage and Family Therapist Board

The Board consists of 15 members, appointed by the governor with the advice and consent of the state senate. Four of the members are licensed as professional clinical counselors or professional counselors. Of these four members, at least two are licensed professional clinical counselors, at least one holds a doctoral degree in counseling and a graduate-level teaching position in a counselor education program, and at least two have received at least a master's degree in counseling. A member may fulfill more than one of these criteria.[1]

Two members of the Board are licensed as independent social workers. Two members are licensed as social workers, at least one of whom holds a bachelor's or master's degree in social work. At all times, the social worker members include one educator who holds a teaching position in a baccalaureate or master's degree social work program.

Two members must be licensed as independent marriage and family therapists who in the past five years have actively engaged in the practice, education, training, or research of marriage and family therapy.

Three members of the Board represent the general public who have not practiced counseling or social work and have not been involved in the delivery of professional counseling or social work services. Not more than eight members of the Board may be members of the same political party or sex. At least one member must be African American, Native American, Hispanic, or Asian American. Terms of office are three years. Members may not serve more than two consecutive terms.[2]

Within the Board, a Counselors Professional Standards Committee, a Social Workers Professional Standards Committee, and a Marriage and Family Therapists Professional Standards Committee have full authority to act on behalf of the Board on all matters concerning counselors, social workers, and marriage and family therapists, respectively.[3]

(B) Licensure

Counselors, social workers, and marriage and family therapists have different educational and experience requirements for licensure.

To be eligible to take the examination for a license as a professional clinical counselor, the applicant must meet the following requirements: (a) be of good moral character; (b) hold a graduate degree in counseling; (c) complete a minimum of 90 quarter hours of graduate credit or semester credit hour equivalents, including courses in the four categories of (i) clinical psychopathology, personality, abnormal behavior; (ii) evaluation of mental and emotional disorders; (iii) diagnosis of mental and emotional disorders; and (iv) methods of prevention, intervention, and treatment of

---

1. OHIO REV. CODE § 4757.03.
2. *Id.*
3. OHIO REV. CODE § 4757.04.

mental and emotional disorders; (d) complete supervised experience as specified by the Board; and (e) pass a field evaluation.[4]

Individuals who wish to take the examination for a license as a professional counselor must meet the following requirements: (a) be of good moral character; (b) hold a graduate degree in counseling; (c) complete a minimum of 90 quarter hours of graduate credit or its equivalent in semester hours in counselor training acceptable to the committee, which the applicant may complete while working toward receiving a graduate degree in counseling or subsequent to receiving the degree; and (d) complete supervised experience as specified by the Board. The Board may issue a provisional license to an applicant who meets all of the requirements to be licensed, pending the receipt of transcripts or action by the Board to issue a regular license.[5]

Applicants for licensure as an independent social worker, must meet the following requirements: (a) be of good moral character; (b) hold a master's degree or a doctorate in social work from an educational institution accredited by the Council on Social Work Education;[6] and (c) complete at least two years of post-master's social work supervised experience.[7]

To be eligible to take the examination for a license as a social worker, the applicant must meet the following requirements: (a) be of good moral character; and (b) hold from a program accredited by the Council on Social Work Education[8] a baccalaureate degree, master's degree, or doctorate degree in social work.[9]

Individuals who wish to be licensed as a marriage and family therapist must hold a master's or doctoral degree in marriage and family therapy, or completed a graduate degree that includes a minimum of 90 quarter hours of graduate coursework in marriage and family therapy that is acceptable to the committee and 300 hours of client contact in a practicum. Graduate instruction must include the following content areas: research, professional ethics, marriage and family studies, marriage and family therapy, human development, appraisal of individuals and families, and systems theory. Applicants must also pass an examination administered by the Board. The Board will exercise a grandparenting provision for two years after the law is implemented by waiving the requirements of the examination and the specific content areas of graduate instruction if the applicant presents satisfactory evidence that he or she has engaged in the practice of marriage and

---

4. Ohio Rev. Code §§ 4757.22(D), 4757-13.
5. Ohio Rev. Code § 4757.22.
6. Ohio Admin. Code § 4757-19-01(C)(1)(g).
7. Ohio Rev. Code § 4757.27; Ohio Admin. Code §§ 4757-1-04, 4757-19.
8. Ohio Admin. Code § 4757-19-01(C)(1)(g).
9. Ohio Rev. Code § 4757.28; Ohio Admin. Code §§ 4757-1-04, 4757-19.

family therapy for a total of not less than five years before the effective date of this law and that at the time of application the applicant is an associate or clinical member of the American Association of Marriage and Family Therapists.[10] Licensees are eligible for a license as independent marriage and family therapists if they complete at least two calendar years of work experience in marriage and family therapy, including at least 1,000 hours of client contact, if 200 of the 1,000 hours have been supervised by a person who is approved by the Board, and if at least 100 hours of supervision have been individual supervision.[11]

Applicants for licensure for any of the three areas of practice whose postsecondary degree is from an institution outside of the United States are reviewed by the respective professional standards committees for counselors or social workers. The committee reviews the applicant's experience, academic program, and command of the English language. If the applicant's background and training are determined to be equivalent, the applicant is permitted to proceed with the examination.[12]

The Board may issue a license to practice to license holders from other states by reciprocal agreement or by endorsement.[13]

The Board may issue a certificate of registration as a social work assistant to applicants who submit an application, pay the required fee, are of good moral character, and hold an associate degree in social service technology or a bachelor's degree that is equivalent to an associate degree in social service technology.[14]

Licenses and certificates for counselors, social workers, and marriage and family therapists must be renewed every two years. The professional standards committees of the Board notify each registrant of the need to renew licenses and certificates. The appropriate committees issue a renewed license to each applicant who pays the renewal fee and has satisfied the continuing education requirements established by the Board.[15] A license or certificate that is not renewed may be restored if the individual applies for restoration within two years, subject to paying the renewal fee and satisfying the continuing education requirements.[16]

To renew a license or certificate from the Board, each registrant must complete a minimum of 30 hours of continuing education in the previous two-year period, at least three hours of which must be in ethics education.[17]

---

10. Ohio Rev. Code § 4757.30.
11. Ohio Admin. Code § 4757.25.
12. Ohio Rev. Code § 4757.17.
13. Ohio Rev. Code § 4757.18.
14. Ohio Rev. Code § 4757.29(A); Ohio Admin. Code §§ 4757-1-04, 4757-19.
15. Ohio Admin. Code § 4757-7-01.
16. Ohio Rev. Code § 4757.32; Ohio Admin. Code § 4757-7-01.
17. Ohio Rev. Code § 4757.33; Ohio Admin. Code § 4757-9.

(B)(1) Exceptions to Licensing

The requirements of licensure and certification do not apply to

1. certified and licensed school psychologists and psychologists;
2. members of other professions who are licensed, certified, or registered by the state while performing services within the scope of their professions;
3. religious leaders when counseling activities are within the scope of their ministerial duties and are performed under the auspices or sponsorship of an established and legally recognized church, denomination, or sect;
4. civil service employees;
5. students while carrying out supervised training activities;
6. individuals who are certified or credentialed by the Department of Alcohol and Drug Addiction Services who are working within the scope of their credentials;
7. individuals employed by the American Red Cross in the performance of their official duties;
8. members of labor organizations who hold union counselor certificates while performing duties in their official capacity; or
9. any individual employed in a hospital or nursing home while providing social services other than counseling and the use of psychosocial interventions and social psychotherapy.[18]

(C) Regulation

(C)(1) Disciplinary Actions

Disciplinary actions may be taken against counselors, social workers, and marriage and family therapists if the individual:

1. violates any provision of the statute;
2. knowingly makes a false statement on an initial application or renewal;
3. accepts referral fees;
4. fails to disclose to clients information about one's practice, education, and fees;[19]
5. is convicted in any state of a felony;

---

18. Ohio Rev. Code § 4757.41.
19. Ohio Rev. Code § 4757.12.

6. is impaired in carrying out one's professional duties as a result of the misuse of alcohol, drugs, or a physical or mental impairment;

7. is convicted in any state of a misdemeanor committed in the course of practice;

8. practices outside one's scope of practice;

9. practices without complying with specified supervision requirements;

10. violates the code of ethics adopted by the Board; and

11. has a license or certification revoked or suspended or surrendered in another jurisdiction for an offense that would be a violation of this Board's rules.[20]

(C)(2) Investigations by the Board

Any person may submit evidence to the Board that appears to show that a registrant has violated the licensure and certification provisions. All licensees, registrants, supervisors, and trainees are obligated to report to the Board any alleged violations of the licensing law and rules. They must also make a report to the Board if they have knowledge or reason to suspect that a colleague or other licensee is incompetent, impaired, or unethical.[21] The Board must investigate all such evidence. Individuals who make such reports to the Board in good faith are not liable for civil damages as a result of the report or later testimony. Information received by the Board pursuant to an investigation is confidential and is not subject to discovery in any civil action.[22]

If a licensee of this Board is convicted of or pleads guilty to one or more drug offenses as specified in the law,[23] the court must transmit a certified copy of the judgment entry of conviction to the Board so that the Board can review the licensee's behavior to determine whether the licensing law has been violated.[24]

The Board may issue subpoenas, examine witnesses, and administer oaths as part of its investigation of any alleged violations. The Board may obtain any information necessary to conduct its investigations.

Registrants may request a hearing when they are under investigation to present and hear information. An attorney may assist the registrant. The Board may appoint one of its own members to act on behalf of the Board for any hearings that may be con-

---

20. Ohio Rev. Code § 4757.36; Ohio Admin. Code § 4757-11.
21. Ohio Admin. Code § 4757-5-01.
22. Ohio Admin. Code § 4757-11-01.
23. Ohio Rev. Code §§ 2925.02–2925.37.
24. Ohio Rev. Code § 2925.38.

ducted.[25] The hearing examiner must submit a report to the Board and to the respondent within 45 days of the hearing with recommendations for the Board.[26]

(C)(3) Penalties for Violations

The professional standards committees of the Board may refuse to issue, refuse to renew, suspend, revoke, restrict, or reprimand the holder of a license or certificate.

Persons whose license or certificate has been suspended or revoked by the Board may apply for reinstatement after one year. The appropriate standards committee may accept or reject the request and may require an examination for reinstatement.[27]

Violations of the statute are considered misdemeanors of the fourth degree on a first offense (punishable by a prison term of up to 30 days and a fine not to exceed $250);[28] subsequent offenses are misdemeanors of the third degree[29] (punishable by a prison term of up to 60 days and a fine not to exceed $500).[30]

25. Ohio Rev. Code § 4757.38.
26. Ohio Admin. Code § 4757-11-04.
27. Ohio Rev. Code § 4757.36(B).
28. Ohio Rev. Code § 2929.21.
29. Ohio Rev. Code § 4757.99.
30. Ohio Rev. Code § 2929.21.

1.7

Certification and Regulation of School Psychologists

The Ohio Department of Education certifies individuals in school psychology who are employed in primary and secondary school settings. The certification is entirely independent of the Board of Psychology, and certified school psychologists are specifically exempted from the regular licensure procedures (see chapter 1.4, Licensure and Regulation of Psychologists).

(A) Certification

A certificate for school psychology may be issued to a person who is recommended by the head of teacher education in a college or university and has completed an examination (called the Praxis series) prescribed by the state Department of Education, who has earned a master's degree with 60 semester hours of graduate coursework, and who has completed a nine-month, full-time internship in a school setting.[1]

(B) Responsibilities

School psychologists link mental health services to learning and behavior problems in the schools. Among their many duties are

---

1. OHIO ADMIN. CODE § 3301-23-12(A); information on becoming a school psychologist, credentialing requirements, and the practice of school psychology is available online at http://www.nasponline.org/certification/becoming_ncsp.html

assessing and diagnosing children's learning problems, designing programs for children at risk of school failure, developing behavior management programs for teachers, and providing psychological counseling for children and families.

1.8

Certification of School Counselors and School Social Workers

The Ohio Department of Education licenses school counselors and social workers. This credential was referred to as a certificate until January 2003, when its title was shifted to a license. The practice of these professionals is limited to the school setting.

(A) Licensure

A school counselor license is available to individuals who are deemed to be of good moral character and who have completed a master's degree in an academic program of preparation approved by the Ohio Department of Education, are recommended by the head of a teacher education program in a college or university, have completed an examination (called the Praxis series) prescribed by the Ohio Department of Education, and have completed one of the following two options of obtaining professional experience: (a) two years of teaching experience and completion of an internship of 600 contact hours in a school setting or (b) an internship of 600 contact hours in a school setting and a one-year induction under the supervision of a licensed school counselor. A person may also obtain a school counselor license with a master's degree and three years of experience as a licensed school counselor in another state.[1]

A school social worker certificate is available to individuals who are recommended by the head of a teacher education program, completed an examination prescribed by the state Board of Education, completed a master's degree or a master's of social

---

1. Ohio Admin. Code § 3301-24-05.

work degree (MSW) and a social work practicum of at least 10 weeks in a school district.[2]

Licenses for school counselors and school social workers must be renewed every five years. To be renewed, applicants must complete six semester credit hours of graduate coursework or 18 continuing education units or other equivalent activities related to their area of licensure.[3]

(B) Responsibilities

School counselors are responsible for delivery of guidance and counseling services for students. School social workers provide services that link home, school, and community agencies. Within these broad parameters, however, school districts establish specific job descriptions for their schools.

---

2. OHIO ADMIN. CODE § 3301-23-12.
3. *Id.*

1.9

Licensure and Regulation of Marriage and Family Counselors

Ohio law does not provide for the separate licensure or regulation of marriage and family counselors. However, marriage and family therapists are licensed by the Counselor, Social Worker, and Marriage and Family Therapy Board (see chapter 1.6, Licensure and Regulation of Counselors, Social Workers, and Marriage and Family Therapists).

1.10

Licensure of Other Types of Mental Health Professionals

In Ohio, individuals may use the title *Chemical Dependency Professional* and related titles if they meet the requirements of the law. The licensure and regulation of chemical dependency professionals is governed by statutory law that establishes the Chemical Dependency Professionals Board, defines terms contained within the act, and establishes qualifications and procedures for licensure. In addition, the Board is authorized to promulgate rules and regulations to carry out the provisions of the statute. The legislature created this Board in December 2002, and the regulations to implement it were not yet available at the time of the writing of this book.

(A) Chemical Dependency Professionals Board

The governor appoints the voting members of the Board, with the advice and consent of the state senate.[1] The Board is composed of 12 voting members as follows: four individuals who hold an independent chemical dependency counselor license (two of whom have achieved at least a master's degree in a field related to chemical dependency counseling), two individuals who hold a chemical dependency counselor III license; one individual who holds a chemical dependency counselor II license; two individuals who hold a prevention specialist II certificate or prevention specialist I certificate; one individual who is licensed to practice

---

1. Ohio Rev. Code § 4758.10(B).

medicine and surgery or osteopathic medicine and surgery (see chapter 1.2, Licensure and Regulation of Psychiatrists) and has experience practicing in a field related to chemical dependency counseling; and two individuals who are public members (at least one of whom must be at least 60 years of age). In addition, the director of the Ohio Department of Alcohol and Drug Addiction Services appoints one representative who serves as an ex officio member of the Board.[2] No more than one half of the voting members of the Board may be of the same gender or members of the same political party. At least two voting members of the Board must be African American, Native American, Hispanic, or Asian American.[3]

(B) Licensure

The regulation of chemical dependency counselors went into effect on December 23, 2002. Before that time, the Ohio Department of Alcohol and Drug Addiction Services issued certificates for the practice of chemical dependency counseling. The Department was required to work with the new Board to enable an orderly transition through the end of 2004.

The Board issues licenses for several categories of people, including independent chemical dependency counselor, chemical dependency counselor III, and chemical dependency counselor II. In addition, the Board issues certificates for individuals as chemical dependency counselor I, chemical dependency counselor assistant, certified prevention specialist II, and certified prevention specialist I.[4] Effective December 23, 2002, the Board does not issue an initial certificate to practice as a chemical dependency counselor I, even though such certificates had been issued by the Department, although the Board may issue continuing certificates.[5] After December 23, 2008, however, the law specifies that the title of chemical dependency counselor I will cease and persons may not represent themselves to the public or engage in counseling as a chemical dependency counselor I.[6]

The Board issues a license or certificate to applicants who submit an application on a form provided by the Board, pay a fee, are of good moral character, meet the educational and supervised experience requirements, and pass an examination selected by

---

2. OHIO REV. CODE § 4758.10(C).
3. OHIO REV. CODE § 4758.10(D).
4. OHIO REV. CODE § 4758.02(A).
5. OHIO REV. CODE § 4758.24(B).
6. OHIO REV. CODE § 4758.02(B).

the Board. The educational and training requirements vary by type of licensure and certification and can be met either based on already possessing a relevant certificate issued by the Department of Alcohol and Drug Addiction Services and having attained a specified amount of education and supervised training or, lacking such a certificate, based on meeting educational and supervised experience requirements. For example, the independent chemical dependency counselor license, for a licensee who is authorized to practice independently without supervision, requires the applicant to hold a master's degree in a behavioral science area, have not fewer than 4,000 hours of compensated work experience in relevant chemical dependency services, and have at least 270 hours of training in chemical dependency.[7] In contrast, an individual seeking a chemical dependency counselor II license must hold an associate's degree in a behavioral science or a bachelor's degree in any field and have not fewer than 5,000 hours of compensated, volunteer, or practicum work.[8] Each level of license and certification has specific education and supervised experience requirements.[9]

The Board may enter into a reciprocal agreement with any state that regulates individuals practicing in similar capacities if the Board finds that the state has substantially equivalent requirements. The Board may also issue licenses and certificates by endorsement to a resident of another state if the Board finds that the state has requirements substantially equivalent to the requirements of Ohio for receipt of the license or certificate.[10]

Licenses and certificates expire two years after being issued. The Board notifies each registrant that the license or certificate is about to expire, and the registrant is invited to submit a renewal form, pay a fee, and indicate that he or she has satisfied the continuing education requirement that consists of 40 clock hours of instruction.[11]

(B)(1) Exceptions to Licensing

Three categories of individuals are exempt from this law. First, all individuals who hold a license, registration, certificate, or other credential issued under another chapter of the *Revised Code* while performing services within the scope of practice of that individual's profession are exempt. This would include all licensed MHPs. Second, any individuals who perform pastoral counseling services

---

7. OHIO REV. CODE § 4758.40.
8. OHIO REV. CODE § 4758.42.
9. OHIO REV. CODE §§ 4758.41, 4758.43, 4758.44, 4758.60.
10. OHIO REV. CODE § 4758.25.
11. OHIO REV. CODE § 4758.51(A).

when the chemical dependency counseling activities are within the scope of the performance of ministerial duties are exempt. Third, students are exempt while carrying out activities that are part of the person's prescribed course of study, if the activities are supervised, as required by the educational institution.[12]

(C) Regulation

The Board is empowered to refuse to issue a license or certificate; refuse to renew a license or certificate; suspend, revoke, or restrict a license or certificate; or reprimand an individual holding a license or certificate.[13]

(C)(1) Disciplinary Actions

The Board has the power to take disciplinary action against a chemical dependency counselor who:[14]

1. violates any provision of the statutes or its regulations;
2. knowingly falsifies an application for a license or certification;
3. accepts a commission or rebate for referring an individual;
4. is convicted in any state of a crime that is a felony;
5. is convicted in any state of a misdemeanor committed in the practice of chemical dependency counseling;
6. is unable to practice because of abuse of or dependency on alcohol or other drugs or other physical or mental conditions;
7. practices outside his or her scope of practice;
8. practices without complying with supervision requirements as specified by the license or certificate;
9. violates the code of ethical practice and professional conduct; and
10. has a license or certificate in another state revoked or suspended for an offense that would violate the Ohio law for chemical dependency counselors.

(C)(2) Investigations by the Board

The Board may obtain any information necessary to conduct an investigation. All records pertaining to an investigation remain

---

12. Ohio Rev. Code § 4758.03.
13. Ohio Rev. Code § 4758.30.
14. Ohio Rev. Code § 4758.30(A).

confidential during the investigation. After the investigation, the records are considered pubic records.[15]

If a chemical dependency counselor is convicted of or pleads guilty to one or more drug offenses as specified in the law,[16] the court must transmit a copy of the judgment entry of conviction to the Board so that it can determine whether the person has violated the licensing law.[17]

(C)(3) Penalties for Violations

The Board has the power to limit, reprimand or place on probation, suspend, and revoke a chemical dependency counselor's license.[18]

Individuals who practice chemical dependency counseling without an appropriate license or certificate are guilty of a misdemeanor of the fourth degree on a first offense; on each subsequent offense, the individual is guilty of a misdemeanor of the third degree.[19]

---

15. OHIO REV. CODE § 4758.31.
16. OHIO REV. CODE §§ 2925.02–2925.37.
17. OHIO REV. CODE § 2925.38.
18. OHIO REV. CODE § 4758.30.
19. OHIO REV. CODE § 4758.99.

1.11

Licensure and Regulation of Hypnotists

Ohio law does not provide for the separate licensure or regulation of hypnotists. However, hypnosis is an acceptable treatment option for psychologists and other MHPs treating mental and emotional disorders. The use of hypnotically induced testimony is admissible in Ohio courts under certain circumstances (see chapter 6.8, Hypnosis of Witnesses).

The state Board of Psychology identifies hypnosis as a procedure that the Board judges to be a serious hazard to mental health. Individuals may not use hypnosis for diagnostic, treatment, or other psychotherapeutic purposes without being licensed by one of the health care licensure boards (see chapter 1.4, Licensure and Regulation of Psychologists).

1.12

Licensure and Regulation of Polygraph Examiners

Ohio law does not provide for the separate licensure or regulation of polygraph examiners. However, the conduct of polygraph examinations is included as one of the activities of private investigation and security services, which are licensed,[1] and a voluntary certification program, administered by the Ohio Association of Polygraph Examiners, is available.[2] Certification requirements include: (a) graduation from a polygraph school recognized by at least one national polygraph association; (b) completion of four years of polygraph experience and documentation of 32 hours of continuing education since graduation from polygraph school; (c) completion of at least 200 polygraph examinations, at least 20 of which have been conducted in the year immediately before application to become a certified polygraphist; and (d) being of sound moral character and having no adult felony convictions or serious misdemeanor convictions.

---

1. OHIO REV. CODE ch. 4749.
2. See Web page for certification requirements: http://www.polygraph.org/states/oape/certification.htm

1.13

Regulation of Unlicensed Mental Health Professionals

Ohio regulates MHPs through separate boards. Ohio does not provide an overarching board or department that is empowered to receive and investigate complaints about unlicensed MHPs who engage in any prohibited conduct. Instead, complaints are routed to the appropriate board. For example, conduct that violates the psychology licensing law is referred to the Board of Psychology (see chapter 1.4, Licensure and Regulation of Psychologists), which is empowered to investigate and enforce its statute and regulations and to impose penalties on individuals who practice psychology without a license.

With the exception of the licensing law for medicine (see chapter 1.2, Licensure and Regulation of Psychiatrists), the statute for each profession that provides for licensure of MHPs permits certain unlicensed individuals to engage in that profession's activities, as long as the activities are within the scope of practice of the excepted person's profession. For example, priests, ministers, rabbis, and members of the clergy of any religious sect may do work of a psychological nature (see chapter 1.4, Licensure and Regulation of Psychologists) and perform social work or counseling (see chapter 1.6, Licensure and Regulation of Counselors, Social Workers, and Marriage and Family Therapists) without a license as long as these activities are within the scope of practice of their regular ministerial duties. Nursing care also is permitted without a license when given in connection with religious beliefs (see chapter 1.3, Licensure and Regulation of Psychiatric Nurses).

1.14

Sunset of Credentialing Agencies

A sunset law is the means by which legislatures review and revise most facets of state government, from entire departments to small commissions. Such laws work by automatically terminating the authority of an agency to continue to operate unless the legislature, after a mandatory review of the entity's past work, extends the termination date. Thus, this law affects the licensing of MHPs.

(A) Operation of the Law

Ohio law requires that each state agency assign a review date to each of its rules and notify the Joint Committee on Agency Rule Review of the review dates. Review dates must be established that are not later than five years after the effective date of the rule.[1] Before the review date of the rule, the agency must review the rule to determine all of the following:[2]

1. whether the rule should be continued without amendment, be amended, or be rescinded;

2. whether the rule needs to be amended or rescinded to give more flexibility at the local level;

3. whether the rule needs to be amended or rescinded to eliminate unnecessary paperwork; and

4. whether the rule duplicates, overlaps with, or conflicts with other rules.

---

1. Ohio Rev. Code § 119.04(A).
2. Ohio Rev. Code § 119.04(C).

In making the review, the agency also is asked to consider any complaints or comments received about the rule and any relevant factors that have changed in the subject matter areas affected by the rule.[3] If the agency determines that the rule does not need to be changed or rescinded, the agency files information with the Joint Committee, the secretary of state, and the director of the Legislative Service Commission. The Joint Committee provides public notice in the *Register of Ohio* of the agency's review of its rules and it accepts public comments. The Joint Committee may recommend invalidating the rule if the Committee determines that the agency either improperly applied the criteria in reviewing the rule or the agency failed to file proper notice with the Committee. If the Joint Committee does not recommend invalidating the rule, the rule continues in effect without amendment until it is reviewed in the next cycle. The agency may also recommend to the Joint Committee that a rule be amended or rescinded. The Joint Committee then reviews the proposed changes and oversees the legislative review and approval process that is followed for any rule additions or changes.[4]

---

3. Ohio Rev. Code § 119.04(D).
4. Ohio Rev. Code § 119.04(E).

Business Matters

2.1

Sole Proprietorships

Mental health professionals (MHPs) who practice alone and without any formal organization are termed *sole proprietors*. Unlike partnerships and professional corporations (see chapters 2.2, Professional Corporations, and 2.3, Partnerships), there is no law directly regulating this type of business entity. Rather, sole proprietors must abide only by the laws regulating businesses in general.

The major advantages for an MHP doing business as a sole proprietor are that this is the simplest form of business organization, the practitioner is in full control of the practice, no complex business relationships are established, start-up costs are minimal, and it is fairly easy to terminate the business.

The major disadvantages of this form of business are that the practitioner is personally liable for the obligations and debts of the practice. The practice's assets and liabilities are the owner's assets and liabilities. All taxable income and deductions of the practice are reported by the owner on his or her personal tax return. This may be an economic advantage or disadvantage, depending on the practitioner's circumstances.

2.2

Professional
Corporations

MHPs who do not work for an employer typically organize their businesses in one of three forms: sole proprietorship (see chapter 2.1, Sole Proprietorships), partnership (see chapter 2.3, Partnerships), or professional corporations. In Ohio, a professional corporation is called a *professional association* (PA). The advantage of the professional association is that it offers many of the tax and practice benefits of regular incorporation.

(A) Benefits of Incorporation

The primary advantage of incorporating a professional practice is limited liability. The professional may shield personal assets from the creditors of the business. A shareholder of a PA has no responsibility for satisfying claims against the association beyond the amount that he or she invested in the association.

In a PA, the individual professional is not liable for the malpractice of other professionals in the association but is liable for his or her own malpractice or other negligent actions committed within the scope of his or her employment.[1]

Some tax advantages exist for a PA. For example, PAs can deduct some premium payments for health and accident insurance and for reimbursement of medical expenses, and these payments are not considered to be taxable income to the employee.

Another advantage of a PA over a partnership is the relative ease with which its ownership can be changed and members added or removed. A shareholder of a PA may sell or transfer

---

1. OHIO REV. CODE § 1785.04.

shares to another individual who is licensed or otherwise authorized to render the same professional service.[2] Such changes do not require reformation of the PA. The PA must, however, furnish a statement to the secretary of state each year that lists the names and addresses of all shareholders and certifies that all shareholders are licensed or otherwise authorized to practice the relevant profession in Ohio.[3]

The major disadvantages of a PA are that its earnings may be subject to two levels of taxation. Ordinarily, a corporation's earnings are subject to income tax when the income is earned by the corporation and then are taxed again when the individual shareholders receive dividends. A second disadvantage of a PA is the need to observe certain legal and operational formalities. For example, PAs must file with the secretary of state articles of incorporation, subsequent amendments, and annual reports. Annual meetings must be held for the election of officers and directors.

(B) Incorporation and Operation Procedures

MHPs who wish to incorporate may do so under the regular incorporation laws of Ohio.[4] Psychiatrists, psychologists, and registered nurses also have the option to incorporate as a professional association.[5] If the regulations of a PA conflict with those for a general corporation, then the PA requirements apply.[6]

Incorporating requires filing articles of incorporation with the secretary of state. Among other requirements, the articles must specify a name (including the words *company, corporation, incorporated,* or an abbreviation) and the purpose of the corporation, and identify an agent with a business address in the state of Ohio on whom any process, notice, or demand may be served. A PA must have one specific purpose spelled out in the articles of incorporation, and that must be to practice the relevant profession. The PA may not engage in any other business, although it may invest its funds in real estate, stocks, bonds, and so forth.

A PA may issue its stock only to licensed or otherwise legally authorized members of the relevant profession,[7] and only licensed

---

2. OHIO REV. CODE § 1785.07.
3. OHIO REV. CODE § 1785.06.
4. OHIO REV. CODE ch. 1701.
5. OHIO REV. CODE § 1785.
6. OHIO REV. CODE § 1785.08.
7. OHIO REV. CODE § 1785.05.

or supervised personnel may render mental health services within a PA.[8] This requirement does not apply to secretaries, book-keepers, and other support assistants who are not ordinarily considered to be rendering professional services for the association.[9]

(C) Liability and Accountability

Incorporating as a professional association does not alter the professional relationship of MHPs with their patients receiving services, including liability arising out of the delivery of services.[10] Directors are liable for actions they take or fail to take as directors only if their actions have been taken with deliberate intent to harm the corporation or reckless disregard for the best interests of the corporation.[11]

(D) Termination of the Professional Association

A professional association may be terminated at a predetermined date if this is specified in the articles of incorporation,[12] or it may continue until voluntarily or involuntarily terminated following the provisions of the general corporation laws of Ohio. A professional association may be voluntarily terminated by notifying the secretary of state that the association plans to dissolve. The secretary of state may dissolve the PA if it fails to file the annual report. In such instances, the secretary of state gives notice to the PA of the failure by certified mail and, if the report is not filed within 30 days, the secretary of state will cancel the articles of incorporation and give notice of the cancellation to the PA by mail. The PA whose articles have been cancelled may be reinstated by filing an application for reinstatement, together with the required annual report, and by paying a reinstatement fee of $10.[13]

---

8. Ohio Rev. Code § 1785.03.
9. Id.
10. Ohio Rev. Code § 1785.04.
11. Ohio Rev. Code § 1701.59.
12. Ohio Rev. Code § 1701.04(B).
13. Ohio Rev. Code § 1701.07.

2.3

Partnerships

A partnership is formed when two or more individuals, each of whom is a co-owner, enter into a for-profit agreement. It allows the partners to pool their resources to undertake projects that would be financially difficult for one person. However, the law may find that any joint endeavor is a partnership, whether or not the persons labeled it as such. Such a finding could result in a forced sharing of profits and debts. Thus, MHPs should be aware of this form of business whether they intentionally form a partnership or merely work in a close business relationship with other individuals that could be construed as a partnership. In Ohio, partnerships are governed by the Ohio Uniform Partnership Law.[1]

(A) Formation of a Partnership

A partnership is defined as an association of two or more people who agree to operate as co-owners of a business for profit.[2] A partnership may be formed by verbal agreement, but it is preferable to set out the rights and duties of the partners in a written partnership agreement. The agreement describes the roles and responsibilities of the partners and outlines the rules for the operation of the partnership.

---

1. OHIO REV. CODE ch. 1775.
2. OHIO REV. CODE § 1775.05.

(B) Rights and Duties Between Partners

In general, each partner is fully responsible for all liabilities of the partnership. Partnership liability is joint and several, meaning that a client may sue each partner separately or as a group. This means that each partner is potentially responsible for the full amount of damages, regardless of his or her personal activities in the partnership.

The major advantages of a partnership are tax-related. Partnerships are considered "invisible" for tax purposes; that is, income earned by them is not separately taxed but instead the income is taxed directly to the partners at their individual tax rates in a manner similar to that of a sole proprietorship.

The major disadvantage of a partnership is the unlimited liability. Each partner is personally liable for the debts, obligations, and wrongful acts of any of the partners.[3]

(C) Dissolution of a Partnership

The most common way in which a partnership is dissolved is through a change in the partners. The withdrawal or addition of a new partner results in termination of the original partnership and requires the creation of a new one.

When a partnership dissolves, several steps may be necessary to dissolve the obligations of the partnership. Dissolution includes completing transactions unfinished at dissolution, selling or distributing assets, and paying debts.[4]

---

3. OHIO REV. CODE § 1775.14.
4. OHIO REV. CODE § 1775.34.

2.4

Health Maintenance Organizations

A health maintenance organization (HMO) is a health care program in which an individual or a group pays a single fee, usually annually, to receive health care services at little or no additional cost. The services are provided by HMO employees or by professionals who contract with the organization on a fee-for-service or capitated basis. In theory, the overall costs are kept lower by limiting the organization's expenses to the prepaid amount and by centralized administration. Some states require employers with 25 or more employees to offer HMO plans. Ohio does not have such a requirement, so small employers are free to offer an HMO option or not.

(A) Benefits for Mental Health Services

Insurance coverage for mental health benefits is optional in Ohio, but there are standards in place that must be followed if a policy does provide mental health coverage. Specifically, every health insurance policy that provides coverage for inpatient mental or emotional disorders must also provide benefits for services on an outpatient basis for each eligible person under the policy that are equal to at least $550 in any 12-month period.[1]

---

1. Ohio Rev. Code § 3923.28(A).

(B) Professional Services

Mental health services may be provided by licensed physicians, including psychiatrists, and licensed psychologists in inpatient and outpatient facilities, so long as the facility is approved by the Joint Commission on Accreditation of Healthcare Organizations, the Council on Accreditation for Children and Family Services, or the Rehabilitation Accreditation Commission.[2] Outpatient benefits are subject to reasonable contract limitations, deductibles, and out-of-pocket expenses.

For services performed under the clinical supervision of a physician or psychologist to be reimbursable, the services must be performed in accordance with a treatment plan that describes the expected duration, frequency, and type of services to be performed, and the plan must be reviewed and approved by the physician or psychologist every three months.[3]

---

2. OHIO REV. CODE § 3928.28(A).
3. OHIO REV. CODE § 3923.28(E).

2.5

Preferred Provider Organizations

A preferred provider organization (PPO) comprises a group of health care providers or hospitals that contracts with employers, unions, or third-party payers (such as Blue Cross/Blue Shield) to provide services to the employees, members, or insureds for a discounted fee in return for an exclusive service arrangement. The service providers see the patients in their own offices or facilities. There is no law regulating the formation, organization, or operation of PPOs in Ohio. The law neither expressly permits nor forbids such organizations.

2.6

Individual Practice Associations

An individual practice association (IPA) is a group of health care providers who individually contract to provide health care services for an organization that provides a prepaid health plan, frequently an HMO. The members of the IPA practice independently but are compensated by the organization on a fee-for-service or fee-per-patient basis. Ohio law does not address IPAs.

2.7

Hospital, Administrative, and Staff Privileges

The law in many states governs which classes of MHPs are eligible for agency and hospital staff and administrative privileges.

(A) Agency and Administrative Positions

Ohio law provides for hospital staff membership and professional privileges, which permit medical specialists and psychologists to provide services in the hospital, within the scope of the applicant's respective license.[1]

(B) Hospital Staff Privileges

Psychologists do not have admitting privileges in Ohio;[2] only psychiatrists may admit patients to hospitals. Hospitals are not required to provide psychological services, but if psychological services are provided, then psychologists are permitted to carry them out within the scope of the psychology licensing law. Staff privileges for other MHPs are not addressed in Ohio law.

---

1. Ohio Rev. Code § 3701.351(B).
2. Id.

2.8

Zoning for Community Homes

Zoning regulations are the laws by which state and local governments guide the rate and type of growth of communities, including their residential and commercial buildings. These laws can be, and have been, used to exclude certain classes of people thought to be undesirable from particular communities or areas within communities in some states. For example, some zoning boards have prohibited community homes for people with mental disorders from locating in single-family residential neighborhoods, even though such a placement would be in the best interests of the community home residents.

In Ohio, adult family homes for three to five unrelated adults that provide supervision and personal care services to at least three of those adults for mental health and related problems (but not substance abuse problems) may be located in any residential zone, including any single-family residential zone. The facility may be required to comply with area, height, yard, and other requirements that are imposed on other residences within the zone.

Group homes, providing accommodations to 6 to 16 unrelated adults and personal care services to at least three of the unrelated adults for mental health or related problems (but not substance abuse problems) may be located in any multiple-family residential zones. The facility may be required to comply with the housing requirements established for other residences within the zone.[1]

---

1. OHIO REV. CODE § 3722.03.

Insurance Reimbursement for Services

Health insurance carriers (insurers) typically have provisions providing reimbursement for mental health services. The policies frequently limit reimbursement to certain classes of health care providers, usually physicians, and to particular types of services. Ohio law provides that insurers must reimburse psychiatrists and psychologists in certain situations. There are no laws pertaining to services by other MHPs, which means that insurers may deny claims by them or their clients if they are not specifically included in the policy.[1]

(A) Types of Insurance Affected

Ohio law mandates that every health insurance policy for sickness and accident insurance must provide coverage for services for alcoholism,[2] both inpatient and outpatient, and must provide coverage for outpatient mental health services if the policy provides any coverage for inpatient mental health services.[3] Self-insured health care plans are generally not covered by the same mandate.

1. OHIO REV. CODE § 3923.28.
2. OHIO REV. CODE § 3923.29(A).
3. OHIO REV. CODE § 3923.28(A).

(B) Required Coverage of Psychiatric Services

Ohio law mandates that every policy for sickness and accident insurance providing coverage for inpatient hospital, surgical, or medical expenses and coverage for mental or emotional disorders must also provide benefits for services for mental or emotional disorders on an outpatient basis that are equal to at least $550 per 12-month period. The services may be provided by, or under the supervision of, a physician, including a psychiatrist or a psychologist. Outpatient benefits are subject to reasonable contract limitations and reasonable deductibles and out-of-pocket payments, and providers are reimbursed at rates that are usual, customary, and reasonable. To qualify for reimbursement for mental health services, facilities must have in effect a plan for review of service utilization and a plan for review of the quality of services of its providers.[4]

Ohio law also mandates that every policy for sickness and accident insurance providing hospital, surgical, or medical expense coverage must provide outpatient, inpatient, and intermediate primary care benefits for alcoholism that are equal to at least $550 in a 12-month period. The services may be provided under the clinical supervision of physicians or psychologists. As with coverage for mental health services, coverage for services for alcoholism are subject to reasonable contract limitations and deductibles and coinsurance costs, and providers are reimbursed at rates that are usual, customary, and reasonable. Facilities must have in place a plan for utilization review and a plan for peer review.[5]

(C) Prohibiting Denial of Reimbursements for Psychological Services

If an insurance policy for accidents and sickness provides coverage for services that can be performed by a psychologist, reimbursement may not be denied for the services of a licensed

---

4. OHIO REV. CODE § 3923.28.
5. OHIO REV. CODE § 3923.29(C), (F).

psychologist who has a doctorate of psychology or has a minimum of five years clinical experience.[6]

(D) Prohibiting Denial of Reimbursements for Social Work Services

Ohio law is silent on this issue.

---

6. OHIO REV. CODE § 3923.231.

Mental Health Benefits in State Insurance Plans

In some states, the law mandates that any health insurance plan provided for state government employees must include certain mental health benefits. Ohio law does not specify which health benefits must be offered to state employees whose coverage is provided by a health insurance company. The law does, however, require that self-insured health care plans for government employees must include the following benefits:[1]

1. If the plan provides payment for the treatment of mental or nervous disorders, then the plan must provide benefits for services on an outpatient basis for each eligible employee and dependent for mental or emotional disorders, or for evaluations, that are equal to at least the following:
    a. payments are not less than $550 in a 12-month period for services delivered by a physician or psychologist in an approved facility;
    b. benefits are subject to reasonable limitations, deductibles, and out-of-pocket payment obligations;
    c. each treatment facility must have a plan for utilization review to monitor the use of, or evaluate the necessity and efficacy of, services and peer review to monitor and evaluate the effectiveness of providers;
    d. payment for benefits shall not be greater than usual, customary, and reasonable fees;
    e. services performed under the clinical supervision of a physician or psychologist must be performed in accordance with a treatment plan that describes the expected duration, frequency, and type of services to be performed, and the

---

1. OHIO REV. CODE § 3923.30.

treatment plan must be reviewed and approved by a physician or psychologist every three months. Reimbursement for mental health services performed under supervision may not be restricted to just those services described in the treatment plan.

2. Payments for benefits for alcoholism treatment are basically similar to those outlined for mental health services, except that the law is silent about payment for services provided under the supervision of physicians and psychologists.

Permanent full-time and permanent part-time employees of the state of Ohio and their dependents are eligible to participate in a health insurance plan provided for state government employees called the State Employee Health Benefit Fund. State law does not specify the benefits that must be available under this plan. Rather, the director of the fund determines the benefits, deductibles, copayments, and limitations of benefits.[2]

---

2. Ohio Admin. Code § 125-1-03.

2.11

Tax Deductions for Services

Payments for mental health services may be deductible as either an individual medical deduction or a business expense, depending on the nature of the service and the use by the recipient taxpayer.

(A) Mental Health Services as a Medical Deduction

Ohio law provides that taxpayers may take a state income tax deduction for medical expenses paid during the year, not compensated, if these expenses exceed 7.5% of the person's gross income. Costs for prescription medications are included. The medical care must be intended for the treatment of an illness.[1]

(B) Mental Health Services as a Business Deduction

Mental health services may qualify as a business deduction for federal tax purposes in very limited circumstances. If mental health services are received for educational purposes, they are deductible if the education is undertaken to maintain or improve skills for one's business. They are not deductible, however, if they

---

1. Ohio Rev. Code § 5747.01(A)(11)(b).

are undertaken to obtain a new position or to meet requirements of an unrelated business.[2]

(C) Mental Health Services Received by MHPs

Mental health services received by MHPs are deductible as a medical expense if received for treatment (see earlier section), as would be true for any other citizen who received the services.

Mental health services received by MHPs are deductible as a business expense if received for the purpose of maintaining or improving business skills (see earlier section).

---

2. Namrow v. Commissioner of Internal Revenue, 288 F.2d 648 (1961). The court held that two psychiatrists undergoing psychoanalysis to qualify to be psychoanalysts could not deduct expenses of treatment as either a business expense or a medical expense.

2.12

Limited Liability Companies

A limited liability company (LLC) may be formed under Ohio law for the purpose of rendering services.[1] Ohio has no limitations on any professional groups setting up LLCs. Its members, employees, or other agents each must be licensed to practice, under Ohio law, the services provided by the company. A LLC combines some of the features of a partnership and a corporation. The LLC allows owners to enjoy the limited liability of the corporate structure while being taxed as a partnership (or a sole proprietor if only one person forms the LLC).

(A) Formation and Operation Procedures

One or more individuals, without regard to residence, may form an LLC. An LLC is formed by signing and filing with the secretary of state articles of organization that set forth, among other things, the name and address of the company and any provisions that the members elect to set out for the regulation of the company. All members must be licensed to practice in the same field. If the articles of organization do not set a termination date for the company, its duration is perpetual.[2] The articles of organization must identify a person to contact to deliver legal documents (called an "agent for service of process").[3]

---

1. Ohio Rev. Code ch. 1705.
2. Ohio Rev. Code § 1705.04(A).
3. Ohio Rev. Code § 1705.06.

Unless otherwise specified in the operating agreement, the management of the LLC is vested in its members in proportion to their respective contributions to the capital of the company.[4]

(B) Liability and Accountability

The provisions of an LLC do not alter the professional relationship between the MHP and the person receiving services in terms of liability arising out of the relationship.[5] Members of the LLC have no personal liability for the acts and omissions of the company solely by reason of their being members, but MHPs are liable for their own personal actions.[6]

(C) Termination of the LLC

If the articles of organization do not establish an ending date for the LLC, its duration is perpetual. Nonetheless, an LLC is dissolved when any of the following events occurs: (a) an event specified in the operating agreement causes dissolution; (b) the members unanimously agree in writing to dissolve the company; (c) a member of the company withdraws, unless the operating agreement specifies that the remaining members of the company may continue it and the remaining members are in agreement to do so; or (d) a decree of judicial dissolution is filed.[7]

A dissolved LLC continues in existence until the closing of its affairs has been completed.[8]

---

4. OHIO REV. CODE § 1705.24.
5. OHIO REV. CODE § 1705.48(D).
6. OHIO REV. CODE § 1705.48.
7. OHIO REV. CODE § 1705.43.
8. OHIO REV. CODE § 1705.45.

Limitations on and Liability for Practice

3.1

Informed Consent for Services

Informed consent ordinarily must be obtained before administering services, disclosing information concerning the client to a third party, or taking any other action that has an impact on the client. The failure of mental health professionals (MHPs) to obtain consent may be considered professional misconduct by a licensing board (see chapters 1.2, Licensure and Regulation of Psychiatrists, 1.3, Licensure and Regulation of Psychiatric Nurses, 1.4, Licensure and Regulation of Psychologists, and 1.6, Licensure and Regulation of Counselors, Social Workers, and Marriage and Family Therapists) and it renders MHPs liable to a malpractice suit (see chapter 3.10, Malpractice Liability).

(A) Legal Definition of Informed Consent

The general principle of informed consent to treatment is that the professional must disclose to the client the benefits and risks inherent in the proposed treatment. How much information must be disclosed to the client is difficult to quantify, but the general rule is that material information must be shared, such that a reasonable client would be able to come to an informed decision about accepting or rejecting the proposed treatment. The MHP also must inform the client about alternatives to the proposed treatment, including the potential outcome of doing nothing. In exceptional situations, the amount and type of information that must be shared may be modified if the client's well-being would be unduly disturbed by such disclosure. Consent is not necessary in an emergency.

Ohio has not codified requirements regarding informed consent to treatment for MHPs, with the following exceptions:

1. The Board of Psychology has promulgated rules of conduct for licensed psychologists and school psychologists that specify that they must give a "truthful, understandable, and reasonably complete account of a client's condition" and "shall keep the client fully informed as to the purpose and nature of any evaluation, treatment, or other procedures, and of the client's right to freedom of choice regarding services provided."[1]

2. The Counselor, Social Worker and Marriage and Family Therapist Board specifies that licensees must inform clients about the extent and nature of services, as well as the limits, rights, opportunities, and obligations available to them.[2] Providers must use clear and understandable language to inform clients about their services, as well as the limits to the services, relevant costs, reasonable alternatives, and the client's right to refuse or withdraw consent. Providers who extend services via electronic means must inform clients of the limitations and risks associated with such services, such as threats to confidentiality.

3. Written consents to medical procedures (including psychiatric procedures) are presumed to be valid and effective if they have set forth in general terms the nature, purpose, and intent of the procedures; identified the reasonably known risks; identified the physician who will perform the procedures; and the client, or someone with legal authority for the client, signs the consent form and acknowledges that the disclosure of information has been made and all questions have been answered. These requirements do not eliminate the right of a physician to obtain the oral or implied consent of a client for a medical procedure.[3] A client's consent may be given either orally or in writing.[4]

4. For clients receiving treatment in mental hospitals, the chief clinical officer or, in a nonpublic hospital, the attending physician responsible for the client's care must provide information, including expected outcomes, to enable the client to give "a fully informed, intelligent, and knowing consent." The client also must be afforded the opportunity to consult with independent specialists and legal counsel and must be granted the right to refuse consent for several forms of treatment, including

---

1. Оніо Аdmin. Code § 4732-17-01(C)(3).
2. Оніо Аdmin. Code § 4757-5-01(B).
3. Оніо Rev. Code § 2317.54.
4. Cardinal v. Family Foot Care Centers, Inc., 40 Ohio App.3d 181, 532 N.E.2d 162 (1987).

convulsive therapy, major aversive interventions, and psycho-surgery.[5]

5. Clients who are treated for alcohol and drug addictions may not be experimented on with treatments that are not accepted as good medical practice unless they have given informed consent.[6]

6. Residents of institutions for the mentally retarded are not to be subjected to surgery, convulsive therapy, major aversive interventions, sterilization, experimental procedures, or other unusual or hazardous treatment procedures without the resident's informed consent. If the resident has been adjudicated incompetent to make such decisions, the consent must be sought from the resident's natural or court-appointed guardian.[7]

In addition, the Ohio supreme court has clarified that a lack of informed consent may be established in cases involving medical care when (a) the physician fails to inform the client about the risks and dangers inherent in the proposed treatment, (b) the unrevealed risks that should have been discussed actually materialize and are the proximate cause of an injury to the client, and (c) a reasonable person would have decided against the treatment had the risks and dangers been disclosed before the treatment.[8]

Ohio courts have not addressed the question of whether any different criteria might be appropriate for mental health care.

---

5. OHIO REV. CODE § 5122.271.
6. OHIO REV. CODE § 3793.14.
7. OHIO REV. CODE § 5123.86.
8. Nickell v. Gonzalez, 17 Ohio St. 3d 136, 477 N.E.2d 1145 (1985).

3.2

Extensiveness, Ownership, Maintenance, and Access to Records

An MHP's records are an important, required part of a practice. Because the law does not speak expressly to the issue, it is assumed that MHPs own the physical records but patients have the right to control access to them. Ohio law, however, does regulate other issues relating to a psychologist's, psychiatrist's, nurse's, counselor's, and social worker's records. It also is important to note that many insurance companies and governmental entities have their own requirements for record keeping for MHPs submitting requests for reimbursement.

Under Ohio law, a "medical record" includes any data in any form pertaining to a client's medical history and care and that is developed and maintained by a health care provider.[1] Ohio law specifies that psychiatrists, psychologists, professional clinical counselors, professional counselors, social workers, independent social workers, and social work assistants are included as health care providers for purposes of regulations regarding medical records in medical settings.[2]

Some MHP licensure boards provide guidance to licensees on record keeping. For example, the state Board of Psychology regulations provide guidance to psychologists regarding record development and maintenance (see later in this chapter).[3]

The Counselor, Social Worker and Marriage and Family Therapist Board has established a code of ethical practice that addresses record keeping.[4] The licensure laws pertaining to the other

---

1. OHIO REV. CODE § 3701.74(A).
2. OHIO REV. CODE §§ 3701.74; 3729.01, 4769.01.
3. OHIO ADMIN. CODE § 4732-17-01(B)(6).
4. OHIO ADMIN. CODE § 4757-5-01(I).

MHPs are silent regarding development and maintenance of client records.

Agencies may develop their own record-keeping standards, often guided by third-party payers, and MHPs are also subject to these standards.

(A) Extensiveness of Records

The law in Ohio does not specify the medium in which records must be kept, although the administrative code sections for counselors and social workers[5] and for psychologists and school psychologists[6] make it clear that their records may be kept in electronic or other formats. As a consequence, it would appear to be appropriate to store records either in paper form or in electronic or microfilm media, or both.

Licensure laws pertaining to some MHPs have specific requirements that address the content of records. The law specifies that records of psychologists and school psychologists must include a summary of the presenting problem, the dates and purpose of each client contact, the fee arrangement, test data and other evaluative results and accompanying reports, notations about formal contacts with other providers, and authorizations by the client for release of information.[7]

The administrative code section for counselors and social workers specifies that each client's record must contain information about dates of service, types of services, and termination of services, as well as billing information.[8]

(B) Maintenance of Records

Psychologists and school psychologists are required to maintain their records for a period of not fewer than five years after the last date of service. A summary of the record, or the full record, must then be kept for not fewer than seven additional years after the last date of service, for a total of 12 years. The law also specifies that records must be kept longer if other provisions require it, such as might be found in contracts with insurance companies or the regulations of state or federal funding agencies. Furthermore,

---

5. OHIO ADMIN. CODE § 4757-5(B).
6. OHIO ADMIN. CODE § 4732-17-01(B)(6)(c).
7. OHIO ADMIN. CODE § 4732-17-01(B).
8. OHIO ADMIN. CODE § 4757-5-01(I).

records are to be stored and disposed of in ways that ensure their confidentiality. Each licensee must report to the Board of Psychology on the biennial renewal form the name and telephone number of a person who is knowledgeable about the psychologist's records in the event of the licensee's absence, emergency, or death.[9]

Counselors, social workers, and marriage and family therapists are required to maintain their records for five years after the last contact with the client.[10]

Licensure law does not specify how long physicians, including psychiatrists, must keep their mental health records. Nonetheless, licensed health care facilities must maintain medical records for at least six years from the date of discharge.[11]

Practitioners who practice in institutions or agencies also must follow the requirements of the setting in which they are employed. Similarly, practitioners may agree by contract to maintain records for periods of time specified by preferred provider plans (see chapter 2.5, Preferred Provider Organizations) and health maintenance organizations (see chapter 2.4, Health Maintenance Organizations).

(C) Client Access

Effective April 2003, clients of all MHPs have broad access to their health records.[12] The law states that a client or the client's representative may, on submitting a written request, examine or obtain a copy of his or her medical record. Physicians, including psychiatrists, and chiropractors who determine that disclosure of the record is likely to have an adverse effect on the client, may provide the record to another physician or chiropractor designated by the client. That provider may then determine whether to share the record with the client. The law is silent on whether the client has any additional recourse if the second provider determines that sharing the record with the client would have an adverse effect, and no court cases have as yet provided clarification. No right to have the record provided to another provider is granted in the law for clients of any other MHPs. This law overrides all contrary ethical rules that have been approved by the MHP licensing boards.

---

9. OHIO ADMIN. CODE § 4732-17-01(B).
10. OHIO ADMIN. CODE § 4757-5-01(I).
11. OHIO ADMIN. CODE § 3701-83-11(E).
12. OHIO REV. CODE § 3701.74(B).

If the licensee does not provide a record as requested, the client or the client's representative may bring a civil action to enforce the client's right of access.[13]

This right of client access does not apply to medical records whose release is covered by federal regulations for protection of alcohol and drug abuse client records,[14] records of clients in nursing homes and residential care facilities,[15] records of patients in mental hospitals or who receive care in public community mental health centers,[16] or records created by quality assurance and utilization committees[17] and peer review committees.[18]

(D) Access by Regulatory Departments and Boards

The law specifies that records of hospitalized clients are confidential and not to be released without the client's consent except under the following conditions:

1. in response to a court order;

2. to obtain reimbursement from an insurer;

3. to share information with other inpatient and outpatient agencies within the Department of Mental Health and with the Board of Alcohol, Drug Addiction, and Mental Health Services;

4. to ensure continuity of care for inmates who are also receiving mental health services from the Department of Rehabilitation and Correction;[19] and

5. for purposes of quality assurance review, conducted by the facility to ensure that services are appropriate and effective.[20]

The medical records of a client may be reviewed by a representative of the office of the state long-term care ombudsman program, which is empowered to investigate complaints about client care. Ordinarily, the client's consent, or that of the client's guardian or legal representative, would be obtained for such an investigation. However, a representative of the ombudsman program may access the records without the client's consent in instances such

13. Оню Rev. Code § 3701.74(C).
14. Оню Rev. Code § 3701.74(D); see 42 C.F.R. pt. 2; 42 C.F.R. § 483.10.
15. Оню Rev. Code § 3721.13.
16. Оню Rev. Code ch. 5122.
17. Оню Rev. Code § 2305.24.
18. Оню Rev. Code § 2305.25.
19. Оню Rev. Code § 5122.31.
20. Оню Rev. Code § 5122.32.

as when the client has not refused access to the records but is not able to consent and there is no legal representative or guardian available or when the ombudsman representative has reason to believe the guardian or legal representative is not acting in the best interests of the client.[21]

Licensure boards for MHPs may access client records in response to a complaint against the practitioner (see chapters 1.2, Licensure and Regulation of Psychiatrists, 1.3, Licensure and Regulation of Psychiatric Nurses, 1.4, Licensure and Regulation of Psychologists, and 1.6, Licensure and Regulation of Counselors, Social Workers, and Marriage and Family Therapists).

(E) Hospital Utilization Review

Client records made available for hospital utilization review purposes, such as to review medical necessity and effectiveness of treatments, are confidential and are to be used by the hospital committee and its members only for utilization review purposes.[22]

Records created by review committees also are confidential and are not subject to inquiry, review, or other use in civil actions against a provider, a hospital, or related groups. Committee members are protected from testifying in any civil action about any information disclosed in the review process,[23] except that a federal district court in Ohio has ruled that confidentiality must give way in federal court to claims involving gender discrimination.[24]

Records created for quality assurance purposes likewise are confidential. Information may not be released except to authorized employees of the Department of Mental Health and to accrediting and licensing agencies or organizations.[25]

(F) Liability for Violation

If a health care provider fails to release a medical record at the request of a client, the client may bring a civil suit to enforce the client's right of access to the record.[26]

---

21. OHIO REV. CODE § 173.20.
22. OHIO REV. CODE § 2305.24.
23. OHIO REV. CODE § 2305.251.
24. LeMasters v. Christ Hospital, 791 F. Supp. 188 (S.D. Ohio 1991).
25. OHIO REV. CODE § 5122.32(E).
26. OHIO REV. CODE § 3701.74.

Members of hospital utilization committees are subject to civil suits for misuse of confidential information in the same way as attending physicians are subject to civil suits from their clients.[27]

MHPs who fail to maintain appropriate records or who breach confidentiality of those records may be subject to civil suits and licensure board complaints (see chapters 1.2, Licensure and Regulation of Psychiatrists, 1.3, Licensure and Regulation of Psychiatric Nurses, 1.4, Licensure and Regulation of Psychologists, and 1.6, Licensure and Regulation of Counselors, Social Workers, and Marriage and Family Therapists).

---

27. OHIO REV. CODE § 2305.24.

3.3

Confidential Relations and Communications

In general, a confidential communication is written or verbal information conveyed by the client to an MHP in the course of a professional relationship. Confidentiality originated in professional ethics codes arising from a belief that effective psychotherapy requires a guarantee from the therapist that no information obtained in the course of evaluation or treatment will be given to others. MHPs may be liable in civil suits initiated by clients who have been harmed by breaches of confidentiality (see chapter 3.10, Malpractice Liability).

Ohio courts have underscored the importance of protecting the confidentiality of mental health records. For example, the Ohio supreme court has recognized that citizens are more likely to avail themselves of mental health care when they are confident that their communications will be kept confidential.[1] Many of the supreme court's decisions addressing confidentiality have done so in the context of balancing the need for confidentiality of records with the need to breach confidentiality when a client poses an imminent threat to another person (see next section in this chapter).

An appellate case is instructive in understanding the importance of maintaining client confidentiality. In this case,[2] a young woman consulted her physician. The physician informed the client that she was pregnant and discussed with her the options she could follow, including the possibility of an abortion. Following this consultation, the physician instructed one of his nurses to

---

1. Littleton v. Good Samaritan Hosp. & Health Center, 39 Ohio St. 3d 36, 529 N.E.2d 449 (1988); Estates of Morgan et al. v. Fairfield Family Counseling Center, 77 Ohio St. 3d 284, 673 N.E.2d 1311 (1997).
2. Hobbs v. Lopez et al., 96 Ohio App.3d 670, 645 N.E.2d 1261 (1994).

call the client to find out what course of treatment she had decided to follow. The nurse called the client's parent's home and told the client's mother about her daughter's pregnancy and that she had consulted the physician about an abortion. The client later sued the physician and the nurse, alleging invasion of privacy, breach of privilege, and infliction of emotional distress. The appellate court followed the standard that a district court[3] had established, namely that (a) private information was made public; (b) the facts disclosed must be about the private life of an individual, not his or her public life; (c) the matter must be one that would be regarded as highly offensive and objectionable to a reasonable person of ordinary sensibilities; (d) the disclosure of private information must have been made intentionally, not negligently; and (e) the publicized information must not be a legitimate concern to the public. The court concluded that the nurse's disclosure of information to the client's mother rose to the level of outrageous conduct sufficient to find intentional infliction of emotional distress.

In 1999, the Ohio supreme court established a new tort regarding the unauthorized release of medical information. In this case,[4] a hospital turned over many of its medical records to its outside attorney to identify clients who might qualify for Social Security Supplemental Security Income (SSI) benefits. The attorney reviewed the files, contacted potentially eligible clients, informed them of this opportunity, and offered to assist them in completing the application. SSI eligibility would provide a means for the hospital to receive payment for services that it would otherwise have to write off as uncollectable accounts. The court concluded that, in the absence of previous authorization by the client, a physician or hospital may disclose confidential information only in special situations in which disclosure is mandated by law or in which disclosure is necessary to protect or further another countervailing interest that outweighs the client's interests in confidentiality. Sharing confidential patient information for the purpose of alerting a small portion of the clients to a possible payment option was not a sufficient countervailing interest.

(A) Duty to Protect or Warn

The law provides that an MHP or a mental health organization may be held liable for serious physical harm or death to third

---

3. Killilea v. Sears, Roebuck & Co., 27 Ohio App.3d 163, 499 N.E.2d 1291 (1985).
4. Biddle v. Warren General Hosp., 86 Ohio St. 3d 395 (1999).

parties resulting from failing to warn or protect from the violent behavior of a mental health patient. However, there is liability only if the patient or a knowledgeable person has communicated to the professional an explicit threat about inflicting imminent and serious physical harm or death to a clearly identifiable victim, the professional or organization has reason to believe that the patient has the intent and ability to carry out the threat, and the professional or organization does *not*:[5]

1. initiate efforts to hospitalize the patient on an emergency basis;

2. have the patient involuntarily or voluntarily hospitalized;

3. develop a written treatment plan that is reasonably calculated to eliminate the possibility that the patient will carry out the threat. The professional also must obtain a second-opinion risk assessment either by the clinical director of the agency or, if in private practice, by another independently licensed mental health professional who is engaged in private practice; or

4. communicate to a law enforcement agency where either the victim or the mental health patient lives and, if possible, communicate to each potential victim information about the identity of the patient making the threat, the identity of each potential victim, and the nature of the threat.

The professional must consider each of these four options and document the reasons for choosing or rejecting each option. Special consideration must be given to those options that would least abridge the rights of the patient. The professional is not required to take an action that would physically endanger the professional or organization, increase the danger to a potential victim, or increase the danger to the patient.[6]

Practitioners subject to this law should review the law in detail when confronted with a potential duty to warn of a situation and consult with their legal counsel.

(B) Psychologists

(B)(1) Psychologists Covered Under These Statutes

The law's provisions for psychologists and school psychologists are identical.[7]

---

5. OHIO REV. CODE § 2305.51(B).
6. OHIO REV. CODE § 2305.51(C).
7. OHIO REV. CODE § 4732.17.

(B)(2) Scope of the Duty

Confidential information includes information revealed by a client or otherwise obtained by a psychologist or school psychologist when there was a reasonable expectation that it was revealed for the purpose of the professional relationship. Such information may not be disclosed without the informed, written consent of the client.[8] Confidentiality continues indefinitely after the professional relationship has ended. The psychologist or school psychologist may share confidential information with other members of a treatment team, but the professional is obligated to clarify to all parties the dimensions of confidentiality. Observation and recording of sessions may not be done without the client's consent. Client information that is used for teaching and research must be appropriately disguised to prevent client identification. In instances of third-party referral, the psychologist and school psychologist must clarify with the client whether information will be shared with the referral source or others. Psychologists and school psychologists must inform clients at the beginning of services of the limitations to confidentiality.[9]

Ohio law specifically exempts psychologists and school psychologists from the general requirement of reporting that a felony has been or is being committed, if the information is gained in the context of a professional relationship.[10] On the other hand, this law permits, but does not require, psychologists and school psychologists to report a felony. If they do make a report, the statute provides them immunity from being sued for breach of privilege (see chapter 3.4, Privileged Communications) or confidentiality.

(B)(3) Limitations on the Duty

The *Ohio Administrative Code*[11] specifies that confidential information may be disclosed by psychologists and school psychologists without the consent of the client in the following circumstances:

1. the client, the client's guardian, or the executor of the client's estate files a legal claim against the psychologist or school psychologist;

2. the psychologist or school psychologist determines that disclosure is necessary to protect against a clear and substantial risk of imminent serious harm to the client or a third party (see earlier section);

---

8. OHIO ADMIN. CODE § 4732-17-01(G)(2)(d).
9. OHIO ADMIN. CODE § 4732-17-01(G).
10. *Id.*
11. OHIO ADMIN. CODE § 4732-17-01(G).

3. the psychologist or school psychologist is served with a court order or is subject to state or federal laws that override confidentiality provisions;

4. the psychologist or school psychologist fulfills the legal obligation to report child abuse[12] (see chapter 4.8, Reporting of Child Abuse, for exceptions) and elder abuse[13] (see chapter 4.7, Reporting of Adult Abuse); or

5. the psychologist or school psychologist contracts with a debt collection agency to collect outstanding fees from the client or former client.

Psychologists and school psychologists are obligated to document in the client's record information about the professional's knowledge or belief that the client has been the victim of domestic violence. This information is not protected by privileged communication rules (see chapter 3.4, Privileged Communications).[14]

(C) Counselors, Social Workers, and Marriage and Family Therapists

(C)(1) Counselors, Social Workers, and Marriage and Family Therapists Covered Under These Laws

The statute and regulations are applicable to all professional clinical counselors, professional counselors, independent social workers, social workers, social work assistants, and marriage and family therapists.[15] (Note that the *Ohio Administrative Code* has not yet been written for marriage and family therapists at the time of this writing.)

(C)(2) Scope of the Duty

Licensees have a "primary obligation" to protect their clients' right to confidentiality. Confidential information may be released to others only with the client's written consent or that of other legally authorized individuals.[16]

(C)(3) Limitations on the Duty

The *Ohio Administrative Code*[17] specifies that counselors and social workers may release confidential client information when failure

---

12. Ohio Rev. Code § 2151.521(A).
13. Ohio Rev. Code § 5101.61(A).
14. Ohio Rev. Code § 2921.22(F).
15. Ohio Rev. Code § 4757.11.
16. Ohio Admin. Code § 4757-5-01(B).
17. Ohio Admin. Code § 4757-5-01(B).

to do so would violate other laws or result in imminent danger to the client or others (see earlier section).

Counselors, social workers, and marriage and family therapists are not exempted, as are physicians and psychologists, from mandatory reporting to law enforcement authorities information about current or past felonies of their clients, except if the information is obtained while working for a program that provides counseling services in drug treatment facilities or in programs established to provide counseling to crime victims or victims of sexual assault.[18]

Counselors, social workers, and marriage and family therapists are obligated to document in the client's record information about the professional's knowledge or belief that the client has been the victim of domestic violence. This information is not protected by privileged communication rules (see chapter 3.4, Privileged Communications).[19]

Counselors, social workers, and marriage and family therapists are mandated reporters of child abuse[20] (see chapter 4.8, Reporting of Child Abuse) and elder abuse[21] (see chapter 4.7, Reporting of Adult Abuse).

(D) Psychiatrists

(D)(1) Psychiatrists Covered Under These Statutes

All physicians, including psychiatrists, are covered under the confidentiality laws.

(D)(2) Scope of the Duty

Ohio law is silent regarding the requirement of physicians, including psychiatrists, to maintain confidentiality, except that the licensing law for physicians states that physicians can be disciplined for willfully betraying a professional confidence.[22]

Psychiatrists are specifically exempted from reporting that a felony is being, or has been, committed when that information was obtained in a professional relationship.[23] On the other hand, this law permits, but does not require, physicians to report a felony. If they do make a report, the statute provides them immunity from being sued for breach of privilege or confidentiality.

---

18. Ohio Rev. Code § 2921.22(G)(5), (6).
19. Ohio Rev. Code § 2921.22(F).
20. Ohio Rev. Code § 2151.421(A).
21. Ohio Rev. Code § 5101.61(A).
22. Ohio Rev. Code § 4731.22(B)(4).
23. Ohio Rev. Code § 2921.22(G).

The *Ohio Revised Code* does not address the issue of a duty to report future felonies, but refer to the previous section in this chapter on the duty to protect or warn.

(D)(3) Limitations on the Duty

Psychiatrists are obligated to document in the client's record the professional's knowledge or belief that the client has been the victim of domestic violence. This information is not protected by privileged communication rules (see chapter 3.4, Privileged Communications).[24]

Physicians are required to make a report to a client's public transportation employer when the physician knows that the employee is abusing nonprescription drugs or has a condition that poses a potential risk of harm to passengers.[25]

Psychiatrists are mandated reporters of child abuse, but they are not required to make a report if the communication is privileged unless the patient, at the time of the communication, is either a child under 18 years of age or a physically or mentally handicapped person under age 21[26] (see chapter 4.8, Reporting of Child Abuse). Physicians also are mandated reporters of elder abuse[27] (see chapter 4.7, Reporting of Adult Abuse).

(E) Nurses

(E)(1) Nurses Covered Under These Statutes

Covered under various sections of this statute are licensed practical nurses, registered nurses, and registered nurses who have earned advanced credentials as advanced practice nurses, certified nurse practitioners, and clinical nurse specialists.

(E)(2) Scope of the Duty

Licensed practical nurses are required to document their nursing assessments and observations about the care being delivered to clients and the client's response to that care.[28] Licensed practical nurses are specifically required to document when they do not follow the directions from a prescribing practitioner in administering a medication or treatment to a client, and they must document that the practitioner was notified of the decision.[29] Licensed practi-

---

24. OHIO REV. CODE § 2921.22(F).
25. OHIO REV. CODE § 2305.33.
26. OHIO REV. CODE § 2151.421(A).
27. OHIO REV. CODE § 5101.61(A).
28. OHIO ADMIN. CODE § 4723-4-06(E).
29. OHIO ADMIN. CODE § 4723-4-04(F).

cal nurses are required to maintain client confidentiality, except that they may share client information with other members of the health care team.[30]

Registered nurses, including those with advanced credentials, are required to document their nursing assessments of client care and the response of the client to that care.[31]

Nurses are specifically exempted from reporting that a felony is being, or has been, committed when that information has been obtained in a professional relationship.[32]

(E)(3) Limitations on the Duty

Licensed practical nurses may not release information without a valid consent by the client, unless acting in accordance with "an authorized law, rule or other recognized legal authority."[33]

Registered nurses, including those with advanced credentials, are expected to share client information with other members of the health care team.[34]

Nurses are obligated to document in the client's record information about the professional's knowledge or belief that the client has been the victim of domestic violence. This information is not protected by privileged communication rules (see chapter 3.4, Privileged Communications).[35]

All nurses are mandated reporters of child abuse[36] (see chapter 4.8, Reporting of Child Abuse) and of elder abuse[37] (see chapter 4.7, Reporting of Adult Abuse).

(F) Liability for Breach of Confidentiality

MHPs may be civilly liable for breaching confidentiality. That is, clients may sue their MHPs for negligence in civil court. In addition, licensure boards may limit, revoke, or suspend a professional's license to practice, refuse to license or relicense a professional, or reprimand or place on probation an MHP who breaches confidentiality.

---

30. OHIO ADMIN. CODE § 4723-4-04(H).
31. OHIO ADMIN. CODE § 4723-4-07(A).
32. OHIO REV. CODE § 2921.22(G).
33. OHIO ADMIN. CODE § 4723-4-04(I).
34. OHIO ADMIN. CODE § 4723-4-07(A).
35. OHIO REV. CODE § 2921.22(F).
36. OHIO REV. CODE § 2151.421(A).
37. OHIO REV. CODE § 5101.61(A).

3.4

Privileged
Communications

Two primary areas of law attempt to protect the client's communications from disclosure. The most well known is confidentiality
law, whose principles originated in professional ethics codes and
have now been incorporated in legislation and court rulings (see
chapter 3.3, Confidential Relations and Communications). Confidentiality law is designed to encourage frank discussion and the
exchange of reliable information and protects the client from improper disclosure of information by the MHP in most situations.
It does not, however, protect the client from court orders requiring the MHP to disclose information. For protection in the courtroom, the communications must be covered under a privileged
communication statute, also known as the testimonial privilege.
Psychologists, psychiatrists, nurses, counselors, social workers,
and marriage and family therapists must be knowledgeable about
this aspect of law so that they can advise their clients of the limits
of confidential information. There are no privileged communication laws for MHPs other than those described; therefore, clients'
disclosures can be revealed in a court hearing if the MHP is
required to testify.

The privileges, assertion and waiver of privileges and limitations on the scope of the privileges are discussed together for
psychologists, school psychologists, and psychiatrists, whose
privilege is identical, and for counselors, social workers, and marriage and family therapists, who also have identical privilege
provisions. This chapter concludes with a discussion of the general liability of mental health professionals for violation of privileged communication statutes.

(A) Psychiatrists and Psychologists

(A)(1) Privilege for Physicians and Psychologists

Psychologists and school psychologists are covered under the same provisions as those created for physicians, including psychiatrists.

In general, privileged communications are those statements made by clients in a professional relationship in which the client consulted the practitioner for diagnosis and treatment. The term "communication" refers to acquiring, recording, or transmitting information concerning facts, opinions, or statements necessary to enable a physician or psychologist to diagnose, treat, prescribe, or act for a patient. "Communications" also include medical charts, letters, memos, laboratory test results, x-rays, photographs, financial statements, diagnoses, and prognoses.[1] The privilege applies only when a client consults a practitioner for diagnosis or treatment and does not extend to situations in which a practitioner is hired to render an opinion in preparation for litigation[2] or the client sought out the practitioner to commit fraud.[3]

In some states, the privilege only applies when the patient sought treatment or evaluation on a voluntary basis. The privilege does not apply in those states when treatment or evaluations are court-ordered. Ohio courts have taken a different direction on this issue. A recent decision by the Ohio supreme court established that the privilege may apply when the treatment was provided in response to a court order.[4] In this case, the court determined that a mother could assert the privilege after she had been ordered by the court to enter treatment as part of a family reunification plan. In a related case, an appellate court ruled that whether mental health treatment or evaluation was sought under voluntary or involuntary circumstances was not a controlling factor; what was important was whether an exception or waiver for the privilege had been invoked by the patient.[5]

---

1. OHIO REV. CODE § 2317.02(B)(4).
2. State v. Fears, 86 Ohio St. 3d 329, 715 N.E.2d 136 (Ohio 1999); In re Jones, 99 Ohio St. 3d, 790 N.E.2d 321 (Ohio 2003).
3. State v. Spencer, 126 Ohio App.3d 335, 710 N.E.2d 352 (Ohio App. 8th Dist. 1998).
4. In re Wieland, 89 Ohio St. 3d 535, 733 N.E.2d 1127 (2000).
5. In re Kyle, No. 2000-P-0014, LEXIS 5619 (Ohio App. 11th Dist. 2000).

(A)(2) Assertion and Waiver of the Privilege

The privilege is intended to encourage open sharing of information by the client and to prevent disclosure of this information to others. As a consequence, the client, not the professional, holds and may assert the privilege.[6] Only the client may waive the privilege or request the professional to testify.[7] An appellate court has concluded that a defendant practitioner could not invoke the client's privilege to shield himself from prosecution.[8]

(A)(3) Limitations on the Scope of the Privilege

The privilege applies to civil actions. The privilege does not apply in the following instances:

1. the patient or legal representative gives consent;
2. if the patient is deceased, the spouse or the executor of the estate gives consent;
3. criminal action concerning test results regarding the presence of alcohol or a drug of abuse in the client relevant to a criminal charge;[9]
4. the client sues the practitioner in either a civil or criminal proceeding;[10]
5. the MHP believes the client is an imminent threat to self or others (see chapter 3.3, Confidential Relations and Communications);[11]
6. the information regards the fact that the practitioner was consulted by a person on a particular date;[12]
7. involuntary commitment proceedings are involved,[13] except a recent district appeals court concluded that, because there was a physician–patient relationship involved (despite the involuntary commitment), the psychiatrist could not testify because the patient had not waived the privilege, there is no legislative exception for commitment hearings, and the attorney for the county mental health board that sought the involuntary commitment conceded that the testimony of the treating psychiatrist was privileged. In upholding the privilege in this case,

---

6. OHIO ADMIN. CODE § 4732-17-01(G)(f)(2).
7. OHIO REV. CODE § 217.02(B).
8. State v. McGriff, 109 Ohio App.3d 668, 672 N.E.2d 1074 (1996).
9. OHIO REV. CODE § 2317.02(B)(1)(b).
10. OHIO REV. CODE § 2317.02(B).
11. OHIO REV. CODE § 2305.51.
12. Jenkins v. Metropolitan Life Ins. Co., 171 Ohio St. 557, 173 N.E.2d 122 (1961).
13. OHIO REV. CODE ch. 5122, and implemented in In re Winstead, 67 Ohio App.2d 111, 425 N.E.2d 943 (1980).

the court encouraged the county mental health board to work with the probate court to develop a protocol for using independent evaluators rather than confronting the question of privilege in cases of involuntary commitment;[14] and

8. a criminal action is brought against the MHP and patients' records related to the action against the MHP are obtained by subpoena, search warrant, or other lawful means.

The statute providing the privilege runs counter to the common law principle established by the courts that all information should be made available to the courts. Therefore, the statute usually is strictly construed. Practitioners who are not specifically identified in the statute may be excluded.[15] For example, an appellate court has ruled that the physician–patient privilege does not apply to chiropractors.[16] Neither the statute nor case law have specified whether the protection is extended to the clients of unlicensed employees and supervisees of psychologists or physicians, but the state attorney general has opined that the protection is extended, similar to the extension that applies to the clerks and other assistants of an attorney.[17] The privilege also has been extended to registered nurses who are working under the supervision of physicians as extenders of the physicians' efforts to treat and diagnose a patient.[18] However, communications made directly by a patient to a nurse, in the performance of his or her hospital duties, are not privileged.[19]

(B) Counselors, Social Workers, Marriage and Family Therapists, and School Guidance Counselors

Counselors, social workers, marriage and family therapists, and school guidance counselors are covered under the same statute.

---

14. In re Angela Washington, 2002 Ohio 2570 (Ohio App.2d Dist., 2002).
15. Mohan J. Durve, M.D., Inc. v. Oker, 112 Ohio App.3d 432, 679 N.E.2d 19 (1996).
16. In re Polen, 108 Ohio App.3d 305, 670 N.E.2d 572 (1996).
17. 1988 Ohio Op. Att'y Gen. No. 88-027, 1988 WL 428809. (Attorney general opinions are not binding on the courts.)
18. Cleveland v. Haffey, 94 Ohio Misc.2d 79, 703 N.E.2d 380 (1998); State v. Napier, No. C-970383, LEXIS 3959 (Ohio App. 1st Dist. 1998).
19. Johnston v. Miami Valley Hospital, 61 Ohio App.3d 81, 572 N.E.2d 169 (1989).

(B)(1) Privilege for Counselors, Social Workers, Marriage and Family Therapists, and School Guidance Counselors

These MHPs may not testify concerning confidential communications received from the client in the context of a professional relationship or concerning the MHP's advice to the client.[20] The privilege applies whether treatment is sought on a voluntary basis or is ordered by a court.[21]

(B)(2) Assertion and Waiver of the Privilege

The client holds the privilege and is the only person who may waive the privilege or request the professional to testify.[22]

(B)(3) Limitations on the Scope of the Privilege

The privilege does not apply when the client gives consent to the testimony or voluntarily testifies or if the professional believes the client is a clear and present danger to self or others (see chapter 3.3, Confidential Relations and Communications), including information about past or present child abuse,[23] or if a court determines in an *in camera* (i.e., private) review that the information communicated by the client is not relevant to the professional relationship.[24] A school guidance counselor may be required to testify in a legal action brought against a school, its administration, or any of its personnel if a court rules after an *in camera* review that the testimony of the school guidance counselor is relevant to the action.[25]

Of concern to many MHPs is whether privilege would apply in instances of marital counseling, when one partner later requests the MHP to testify regarding the contents of counseling but the other partner objects. One appellate court[26] has addressed that issue. In *Eichenberger v. Eichenberger*, the counselor requested that he not be required to testify because one spouse had not waived the privilege, although the other had. The court concluded that courts should seriously consider the good faith assertions of MHPs on the subject of privilege, and the counselor was not required to testify.

---

20. Ohio Rev. Code § 2317.02(G)(1).
21. In re Wieland, 89 Ohio St. 3d 535, 733 N.E.2d 1127 (2000).
22. Ohio Rev. Code § 2317.02(G).
23. *Id.*
24. *Id.*
25. Ohio Rev. Code § 2317.02(G)(f).
26. Eichenberger v. Eichenberger, 82 Ohio App.3d 809, 613 N.E.2d 678 (1992).

(C) Liability for Violation

MHPs who disclose confidential information about their clients without authorization may be subject to both civil action and discipline by their respective licensure boards (see chapters 1.2, Licensure and Regulation of Psychiatrists, 1.3, Licensure and Regulation of Psychiatric Nurses, 1.4, Licensure and Regulation of Psychologists, and 1.6, Licensure and Regulation of Counselors, Social Workers, and Marriage and Family Therapists).

3.5

Search, Seizure, and Subpoena of Records

The search of an MHP's office and seizure of any records may occur within the context of a criminal investigation of the MHP or the client. The discussion in this chapter is limited to the latter situation. If a party, during a civil or criminal action, demands information from an MHP that was obtained during the course of a professional relationship with the client, the request usually will come via a subpoena. Searches and subpoenas are both important to MHPs because they provide major exceptions to confidentiality (see chapter 3.3, Confidential Relations and Communications) and privileged communication law (see chapter 3.4, Privileged Communications). However, the seizure of records does not necessarily mean that they will ultimately be admissible in court. That determination will be made by the court at trial. The same is true for information requested via a subpoena.

(A) Search and Seizure

The Fourth Amendment of the U.S. Constitution prohibits unreasonable searches and seizures. Although the courts have recognized a number of exceptions, the general rule is that searches and seizures are not permitted unless authorized by a judge or magistrate. A search warrant may be authorized when the judge or magistrate is satisfied that there is "probable cause" that a crime has been committed and that evidence is concealed at the place or on the person in question. The warrant must identify the property to be seized or the person to be searched.[1]

---

1. Ohio Rev. Code § 2933.23.

When the warrant has been issued, it is to be given to a law enforcement officer or other authorized individual. The warrant must describe the facts alleged in the request for the warrant and identity the property to be searched for and seized, the place to be searched, and the person to be searched. The search and seizure are to be exercised in the daytime, unless there is necessity for a nighttime search, which must then be ordered. The officer must return the warrant within three days to the judge or magistrate identified on the warrant.[2]

The officer must provide to the person from whom items are taken an inventory of all property taken from the premises. The inventory is to be taken in the presence of the applicant for the warrant and the person from whose possession or premises the property was taken or, if the owner is not available, in the presence of at least one person other than the applicant.[3]

The law enforcement officer may, if necessary, enter a premise without authorization of the owner or individuals occupying the premises, except that the warrant also may specify a waiver for nonconsensual entry[4] if such entry would pose unacceptable risks to the officer.

When MHPs receive a search warrant, they are obligated to comply with its terms or be held in contempt of court. Individuals found to be in contempt of court may be fined or placed in jail, primarily as a way of coercing the person to provide the items identified in the warrant.[5] Confidentiality and privileged communications provisions do not in this case protect client records or the property of the MHP (see chapters 3.3, Confidential Relations and Communications, and 3.4, Privileged Communications).

(B) Subpoena

A subpoena is a request for information or testimony, issued by the clerk of a court or an attorney in a civil lawsuit or criminal prosecution.[6] A subpoena must state the court from which it is issued, the title of the legal action that gives rise to the subpoena, and the documents or individuals who are subject to the request. The subpoena may require that documents be presented or that a person attend and give testimony. A subpoena may be obtained

---

2. OHIO REV. CODE § 2933.24.
3. OHIO REV. CODE § 2933.241.
4. OHIO REV. CODE § 2923.231.
5. OHIO R. EVID. 101.
6. OHIO R. CRIM. P. 17.

on the signature of a clerk of a court or of an attorney on behalf of a court in which the legal action is pending.[7]

A subpoena may be served by a sheriff, coroner, clerk of court, constable, attorney, or any person designated by order of the court. Service of the subpoena must be made to the person (by paper copy or reading) or by leaving it at the person's usual place of residence. Service must include making available on demand the fees for one day's attendance in court and the mileage allowed by law.

MHPs who receive a subpoena must respond to the request at the time and place specified in the subpoena, either by producing the required documents or testifying as requested or by objecting to the subpoena. For example, MHPs should object to producing requested items or testimony if the items or testimony are protected by privilege. Such an objection should be specific with regard to the privilege and the documents and communications that are involved, so that the demanding party is able to contest the objection. The court will then determine whether the privilege applies or the request is valid. If the court determines that the request for information or testimony is appropriate, it will issue an order requiring the information.

Failure to respond to a subpoena may be deemed a contempt of court[8] and the MHP may be fined or placed in jail, primarily to coerce the MHP into complying with the court order.[9]

---

7. Ohio R. Civ. P. 45.
8. Ohio R. Civ. P. 45(E).
9. Ohio R. Evid. 101.

3.6

State Freedom of Information Act

Ohio's freedom of information law[1] permits citizens to access public records in the custody of public officials. The term *public record* is defined broadly, and any record is public and subject to disclosure unless expressly excepted.[2] Certain information is excluded from this act, including medical records[3] and quality assurance and peer review records of hospitalized clients.[4]

Public records are to be stored in a manner that facilitates public access. The law does not specify that requests for records must be made in writing, but it does specify that public records are to be promptly prepared and made available for inspection during regular working hours. Public offices may develop policies and procedures that they will follow in transmitting public records.[5] Copies of records are available at cost.[6]

If a person believes he or she has been inappropriately blocked from access to public records, that person may initiate legal action to obtain a judgment that orders the public office to comply with the law.[7]

---

1. OHIO REV. CODE § 149.43.
2. State ex rel. Toledo Blade Co. v. Telb, 50 Ohio Misc.2d 1, 552 N.E.2d 243 (1990).
3. OHIO REV. CODE § 149.43(A)(1)(a).
4. OHIO REV. CODE § 5122.32(B).
5. OHIO REV. CODE § 149.43(B)(3).
6. OHIO REV. CODE § 149.43(B)(1).
7. OHIO REV. CODE § 149.43(C).

3.7

Right to Refuse Treatment

People who have the capacity to seek voluntary treatment have, by definition, the capacity to refuse such treatment (see chapter 3.1, Informed Consent for Services). However, the right of involuntarily committed clients to refuse treatment has not always been recognized.

Ohio law recognizes the right of clients to refuse treatment.[1] Mentally ill clients may not be subjected to surgery, convulsive therapy, major aversive interventions, sterilization, any unusually hazardous treatment procedures, or psychosurgery unless the client's informed consent is obtained. Court approval is required for clients who have been declared legally incompetent.

The Ohio supreme court has provided some clarity on involuntarily committed clients' rights to refuse medication.[2] The court has ruled that, when an involuntarily committed mentally ill client poses an imminent threat of harm to self or others, the state's interest in protecting its citizens outweighs the client's right to refuse medication. As a consequence, under these circumstances, and when there are no less intrusive means of avoiding the threatening harm, a physician may order the involuntary medication of the client. In addition, when an involuntarily committed mentally ill client does not pose an imminent threat of harm but lacks the capacity to provide informed consent for medication, a court may issue an order permitting a physician to administer antipsy-

---

1. OHIO REV. CODE § 5122.271(A), (B).
2. Steele v Hamilton County Community Mental Health Board, 90 Ohio St. 3d 176, 736 N.E.2d 10 (2000).

chotic medications against the wishes of the client. The court may take such an action when it finds, by clear and convincing evidence, that the client lacks the capacity to give or withhold consent, it is in the best interest of the client to take the medication, and no less intrusive treatments will be as effective.

3.8

Regulation of Aversive and Avoidance Conditioning

Behavioral therapies using aversive stimuli are carefully regulated or prohibited in some states when they are intended for use with developmentally disabled or mentally ill individuals. MHPs using such methods should be aware of legal and institutional limits.

(A) Developmental Disabilities and Aversive Stimuli

Major aversive interventions may not be used with mentally ill hospitalized clients unless the client continues to engage in destructive behavior to self or others and other forms of therapy have been attempted unsuccessfully. Aversive interventions must be approved by the director of the Department of Mental Health. In addition, the director of the Ohio Legal Rights Service[1] must be notified of any proposed aversive treatments before the review by the director of the Department of Mental Health. Aversive treatments may not be administered to voluntarily committed clients without their consent or the consent of a guardian.[2]

Aversive interventions may not be administered to residents living under the auspices of the Department of Mental Retardation and Developmental Disabilities unless the resident continues to engage in behaviors destructive to self or others and other forms of therapy have been tried unsuccessfully. The director of the Ohio Legal Rights Service[3] must be notified of any proposed

---

1. OHIO REV. CODE § 5123.60.
2. OHIO REV. CODE § 5122.271(E).
3. OHIO REV. CODE § 5123.60.

aversive interventions. Aversive treatments may not be administered to voluntarily committed residents without their consent or
the consent of the resident's guardian.[4]

Aversive interventions may not be administered to mentally
ill inmates of correctional facilities of the Department of Rehabilitation and Correction.[5]

---

4. Ohio Rev. Code § 5123.86(F).
5. Ohio Rev. Code § 5120.17(C)(2).

3.9

Quality Assurance for Hospital Care

The law requires that the governing body of every licensed hospital organize health care providers with privileges to practice in the hospital into committees to review the professional practices within the hospital for the purposes of reducing morbidity and mortality and improving care of clients in the hospital.

(A) Peer Review

Peer review includes the work of utilization review committees, quality assurance committees, credentialing committees, and other committees that conduct professional credentialing and quality review activities involving the competence or professional conduct of health care practitioners.[1]

(B) Privilege and Immunity

Any information made available to peer review committees is confidential. Members of peer review committees who breach confidentiality of peer review information are subject to legal action similar to that which a client may bring against a physician for misusing confidential information obtained in the physician–client relationship[2] (see chapters 3.3, Confidential Relations and Communications, and 3.10, Malpractice Liability).

---

1. OHIO REV. CODE § 2305.25(E).
2. OHIO REV. CODE § 2305.24.

Health care entities and individuals who are members of, or work on behalf of, peer review committees for hospitals, state or local societies for physicians and psychologists and other medical professionals, nursing home providers, and insurers are immune from civil liability for any acts, omissions, or decisions made in the course of their duties, so long as they do not act with malice or in bad faith.[3]

---

3. OHIO REV. CODE § 2305.25(D).

Malpractice Liability

A malpractice suit is a civil action in which the plaintiff alleges that he or she suffered damages as the direct consequence of an act or omission by a professional who did not exercise the level of ordinary and reasonable care possessed by the average member of that discipline. Such suits include those against MHPs. Ohio has partially codified the law of malpractice. That is, some aspects of this area of law are codified in statutes and some aspects have been developed by the courts.

(A) Malpractice Law

(A)(1) Who May Be Sued

Under Ohio law, all MHPs may be sued.

Health care professionals, including MHPs, who are volunteers are not liable in damages for providing services at a nonprofit shelter or health care facility to an indigent and uninsured person, unless the acts or omissions constitute willful or wanton misconduct. To qualify for this immunity, the health care professional must obtain the written consent of the client for providing care and informing the client of the immunity.[1]

(A)(2) Standard of Care

For a successful malpractice action based in negligence to succeed, the plaintiff must establish that the practitioner failed to provide to the client the level of care consistent with a comparative standard

---

1. OHIO REV. CODE § 2305.234.

appropriate for the needs of the client and the skills of the profession. In general, the professional's actions are compared with the actions of similar professionals in similar circumstances. At one time, practitioners' conduct was compared only with that of practitioners in similar locations, such that, for example, rural practitioners were compared with rural practitioners and urban practitioners were compared with those who practiced in urban settings. In more recent years, courts in many states, including Ohio, have applied national standards to mental health practitioners.[2] These standards are established through the testimony of expert witnesses and through a review of administrative rules, hospital and agency policies, information from licensure statutes (see chapters 1.2, Licensure and Regulation of Psychiatrists, 1.3, Licensure and Regulation of Psychiatric Nurses, 1.4, Licensure and Regulation of Psychologists, 1.5, Subdoctoral and Unlicensed Psychologists, and 1.6, Licensure and Regulation of Counselors, Social Workers, and Marriage and Family Therapists), and professional codes of ethics. The administrative code for the psychology licensing law specifies that psychologists who undertake practice in a specialty area will be held to the higher standard of care within the specialty.[3]

(A)(3) Proximate Cause

For financial recovery to be granted in a negligence case, the harm or injury to a client must result from or be causally related to a breach of duty by the practitioner. Legally, the breach must be the proximate cause of the harm. *Proximate* means that there was a natural and continuous sequence of events from the practitioner's behavior to the client's injury, without intervening causes, or there was such a major contribution that "but for" the practitioner's behavior the damage to the client would not have occurred. A proximate cause does not necessarily relate to closeness or remoteness in time. No fixed rule exists on how quickly harm must occur to hold a defendant liable.[4] The key issue is the connection between the action, or lack of action, of the practitioner and the harm to the client.

(A)(4) Statute of Limitations

The statute of limitations for civil suits against physicians, including psychiatrists, and registered and practical nurses is one year after the cause of action occurs. However, if before the end of the

---

2. Bruni v. Tatsumi, 46 Ohio St. 2d 127, 346 N.E.2d 673 (1976).
3. OHIO ADMIN. CODE § 4732-17-01(H).
4. Estates of Morgan v. Fairfield Family Counseling Center, 77 Ohio St. 3d 284, 673 N.E.2d 1311 (1997).

one-year period, a claimant who allegedly possesses a medical claim gives written notice that the claimant is considering bringing an action, that action may be initiated any time within an additional 180 days.[5] The time limit is extended for minors until one year after the age of majority (age 18)[6] is attained. For those who are disabled,[7] and thereby unable to commence legal action, the statute of limitations is extended for one year after the removal of the disability. In addition, the statute of limitations may be extended for up to four years for acts or omissions that are not discovered during the one-year limitation but are discovered during the subsequent four-year period.[8]

No statute of limitation is identified by statute for psychologists, social workers, or counselors. However, the Ohio supreme court concluded in 1994 that claims against psychologists, social workers, counselors, and mental health clinics are not medical claims[9] and therefore follow a two-year statute of limitation.[10]

(B) Avoiding Malpractice

MHPs can take steps to reduce the likelihood of being sued for malpractice, although MHPs should recognize that there is some degree of unpredictability in who is sued. No risk management steps can guarantee that one will not be sued.

To minimize the likelihood of being sued for malpractice, MHPs can restrict their practices to areas of competency. Of course, practicing outside of one's areas of competency could be grounds for complaints to licensure boards, too (see chapters 1.2, Licensure and Regulation of Psychiatrists, 1.3, Licensure and Regulation of Psychiatric Nurses, 1.4, Licensure and Regulation of Psychologists, and 1.6, Licensure and Regulation of Counselors, Social Workers, and Marriage and Family Therapists). Good clinical practice is a good risk management strategy. MHPs should be familiar with the laws that pertain to their practices and conversant with the ethics codes of their respective professions. Clients who are well informed about practice procedures and knowingly give their consent are less likely to sue their practitioners. It also is helpful to be aware of, and especially vigilant with, high-risk procedures such as psychotropic medication and electroconvul-

---

5. OHIO REV. CODE § 2305.113.
6. OHIO REV. CODE § 3109.01.
7. OHIO REV. CODE § 2305.16.
8. OHIO REV. CODE § 2305.113.
9. OHIO REV. CODE § 2305.113.
10. Thompson v. Community Mental Health Centers of Warren County, Inc., 71 Ohio St. 3d 194, 642 N.E.2d 1102 (1994).

sive treatment, as well as high-risk clients, including those who have sued other professionals, those who have had many stormy relationships, and those who are threatening harm to themselves or others. Cases in which one party is likely to be disappointed or angered by the outcome of a procedure, such as a child custody evaluation, also are more litigious. Careful and thorough record keeping is essential as a defense for the practitioner.

(C) Malpractice Review Committees

Ohio law does not provide for malpractice review committees, but it does provide for voluntary arbitration options (see later in this chapter).

(D) Voluntary Arbitration

Ohio law provides for voluntary arbitration of complaints brought against medical personnel, including psychiatrists and nurses, and hospitals. Two options are available. In one option the client may enter into a contract with a hospital or medical health care provider before receiving a diagnosis or care.[11] The client has a right to withdraw from this agreement within 30 days by notifying the provider or hospital in writing. Filing a medical claim within the 30 days provided for withdrawal also is considered a withdrawal from the agreement. Such arbitration agreements must specify that the decision of whether or not to sign the agreement is solely a matter for the patient to determine (without pressure from the provider or hospital) and that this agreement constitutes a waiver of any right to a trial. If a dispute then arises, each party to the dispute must select an arbitrator and the two arbitrators select a third, impartial arbitrator. Expenses of the arbitration are shared equally by the two parties.[12]

The second option for arbitration of medical malpractice claims may be accessed whenever all of the parties to the medical claim agree to submit it to nonbinding arbitration. In this option, the court that receives the medical malpractice claim selects three arbitrators, one designated by the plaintiff, one designated by the defendant, and a third person designated by the court. The person designated by the court serves as the chair of the board. If the

---

11. OHIO REV. CODE § 1711.22.
12. OHIO REV. CODE § 2711.23.

decision of the arbitration board is not accepted by all parties, the claim proceeds as if it had not been submitted to nonbinding arbitration. Neither the decision of the arbitration board nor any dissenting opinion written by a board member are admissible into evidence at the trial.[13]

---

13. Ohio Rev. Code § 2711.21.

3.11

Other Forms of Professional Liability

In general, when clients sue MHPs it is for malpractice (see chapter 3.10, Malpractice Liability), which covers suits alleging that a standard of care was violated in diagnosing or treating a client. However, other legal causes of action also may be brought against MHPs. The right to bring suits on alternative legal grounds may be important in some situations because the period for filing a medical malpractice suit is limited to one year after a person realizes that he or she has been harmed as the result of negligence. Other types of legal actions often have a two-year statute of limitations.[1] In general, the rules in Ohio for these forms of liability are the same in the context of the MHP–client relationship as in other contexts.

(A) Intentional Torts

Intentional torts, in contrast to negligent torts, require proof that the actor desired a certain outcome or was certain that it would occur or that the injury to the client was the result of wanton or gross negligence. In lawsuits alleging intentional torts, expert evidence may or may not be necessary to establish the standard of care, depending on the facts of the particular case.

(A)(1) Criminal-Related Actions

When MHPs violate criminal law, a criminal case may be brought by the prosecutor on behalf of the state of Ohio. Violation of the criminal law results in punishment, usually in the form of a fine,

---

1. Ohio Rev. Code § 2305.11(A).

probation, or imprisonment. When an MHP has violated a criminal law, that violation also may become the grounds for a civil suit if the client has been injured. For example, if an MHP were to defame the character of a client, both criminal and civil charges could be filed.

(A)(2) Defamation of Character

Defamation of character includes libel and slander and generally entails the use of false, insulting words that injure someone's reputation. Usually the defendant must have made the communication knowing it was false, although sometimes just being careless in searching for the truth is enough. *Slander* refers to words that are spoken; *libel* refers to words that are published.

(A)(3) Invasion of Privacy

The right to privacy is sometimes described as the "right to be left alone." Mental health treatment inherently involves extensive intrusions into private aspects of a person's life, but liability for invasion of privacy is not likely to be imposed unless the MHP failed to obtain informed consent for treatment (see chapter 3.1, Informed Consent for Services) or for the sharing of information with others about the client (see chapter 3.3, Confidential Relations and Communications). For example, videotaping of therapy sessions without consent of the client or sharing treatment information with others who have no right to know might be grounds for a charge of invasion of privacy.

(A)(4) Malicious Prosecution, False Imprisonment, and Abuse of Process

Malicious prosecution focuses more on proving the malicious intention of the MHP more so than on what the MHP actually did; that is, there must be proof that the MHP lacked probable cause for taking action. For example, if an MHP initiated involuntary commitment proceedings against a client, the client might claim that the MHP acted out of anger or a desire to punish, rather than to assist the client in obtaining treatment.

False imprisonment requires that an MHP wrongfully and intentionally confine a person. The Ohio supreme court has defined false imprisonment as confining another intentionally, without a lawful reason, against the person's consent, within a limited area for any appreciable time, however short.[2] Mental health clients confined in mental hospitals when the rules for such commitment were not followed may bring claims of false imprisonment. Another example would be the continued confinement of a client

---

2. Feliciano v. Kreiger, 50 Ohio St. 2d 69, 362 N.E.3d 646 (1977).

for inappropriate reasons. Placing a patient in restraints without following proper protocol is another possible example of false imprisonment.[3]

Ohio statutory law is silent about claims of abuse of process, but the Ohio supreme court has recognized such claims and has laid out the requirements for them.[4] The requirements are that a legal proceeding has been properly set in motion and with probable cause, the proceeding has been perverted to accomplish an ulterior motive, and direct damage has resulted from the wrongful use of the process. For example, if an MHP initiated an involuntary commitment proceeding against a client, the client might claim that the MHP initiated the proceeding as a way of undermining the client's reputation in the community.

Ohio has established a statute of limitations of one year for bringing a lawsuit in these matters. If the claimant cannot initiate proceedings during this period because he or she is a minor or disabled, a lawsuit may be commenced within two years of attaining majority age (age 18) or removal of the disability. No cause of action for harm that was discovered after the period of one year may be initiated later than four years from the date of the occurrence of the act or omission.[5]

(A)(5) Failure to Commit and Negligent Release

Failure of a psychiatrist or psychologist (the only MHPs who are permitted to petition for an emergency hospitalization)[6] to commit a client who meets the criteria for voluntary or involuntary commitment or releasing a client prematurely may expose the MHP to a lawsuit. In addition, any MHP could face liability for failing to properly assess, diagnose, treat, or refer a patient who should have been hospitalized.

Ohio law is not clear on liability for failure to involuntarily commit or failure to release an involuntarily committed client. This issue was raised before the Ohio supreme court in the context of a duty to protect question.[7] In this case, the court created a duty to protect that was later modified by the Ohio general assembly[8] (see chapter 3.3, Confidential Relations and Communications) but left unclear the status of liability for failure to commit or release an involuntarily committed client. In addition, an MHP

---

3. Barker v. Netcare Corp., 147 Ohio App.3d 1, 768 N.E.2d 698 (2001).
4. Haklevich v. Kemp, Schaeffer & Rowe Co., L.P.A., 68 Ohio St. 3d 294, 626 N.E.2d 115 (1994).
5. Ohio Rev. Code § 2305.11(A).
6. Ohio Rev. Code § 5122.10.
7. Estates of Morgan v. Fairfield Family Counseling Center, 77 Ohio St. 3d 284, 673 N.E.2d 1311 (1997).
8. Ohio Rev. Code § 2305.51(B).

could be found liable for conducting an inadequate examination to determine whether a client met the criteria of involuntary commitment.

Negligent release of voluntarily committed clients has been established as a basis for liability by the Ohio supreme court. The court has established the "professional judgment rule" for determining liability for negligently released clients. The professional judgment rule holds that a psychiatrist will not be held liable for violent acts of a voluntarily hospitalized client who was discharged if (a) the client did not manifest violent propensities while hospitalized and there was no reason to suspect the client would become violent after discharge, (b) a thorough evaluation of the client's propensity for violence was conducted and a good faith decision was made by the psychiatrist that the patient had no violent propensities, or (c) the patient was diagnosed as having violent propensities but a treatment plan was formulated in good faith that balanced the client's interests and the interests of potential victims.[9]

(B) Other Types of Civil Liability

(B)(1) Breach of Fiduciary Duty

MHPs assume a position of superiority in knowledge and skill and must act with good faith, trust, and competence with their clients. The fiduciary duty arises when there is a mutual expectation that the provider will act primarily for the client's needs. This is an obligation implicit in the arrangement and inherent in the relationships that MHPs establish with their clients. Clients are entitled to good faith expectations of their providers, especially because mental health treatment requires clients to share their innermost thoughts and feelings. MHPs must be mindful of a strict duty not to violate the trusting nature of this relationship.

Ethics codes and licensure statutes identify many prohibitions that might violate the fiduciary relationship, including the banning of sexual relationships with clients, breaching confidentiality, and misrepresenting one's services and skills. A breach of fiduciary duty could be alleged by a client when the MHP engages in acts that disrupt the trust that is needed for the relationship to work to the client's benefit.

---

9. Littleton v. Good Samaritan Hospital & Health Center et al., 39 Ohio St. 3d 86, 529 N.E.2d 449 (1988); Griffin v. Twin Valley Psychiatric Systems, 2003 Ohio 7024, LEXIS 6376 (Ohio App. 10th Dist. 2003).

(B)(2) Breach of Contract

The relationship between an MHP and a client is a consensual one usually based on an implied contract, wherein the professional undertakes to provide services in accordance with the applicable standard of care. Beyond this, MHPs should not promise to effect a cure or produce a specific therapeutic result. If an MHP promises a therapeutic result, he or she may be liable for a breach of contract if the outcome is not produced, even if the MHP provided the highest degree of care.

Criminal Liability

Some states have criminal statutes prohibiting MHPs from engaging in certain behaviors (e.g., sexual relations with a client). Ohio has a law classifying sexual relations between MHPs and clients as a form of assault and battery or sexual imposition. The effect of such statutes is to criminalize all sexual activity between MHPs and their clients. In addition, Ohio has three types of criminal laws that could be of relevance to an MHP—namely, sexual offenses other than sexual activity with clients, felonious assault and menacing, and manslaughter.

(A) Assault and Battery Prosecutions Related to Sexual Contact or Conduct

Assault involves a threat of bodily harm in which a potential victim perceives himself or herself to be in imminent peril. *Battery* refers to the unauthorized touching of another person.

(B) Sexual Battery and Sexual Imposition

When a charge of battery involves sexual conduct, it is defined as sexual battery. *Sexual conduct* means vaginal intercourse between a male and female; anal intercourse, fellatio, and cunnilingus between persons regardless of sex; and penetration into the vaginal or anal cavity of another.[1]

Legislation that went into effect in May 2002 extends the statute of limitations for prosecution of assault and battery of one year to two years when the prosecution is brought against an MHP for sexual activity with a client. If the practitioner–client relationship continued after the date of sexual activity, the two-year period does not begin to run until the date on which the treatment relationship was terminated.[2]

The consent of the client to the sexual contact or conduct is not a defense to the claim unless either (a) the plaintiff was the spouse of the MHP or (b) the MHP proves by a preponderance of the evidence that (i) the client was not emotionally dependent on the MHP and (ii) the sexual contact or conduct did not occur because the MHP falsely represented to the client that the sexual behavior was necessary for medical or mental health purposes.[3]

Sexual battery is a felony of the third degree,[4] punishable by one to five years in prison[5] and/or a maximum fine of $10,000.[6]

Sexual imposition refers to unwanted sexual contact with another person or causing other persons to have such contact,[7] such as when an MHP might instruct a staff member to have sexual contact with a client. *Sexual contact* refers to any touching of an erogenous zone of another for the purpose of sexually arousing or gratifying either person.[8]

Ohio law also provides that an MHP is guilty of sexual imposition if the MHP induces a client to engage in sexual contact by falsely representing to the client that the sexual activity is necessary for mental health treatment, even if the client consented to participate.[9]

Sexual imposition is a misdemeanor of the third degree,[10] punishable by a maximum of 30 days in jail[11] and/or a maximum fine of $500.[12]

MHPs may not be convicted of a violation of either sexual contact or sexual conduct solely on the victim's testimony unsupported by other evidence.[13] The Ohio supreme court has added

---

1. OHIO REV. CODE § 2907.01(A).
2. OHIO REV. CODE § 2907.03.
3. *Id.*
4. *Id.*
5. OHIO REV. CODE § 2929.14.
6. OHIO REV. CODE § 2929.18.
7. OHIO REV. CODE § 2907.06(A).
8. OHIO REV. CODE § 2907.01(B).
9. OHIO REV. CODE § 2907.06(A).
10. OHIO REV. CODE § 2907.06(C).
11. OHIO REV. CODE § 2929.21.
12. *Id.*
13. OHIO REV. CODE § 2907.06(A).

some clarity about what additional evidence would be sufficient to support a victim's testimony. It has stated that corroborating evidence need not be independently sufficient to convict the defendant nor address every element of the charge. Even slight circumstances or evidence that supports the victim's testimony is satisfactory.[14]

If an MHP is indicted or charged and bound over to the court for trial, or is convicted of or pleads guilty to a violation of this statute, the prosecuting attorney must send written notice to the applicable licensing board to suspend or revoke the MHP's license.[15]

(C) Sexual Offenses

In addition to the statutes described earlier in this chapter that apply specifically to MHPs, Ohio law prohibits any person from engaging in sexual conduct with another person who is not a spouse whose ability to consent or resist is substantially impaired because of a mental or physical condition or because of advanced age, if the offender is aware of these factors. The mental or physical impairment may be a result of mental retardation or emotional problems. Administering a drug, intoxicant, or controlled substance surreptitiously or by force, threat of force, or deception with the intent to prevent resistance to sexual conduct is specifically prohibited. Sexual conduct with a person younger than 13 years of age, whether or not the offender knows the age, also is prohibited. Violations of this section are defined as rape, which is a felony of the first degree, punishable by a prison term of 3 to 10 years[16] and/or a fine of up to $15,000.[17] The victim need not prove physical resistance to the offender.[18]

(D) Felonious Assault and Menacing

Felonious assault is a felony of the second degree, punishable by a prison term of two to eight years[19] and/or a fine of up to $15,000.[20] It involves knowingly causing serious physical injury to another person. Included in Ohio law as felonious assault are

---

14. State v. Economo, 76 Ohio St. 3d 56, 666 N.E.2d 225 (1996).
15. Ohio Rev. Code § 2907.17.
16. Ohio Rev. Code § 2929.14.
17. Ohio Rev. Code § 2929.18.
18. Ohio Rev. Code § 2907.02.
19. Ohio Rev. Code § 2929.14.
20. Ohio Rev. Code § 2929.18.

(a) engaging in sexual conduct with the knowledge that one has tested positive for HIV without first disclosing this fact to the partner and (b) engaging in sexual conduct with a person under 18 years of age who is not a spouse.[21]

Menacing refers to knowingly causing another person to believe that the offender will physically harm the person or property of the other person or a member of the other person's immediate family. Menacing is a misdemeanor of the fourth degree,[22] punishable by a maximum jail term of 30 days and/or a maximum fine of $250.[23]

(E) Manslaughter

Voluntary and involuntary manslaughter are both felonies in Ohio. *Involuntary manslaughter* includes the accidental causing of the death of another person or the unlawful termination of another's pregnancy as a result of the offender's committing a felony, misdemeanor, or regulatory offense.[24] Involuntary manslaughter is a felony of the first or third degree, depending on the circumstances and punishable by a prison term of 1 to 10 years[25] and a fine up to $20,000.[26] *Voluntary manslaughter* refers to knowingly causing the death of a person or an unlawful termination of another's pregnancy while under the influence of sudden passion or rage brought on by serious provocation by the victim.[27] Voluntary manslaughter is considered a felony of the first degree and is punishable by a prison term of 3 to 10 years[28] and or a fine of up to $20,000.[29]

21. OHIO REV. CODE § 2903.11.
22. OHIO REV. CODE § 2903.22.
23. OHIO REV. CODE § 2929.21.
24. OHIO REV. CODE § 2903.04.
25. OHIO REV. CODE § 2929.14.
26. OHIO REV. CODE § 2929.18.
27. OHIO REV. CODE § 2903.03.
28. OHIO REV. CODE § 2929.14.
29. OHIO REV. CODE § 2929.18.

3.13

Liability of Credentialing Boards

The legislative and judicial branches of government are immune from lawsuits. This status originated from the maxim that "the king can do no wrong" but is now premised on the theory that it cannot be tortious (i.e., wrongful) conduct for a government to govern. This absolute immunity does not extend to all aspects of government, however. This issue is important to MHPs, because they may be personally liable for their wrongful actions as members of a credentialing board.

Ohio licensure laws provide immunity for members, former members, agents (those who carry out the decisions of the Board), and employees of the state Medical Board[1] and the Board of Nursing[2] for any activities or decisions related to official duties. If such individuals are sued, the state provides and pays for the person's defense and pays any resulting judgment or settlement. The state will not pay any part of a judgment that is for punitive or exemplary damages that are assigned when the court concludes that the MHP acted in a careless or deliberately destructive manner.

In addition, other statutes provide immunity for officers and employees of state agencies, boards (including members and employees of the licensure boards for psychologists, counselors, social workers, and marriage and family therapists), and commissions for damage or injury caused in the performance of their duties, unless the actions were manifestly outside the scope of their responsibilities or the employee or officer acted in bad faith, with malicious purpose, or in a reckless manner.[3]

---

1. OHIO REV. CODE § 4730.34.
2. OHIO REV. CODE § 4723.021.
3. OHIO REV. CODE § 9.86.

3.14

Antitrust Limitations to Practice

Antitrust laws were enacted to prevent the formation of monopolies and prevent the abuses of economic power. In recent years, health care providers and their organizations have increasingly become defendants in antitrust litigation. Scrutinized activities include price fixing (an agreement among competitors to establish a common price or a system for setting prices), dividing markets (an agreement among competitors to allocate certain markets to certain participants), boycotting a group (an agreement among competitors to patronize only certain businesses), and making tying arrangements (wherein a party agrees to sell a certain product or service only on the condition that the buyer also purchases a different product). All of these activities fall under the general prohibition of restraint of trade. Most enforcement is through federal law in federal court. However, state law also applies. This chapter is limited to Ohio antitrust law. It applies to any MHP or organization.

(A) Prohibited Activities

A monopoly is a market structure in which one or a few firms dominate the activities in the marketplace for sales of a product or services by engaging in activities that create barriers to competition. Monopoly activities include fixing prices to consumers and agreeing not to buy from, sell to, or provide services to a competitor.[1]

---

1. OHIO REV. CODE § 1331.01.

It is unlawful for a person to engage in antitrust activity or to aid or advise others in doing so. A violation by a person of antitrust activities is a misdemeanor of the first degree and carries with it a term of imprisonment of up to six months and/or a fine of not more than $1,000.[2] The penalties for an organization are fines of not more than $5,000.[3] Each day's violation is a separate offense.[4]

(B) Enforcement of the Law

Ohio law calls for the state's attorney general to conduct investigations into suspected violations of the antitrust act. The attorney general also may appoint special counsel to act as the state's attorney in antitrust cases.

2. OHIO REV. CODE § 2929.21(B).
3. OHIO REV. CODE § 2929.31.
4. OHIO REV. CODE § 331.04.

Families and Juveniles

4.1

Competency to Marry

To marry, many states require a minimum mental status. Ohio, however, does not have such a law. A marriage can be annulled (see chapter 4.4, Annulment) if a party, because of mental illness or retardation, was not able at the time of the marriage to comprehend the significance of the decision to marry. It must be proven that the party was mentally incapable of understanding the nature, effects, and consequences of the marriage. Mental health professionals (MHPs) may be called on to evaluate a party in question and to testify in court.

(A) Standard for Voiding a Marriage

A marriage may be annulled if either party, before the marriage, has been adjudicated to be mentally incompetent, unless the party after being restored to competency cohabited with the other as husband or wife.[1]

---

1. Ohio Rev. Code § 3105.31(C).

4.2

Guardianship for Adults

Individuals who are unable to conduct their day-to-day affairs because of an emotional or cognitive disability may have appointed for them a guardian who will control their lives, much as parents oversee the lives of their children. There are two classes of individuals for whom guardianship generally is obtained: minors and incapacitated persons. This chapter is limited to a discussion of guardianship for incapacitated persons. Guardianship for minors is discussed in chapter 4.11 (Guardianship and Conservatorship for Minors). An MHP may become involved in this process by being asked to evaluate the person and testify about whether the person meets the test for a guardianship or by providing therapeutic services to the person after a guardianship has been imposed.

In some states, guardianship for incompetent individuals (management of the person) is distinguished from conservatorship (management of the estate of the person). In Ohio, guardians may oversee the person, the estate, or both. As a consequence, guardianship and conservatorship are covered together in this chapter. Ohio has separate statutory law for conservators who oversee the functioning and/or estate of competent adults who are physically infirm, and that law is covered in the next chapter (chapter 4.3, Conservatorship for Adults).

(A) Application for Guardianship

The probate court (a court that has jurisdiction over wills and administration of estates and is empowered to appoint guardians and approve adoptions) in the county in which a person resides or in which the person has legal settlement may, on its own initiative or based on the application by an interested party, appoint a guardian. A guardian may be a person, corporation, or association appointed by the probate court to take over the care and management of the incapacitated individual's person, estate, or both. *Guardian* includes a limited guardian, an interim guardian, a standby guardian, and an emergency guardian.[1] If a person applies for appointment as guardian of the estate, the applicant must file with the probate court an application that contains a statement of the whole estate of the person, its probable value, and the likely amount of annual rent of the person's real estate. In addition, the application must include the following information: (a) a statement about whether the applicant has ever been charged with or convicted of any crime involving theft; physical violence; or sexual, alcohol, or substance abuse; and, if the applicant has such a history, the date and place of each charge and conviction; (b) a statement about whether a limited guardianship or full guardianship is sought. If limited guardianship is requested, the application must specify the limited powers that are requested and whether the limited guardianship is requested for a definite or indefinite period of time; and (c) the name, age, and residence of the person for whom the appointment is sought; the facts on which the application is based; and the name, degree of kinship, age, and residence of the next of kin of the alleged incompetent person.[2]

If a professional evaluation is required for determining incompetency, probate courts provide a form that must be completed by either a physician or clinical psychologist and that may be submitted with the application for guardianship. The form requires the physician or psychologist to describe the assessment and diagnosis of the client and to state whether the person is mentally or physically impaired and, if so, the cause of the impairment. In addition, the professional is asked to indicate whether the person can conduct business affairs without the aid of a guardian and can properly care for him- or herself without the aid of a guardian.[3]

(B) Guardianship Hearing

Before the appointment of a guardian for a person found incompetent, the court will conduct a hearing in accordance with the

---

1. Ohio Rev. Code § 2111.01(A).
2. Ohio Rev. Code § 2111.03.
3. Ohio Sup. Ct. R. 51, Form 17.1.

following requirements: (a) the proposed guardian will be present and will swear to fulfill the duties of guardian; (b) the burden of proving incompetency of the person alleged to be incompetent shall be by clear and convincing evidence; and (c) a less restrictive alternative may be proposed and, if proposed, must be considered by the court.

At the hearing, the person alleged to be incompetent has the right to be represented by counsel, the right to have a friend or family member of his or her choice present, and the right to have evidence from an independent expert evaluation introduced.[4]

(C) Appointment, Duties, and Power of the Guardian

The court determines whether a guardian is needed and, if so, selects the person to be the guardian. Once appointed, the guardian takes an oath promising to faithfully perform all duties as guardian. The court specifes the duties and powers of the guardian. In general, the duties are defined so that the incapacitated person is permitted to care for him- or herself and manage his or her property to the extent possible. In general, the court may assign all powers to the guardian of the person that the person would ordinarily have if he or she were not disabled, except the power to make or revoke a will.[5] The court also determines whether to appoint a guardian or a limited guardian. In the case of a limited guardian, the limited duties are spelled out by the court in a letter of authority, and the length of time for which limited guardianship is awarded is specified. In the case of a limited guardian, the incapacitated person retains all of his or her rights in all areas not affected by the court order appointing the guardian. The guardian is responsible for maintaining close contact with the incapacitated person so that appropriate decisions can be made.[6]

The guardian or limited guardian is responsible for making timely and accurate reports to the court at least on a biennial basis. The report must include, among other things, information about the functioning of the person, the approximate number of times the guardian has met with the person and the nature of those contacts, an opinion of the guardian about the necessity for continuing the guardianship, and a statement from a physician

---

4. OHIO REV. CODE § 2111.02(C).
5. OHIO REV. CODE § 2111.50(B).
6. OHIO REV. CODE § 2111.02(C).

or MHP who has examined the person within three months before the date of the report. On review of the guardian's biennial report, the court may direct an investigator to verify aspects of the report and the court may elect to terminate or modify the guardianship.[7]

(D) Termination of the Guardianship

The court does not review the guardianship arrangement on any scheduled basis, although the incompetent person, his or her attorney, or another interested person may request that the court review the guardianship at any time.[8] Following the review, the court may continue, modify, or terminate the guardianship. However, if a guardian is temporarily or permanently removed or resigns and the matter requires immediate attention, the court may, with or without notice to the incapacitated person or interested parties, appoint an interim guardian for up to 15 days. The court may extend the interim guardianship for another 30 days if the situation requires it to protect the person or property.[9]

---

7. Ohio Rev. Code § 2111.49.
8. Id.
9. Ohio Rev. Code § 2111.02(B)(2).

4.3

Conservatorship for Adults

In addition to authorizing appointment of a guardian (see chapter 4.2, Guardianship for Adults), the law authorizes the court to appoint a conservator to manage the person and estate (e.g., property, financial resources, and business enterprises) of a competent adult who is physically infirm. This chapter focuses on adult wards. Conservatorship for minors is discussed in chapter 4.11 (Guardianship and Conservatorship for Minors). MHPs may become involved in this process by being asked to evaluate the infirm person and to testify about that person's capacity to manage his or her estate and to provide therapeutic services to the infirm person after a conservatorship has been imposed.

(A) Application for Conservatorship

The application or petition for conservatorship is filed by the infirm adult. The applicant may request that the care of his or her person and/or any or all of his or her real or personal property be placed by the court under a conservatorship with the court. The petitioner may grant specific powers to the conservator or court and must identify the proposed conservator.[1]

---

1. Ohio Rev. Code § 2111.021.

(B) Conservatorship Hearing

The court holds a hearing to determine that the petition was voluntarily filed and that the proposed conservator is suitable. If those findings are made, the court orders the conservatorship.

(C) Appointment, Duties, and Power of the Conservator

The duties and powers of the conservator are similar to those of guardians (see chapter 4.2, Guardianship for Adults), except those areas that were specifically limited by the petitioner. The petitioner may request the court to change the powers of the conservator at any time.

(D) Termination of the Conservatorship

The court may terminate a conservatorship because of incompetency or death of the petitioner or by a written termination notice by the petitioner. If the petitioner terminates the conservatorship, the petitioner must file a notice with the court within 14 days for the termination to be valid.[2]

---

2. *Id.*

4.4

Annulment

Whereas a divorce dissolves what was once a valid, functioning marriage, annulment is the process whereby a marriage is declared void and is legally held never to have existed. This result can have legal significance. For instance, a widowed spouse of a worker receives compensation benefits until the widow remarries, and if the second marriage ceases by virtue of an annulment rather than divorce, the person regains the benefits. MHPs may be involved in an annulment proceeding directly through evaluation and testimony or indirectly when they are working with individuals who are contemplating dissolving their marriage.

(A) Grounds for Annulment

A marriage may be annulled if any of the following circumstances existed at the time of the marriage:[1] (a) the party seeking the annulment was under the age of 18 for males and 16 for females,[2] unless after attaining this age the party cohabited with the other as husband and wife; (b) another marriage was still in effect for one of the parties; (c) either party was adjudicated, before the marriage, to be mentally incompetent (neither the statute nor case law has clearly defined this condition for this purpose), unless this person was restored to competency and then lived with the partner as husband or wife; (d) the consent of either party was obtained by fraud, unless the defrauded party afterward, with full knowledge of the fraud, continued to live with the other party

---

1. Ohio Rev. Code § 3105.31.
2. Ohio Rev. Code § 3101.01.

as husband and wife; (e) the consent to marriage was obtained by force unless the parties afterward lived together as husband and wife, or (f) the marriage was never consummated.

In any request for annulment, the court may, on its own accord or at the request of one of the parties, order the couple to participate in counseling for up to 90 days. If children are involved, the court may require the parties to participate in family counseling during the course of the proceeding or for any reasonable period of time as directed by the court.[3]

---

3. Ohio Rev. Code § 3105.091.

4.5

Divorce

At one time, divorce laws in many states required the petitioning party to allege fault by the other spouse. More recently many states, including Ohio, added a no-fault divorce provision to the divorce law. Now, if the parties have reached a voluntary separation agreement, litigation typically will center around property division, child support, spousal maintenance, or child custody (see chapter 4.6, Child Custody After Marital Dissolution). Aside from custody assessments, MHPs become involved in divorce issues by providing counseling and psychotherapy to individuals, couples, and families who are contemplating, participating in, or recovering from a divorce.

(A) Divorce Procedure

The court of common pleas (a state court found in each county) may grant divorces[1] and legal separations[2] on certain grounds. The following grounds are available for both divorce and legal separation: (a) either party had another living spouse at the time of the marriage, (b) willful absence for at least one year by one party, (c) adultery, (d) extreme cruelty, (e) fraudulent contract, (f) any gross neglect of duty, (g) habitual drunkenness, (h) imprisonment of one party, (i) living apart by agreement for one year without cohabitation, and (j) incompatibility unless denied by either party (essentially the equivalent of no fault).[3] In addition,

---

1. OHIO REV. CODE § 3105.01.
2. OHIO REV. CODE § 3105.17.
3. OHIO REV. CODE § 3105.01.

a divorce may be granted in Ohio if one of the parties has obtained a divorce outside of Ohio.[4]

Either party to the marriage may file a complaint for divorce or legal separation, and the other party may file a counterclaim.[5] The court may order the parties to undergo counseling for a period not to exceed 90 days. If children are involved, the court may order the parties to participate in family counseling during the time of the proceedings or for any reasonable period of time. If counseling is ordered, the court may not grant the divorce or legal separation until the counseling has concluded and the results are reported to the court.[6]

With a few exceptions, the *Rules of Civil Procedure* (a set of procedures that guide civil court proceedings in Ohio) apply in actions for divorce.[7] When a complaint for divorce or legal separation is filed and children are involved, the court may require an investigation to be made regarding the character, family relations, past conduct, earning ability, and financial worth of each parent, including medical, psychiatric, and psychological examinations of parents and child.[8] The report of the investigation must be made available to both parties not less than seven days before trial if the information from the investigation is going to be used by the court.[9] The court may subpoena either party within the state to appear and testify. The court also may appoint a guardian *ad litem* (a person who represents the interests of a child) and legal counsel for the child. If child support is ordered, the court may make the employer of the person ordered to pay child support a party defendant whereby the employer deducts money from the employee's pay and transfers it to the recipient of the support.

Final judgment on the complaint for divorce or legal separation may not be granted unless the court also has addressed in some manner issues of property division, spousal support, and, if children are involved, matters of payment of child support and parental rights and responsibilities, including the option of shared parenting.[10]

The court may issue a temporary restraining order to prevent a party to divorce from disposing of property to reduce spousal support, or when the court is convinced that a child or party to

---

4. OHIO REV. CODE § 3105.01(I); Rousculp v. Rousculp, 17 Ohio App.2d 101, 244 N.E.2d 512 (1968).
5. OHIO REV. CODE § 3105.17(A).
6. OHIO REV. CODE § 3105.091.
7. OHIO R. CIV. P. 75.
8. OHIO REV. CODE § 3109.04(C).
9. OHIO REV. CODE § 2317.39; Sayre v. Hoelzle-Sayre, 100 Ohio App.3d 203, 653 N.E.2d 712 (1994).
10. OHIO R. CIV. P. 75(F).

the divorce is about to suffer abuse or injury by the other party. The temporary restraining order may be issued without notice and remains in force during the procedures unless the court terminates it.[11]

A waiting period of 42 days after the service of process (notice given to the spouse) or 28 days after the last publication of notice of the complaint or counterclaim is required before a complaint for divorce or legal separation may be settled.[12] Publication of notice is required in a divorce when the residence of the defendant is unknown. Service by publication is made by mailing the notice to the last known address of the defendant and by posting the notice in three public places, including in the courthouse and two other public places that have been designated by local rule. The notice must be posted for six successive weeks.[13]

A judgment for a divorce or legal separation may not be granted solely on the basis of testimony or admission by one party without support from other credible evidence. The court also will not accept evidence that it has reason to believe was obtained by fraud, coercion, or other improper means. Both parties, regardless of the quality of their relationship, are competent to testify in the proceeding.[14]

---

11. Ohio R. Civ. P. 75(I).
12. Ohio R. Civ. P. 75(K).
13. Ohio R. Civ. P. 4.4.
14. Ohio R. Civ. P. 75(M).

Child Custody After Marital Dissolution

Child custody determinations can result from four types of changes in the legal status of the marriage: annulment, legal separation, divorce, and modification of a divorce decree. MHPs may become involved in this determination in one of two ways. First, the judge or a party may request an evaluation of the mental status of a parent, proposed parent, or child, possibly culminating in a court appearance as an expert witness. Second, an MHP who has provided services to the family unit, whether diagnostic or therapeutic, may be subpoenaed by either party to present evidence as a witness.

(A) Criteria to Establish Court Jurisdiction

The court may establish jurisdiction to decide the custody of a child in a variety of ways:[1]

1. Ohio is the home state of the child at the time the custody proceedings were initiated, or Ohio had been the child's home state within six months before the proceedings began and the child is now absent because one parent or another person has moved the child to another state while claiming custody, as long as one parent continues to live in Ohio;

2. the court determines that it is in the best interest of the child that Ohio assume jurisdiction;

---

1. Ohio Rev. Code § 3109.22(A).

3. the child is living in Ohio and either has been abandoned or establishing jurisdiction is necessary because of an emergency involving the child's safety; or

4. no other state would have jurisdiction or a court in another state has declined to exercise jurisdiction on the ground that Ohio is the more appropriate forum.

(B) Legal Standards in Custody Determinations

The best interest of the child standard is used to determine custody. The court must consider all relevant factors, including, but not limited to:[2]

1. the wishes of the child's parents;

2. the wishes and concerns of the child if the court deems the child to be able to express a preference and the court has interviewed the child;

3. the child's interaction and relationships with his or her parents, siblings, and others who may affect the child's best interest;

4. the child's adjustment to his or her home, school, and community;

5. the mental and physical health of everyone involved in the situation;

6. the parent more likely to honor and facilitate visitation and companionship rights ordered by the court;

7. whether either parent has failed to make support payments;

8. whether either parent previously has been convicted of or pleaded guilty to a criminal offense involving child abuse;

9. whether the parent with whom the child resides or one of the parents in a shared parenting arrangement has denied the other parent the right to visitation; and

10. whether either parent has established, or plans to establish, a residence outside of Ohio.

In addition, if shared parenting is an option, the court also must consider the following factors:[3]

---

2. Ohio Rev. Code § 3109.04(F)(1).
3. Ohio Rev. Code § 3109.04(F)(2).

1. the ability of the parents to cooperate and make joint decisions about the children;

2. the ability of the parents to encourage the sharing of love, affection, and contact between the child and the other parent;

3. any history of, or potential for, child abuse, spouse abuse, domestic violence, or kidnapping by either parent;

4. the geographical proximity of the parents to each other; and

5. the recommendation of the guardian *ad litem* (person identified by the court to represent the child's interests) if one is available.

(C) Mental Health Evaluations

Before making a determination about child custody, the court may require an investigation into the character, family relations, past conduct, earning ability, and financial worth of each parent and may order the parents and minor children to submit to medical, psychological, and psychiatric examinations.[4]

The evaluation report is provided to each parent or his or her counsel, on written request, not less than five days before trial. If the report is to be used by the court, the report must be made available to each party before it is considered by the court. On the other hand, although the investigation report may be requested by the court and may provide the court with valuable information, the court may not make its custody decision solely on the basis of such an investigation while excluding other available evidence.[5] The examiner is subject to cross-examination by either parent.[6]

(C)(1) Confidentiality and Privileged Communications

MHPs who conduct these evaluations for the court are entitled to qualified immunity. The MHP can be held liable only on a theory such as malpractice for failure to conduct an adequate and complete examination. That is, in an effort to encourage participants in judicial proceedings to speak freely and candidly, the court prohibits civil actions based on reports and statements by the participants. However, MHPs could be held liable for negligence in the administration of the psychological evaluation.[7]

---

4. Ohio Rev. Code § 3109.04(C); Stone v. Stone, 9 Ohio App.3d 6, 457 N.E.2d 919 (1983).
5. Hillard v. Hillard, 29 Ohio App.2d 20, 277 N.E.2d 557 (1971).
6. Ohio Rev. Code § 3109.04(C).
7. Elling v. Graves, 94 Ohio App.3d 382, 640 N.E.2d 1156 (1994).

4.7

Reporting of Adult Abuse

The law requires certain individuals who have reasonable cause to believe that a person is being abused, mistreated, or neglected to make a report. In some states, this reporting requirement applies to adults living in nursing homes or residential health care facilities. In Ohio, the reporting requirement applies to adults living in an independent living arrangement, including but not limited to a private home, apartment, trailer, rooming house, licensed community alternative home, and licensed adult care facility. The reporting requirement does not apply to adults living in institutions or facilities licensed by the state in which the adult resides as a result of voluntary, civil, or criminal commitment.[1]

(A) Who Must Report

Adults are defined by the law for purposes of reporting adult abuse as any individuals 60 years of age or older who are handicapped by infirmities of aging or who have a physical or mental impairment that prevents them from providing for their own care and protection and who are living in an independent living arrangement.[2]

Any of the following individuals who has reasonable cause to believe that an adult is being abused, neglected, or exploited, or is in a condition that is the result of abuse, neglect, or exploitation, must immediately make a report to the county Department of Job and Family Services: any attorney, physician (including a

---

1. OHIO REV. CODE § 5101.60(B).
2. OHIO REV. CODE § 5101.60.

psychiatrist), osteopath, podiatrist, chiropractor, dentist, psychologist, or nurse; any employee of a hospital, ambulatory health facility, home health agency, adult care facility, community alternative home, nursing home, residential care facility, or home for the aging; any senior service provider, peace officer, coroner, member of the clergy, employee of a community mental health facility, or any person engaged in social work or counseling.[3]

Other individuals who are not members of these professional groups who have a reasonable belief that an adult is suffering abuse, neglect, or exploitation *may* voluntarily make a report to the Department, but they are not required to do so.[4]

In addition, reports must be made by members of several professional groups if they have reason to believe that a mentally retarded or developmentally disabled adult (18 years of age and older) has suffered a wound, injury, disability, or condition that reasonably indicates abuse or neglect. Included as mandatory reporters are the following professionals: physicians (including interns and residents), dentists, podiatrists, chiropractors, practitioners of limited branches of medicine, hospital administrators and employees, and nurses; employees of ambulatory health facilities, home health agencies, adult care facilities, and community mental health facilities; school teachers and school authorities, social workers, psychologists, attorneys, peace officers, coroners, members of the clergy, residents' rights advocates, superintendents, board members and employees of county boards of mental retardation and developmental disabilities, administrators, board members, and employees of public and private residential facilities, members of citizen advisory councils, and individuals who, while acting in an official or professional capacity, render spiritual treatment.[5]

In addition, any other individuals having reasonable cause to believe that a mentally retarded or developmentally disabled adult has suffered abuse or neglect *may* voluntarily report the belief to a law enforcement agency or the county Board of Mental Retardation and Developmental Disabilities, although they are not required to do so.[6]

---

3. Ohio Rev. Code § 5101.61(A).
4. Ohio Rev. Code § 5101.61(B).
5. Ohio Rev. Code § 5123.61(C).
6. Ohio Rev. Code § 5123.61(F).

(B) When Must a Report Be Made?

Reports regarding abused adults and mentally retarded or developmentally disabled adults must be made immediately,[7] although the meaning of "immediately" is not defined in the statutes.

(C) How a Report Must Be Made

Reports on abused adults may be made either orally or in writing, although oral reports must be followed by written reports if requested by the Department of Job and Family Services. The statute specifies that the written report must contain the name, address, and approximate age of the adult who is the subject of the report; the name and address of the person responsible for the adult's care; the nature and extent of the alleged abuse, neglect, or exploitation; and the basis of the reporter's belief that the adult has been abused, neglected, or exploited.[8]

Reports regarding mentally retarded or developmentally disabled adults also must be made immediately by telephone or in person and must be followed by a written report. The report must be made to a law enforcement agency or to the county Board of Mental Retardation and Developmental Disabilities. If the report concerns a resident of a facility operated by the Department of Mental Retardation and Developmental Disabilities, the report must be made either to a law enforcement agency or the Department. The statute specifies that the report must contain (a) the names and addresses of the mentally retarded or developmentally disabled adult and the adult's custodian, if known; (b) the adult's age and the nature and extent of the person's injuries or neglect; and (c) any other information that might be helpful in establishing the cause of the injury, abuse, or neglect.[9]

Physicians, including psychiatrists, who are members of the staff of a hospital and who have reason to believe that a mentally retarded or developmentally disabled adult has suffered abuse, injury, or physical neglect must notify the person in charge of the institution or the client's designated delegate, who then must make the report.[10]

---

7. Ohio Rev. Code §§ 5101.61(D), 5123.61(C).
8. Ohio Rev. Code § 5101.61(C).
9. Ohio Rev. Code § 5123.61(D).
10. Ohio Rev. Code § 5123.61(E).

(D) Immunity From Liability

Individuals who make these reports or who participate as witnesses in subsequent proceedings are immune from civil and criminal liability, except for liability for deliberately lying about the abuse, neglect, or exploitation, or unless they acted in bad faith or with maliciousness in making the report.[11]

(E) Confidentiality and Privilege

Reports made under these laws are considered confidential and are not public records (see chapter 3.6, State Freedom of Information Act). Information contained in these reports is made available on request to the adult who is the subject of the report, to his or her legal counsel, and to agencies authorized to receive information in the report.[12]

The physician–patient privilege may not be used to exclude information regarding a mentally retarded or developmentally disabled adult's injuries or neglect in any proceeding that results from a report[13] (see chapter 3.4, Privileged Communications).

The law regarding abused adults is silent regarding testimonial privilege in proceedings that may result from a report.

(F) Failure to Report

Failure by a mandated reporter to report adult abuse may result in a fine of not more than $500. Failure to report is not labeled as a misdemeanor or felony.[14]

Penalties for failure by a mandated reporter to report abuse of a mentally retarded or developmentally disabled adult vary depending on the setting in which the abuse allegedly occurred.[15] Failure to report abuse of an adult in a supported living setting is a misdemeanor of the first degree[16] and is punishable by a fine up to $1,000,[17] a jail term up to 180 days,[18] and/or probation (called "community control sanction" in Ohio law).[19] Failure to report

---

11. OHIO REV. CODE §§ 5101.61(D), 5123.61(K).
12. OHIO REV. CODE §§ 5101.61(F), 5123.61(M).
13. OHIO REV. CODE § 5123.61(N).
14. OHIO REV. CODE § 5101.99.
15. OHIO REV. CODE § 5123.99.
16. OHIO REV. CODE § 5123.99(A).
17. OHIO REV. CODE § 2929.28.
18. OHIO REV. CODE § 2929.24.
19. OHIO REV. CODE § 2929.26.

abuse in other settings is punishable by a fine of not more than $500.[20]

Failure to report abuse of a mentally retarded or developmentally disabled adult in other settings is not listed as a misdemeanor, but the law provides for a fine up to $500.[21]

---

20. OHIO REV. CODE § 5123.99(B).
21. *Id.*

4.8

Reporting of Child Abuse

The law requires MHPs to report known or suspected incidents of child abuse. Although the initial duty to report is discharged once the report is properly filed, the MHP may also have to appear in court proceedings as a witness on this issue (see chapter 4.10, Termination of Parental Rights).

(A) Who Must Report

Included as mandated reporters are all of the following when they are acting in their official or professional capacity: attorneys, physicians (including psychiatrists, hospital interns, and residents), dentists, podiatrists, practitioners of a limited branch of medicine, registered nurses, licensed practical nurses, visiting nurses, other health care professionals, psychologists and school psychologists, speech pathologists and audiologists, coroners, administrators or employees of a child day care center, administrators or employees of a residential camp or child day camp, administrators or employees of a certified child care agency or other public or private children services agency, school teachers, school employees, school authorities, social workers, professional counselors, and individuals rendering spiritual treatment through prayer.[1]

A physician is not required to make a report, however, if the suspicion of abuse is based on a communication that is privileged (see chapter 3.4, Privileged Communications), unless the patient, at the time of the communication, is either a child under 18 years

---

1. OHIO REV. CODE § 2151.421(A).

of age or a physically or mentally handicapped person under age 21 and the physician knows or suspects that the patient has suffered or faces a threat of suffering abuse or neglect.[2] The statute is not clear about whether psychologists also are exempt from child abuse reporting in circumstances in which privileged communication rules apply. Two Ohio courts have addressed somewhat related issues. In one case, the Ohio supreme court[3] ruled that psychologists have no duty to report regarding persons outside the psychologist–patient relationship. A more recent ruling by an appellate court, with a different set of circumstances, came to the same conclusion.[4] Neither of these cases provides clarity, however, about whether a psychologist must make a child abuse report if the patient is an adult who admits to abusing a child, when the child is not the patient. Finally, the Ohio attorney general has rendered an opinion in which she noted that attorneys and physicians are exempt from the reporting requirement as noted earlier, and she noted that this exemption does not extend to counselors or social workers.[5]

Another question that sometimes is asked by MHPs is whether professionals listed in the statute as mandatory reporters must make a report when the previously abused person is no longer a child under 18 years of age. The Ohio attorney general reviewed related statutes and case law and advised that counselors and social workers are not obligated to make reports when the abused person is no longer a child. She also advised, however, that a report must be made when there is reason to believe that another person who is still a child is at risk of child abuse (e.g., another child in the home or a grandchild).[6]

The report is to be made by the previously mentioned individuals whenever they know or suspect that a child under the age of 18 or a mentally retarded, developmentally disabled, or physically impaired child under the age of 21 has suffered abuse or faces a threat of abuse.[7]

In addition, anyone who is not identified by statute as a mandated reporter who knows or suspects that a child under 18 or a mentally retarded, developmentally disabled, or physically impaired person under 21 has suffered or faces threats of abuse

---

2. Ohio Rev. Code § 2151.421(A).
3. Brodie v. Summit Cty. Children Serv. Board, 51 Ohio St. 3d 112, 554 N.E.2d 1301 (1990).
4. Hite v. Brown, 100 Ohio App.3d 606, 654 N.E.2d 452 (1995).
5. Op. Att'y Gen. 205 (2001-035). (Opinions of the attorney general are not binding on courts.)
6. Id.
7. Ohio Rev. Code § 2151.421(A).

may voluntarily report the information to the public children services agency or to a municipal or county peace officer.[8]

(B) When Must a Report Be Made?

Reports must be made immediately.[9]

(C) How a Report Must Be Made

Reports are to be made to the public children services agency or a municipal or county peace officer in the county in which the child resides or in which the abuse or neglect is occurring or has occurred. Municipal or county peace officers who receive such reports must refer the report to the public children services agency.[10] Reports may be made by telephone or in person and must be followed by a written report if requested by the receiving agency or officer. The written report must include the names and addresses of the child and the child's parents or the person having custody of the child, the child's age and the nature and extent of the child's suspected abuse or threats of abuse, and any other information that might be helpful in establishing the cause of abuse. Mandated reporters also may take photographs of visible trauma on a child and, if medically indicated, may have radiological examinations performed.[11]

(D) Immunity From Liability

Anyone making a report of child abuse, whether a mandated reporter or a voluntary reporter, is immune from civil or criminal liability for making the report or for participating in good faith in subsequent judicial proceedings. Individuals who knowingly make false reports or cause others to make false reports are guilty of a misdemeanor of the first degree.[12] Penalties may include a jail term of up to 180 days,[13] a fine up to $1,000,[14] or a period of community controlled sanction (probation).[15]

---

8. Ohio Rev. Code § 2151.421(B).
9. Ohio Rev. Code § 2151.421(C).
10. Ohio Rev. Code § 2151.421(D).
11. Ohio Rev. Code § 2151.421(C).
12. Ohio Rev. Code § 2921.14.
13. Ohio Rev. Code § 2929.24.
14. Ohio Rev. Code § 2929.28.
15. Ohio Rev. Code § 2929.26.

(E) Confidentiality and Privilege

Reports made to a public children services agency and to a municipal or county peace officer are confidential. The information in the report and the name of the person who made the report may not be released and may not be used as evidence in any civil action brought against the person who made the report. The report is admissible, however, in a criminal proceeding that arises from the report, and the person who made the report may be questioned by attorneys as they prepare their case.[16]

The public children services agency may not provide to the alleged perpetrator of the abuse the name or identity of the person or agency who made the report or who made statements to the police.[17] These records are not public records (see chapter 3.6, State Freedom of Information Act).[18]

(F) Failure to Report

Failure of any cited professionals to make a report is a misdemeanor of the fourth degree and may be punishable by a maximum jail term of 30 days,[19] a fine up to $250,[20] and/or a period of community control sanction (probation).[21]

---

16. Ohio Rev. Code § 2151.421(H).
17. Ohio Rev. Code § 2151.421(H)(5).
18. Ohio Rev. Code § 2151.421(H).
19. Ohio Rev. Code § 2929.24.
20. Ohio Rev. Code § 2929.28.
21. Ohio Rev. Code § 2929.26.

4.9

Abused and Neglected Children

Procedures for handling child abuse and neglect cases typically involve three stages: taking the child into protective custody, holding a fact-finding hearing, and holding a dispositional hearing. It generally is a hierarchical process that may stop at any point if the allegations are unfounded or on a showing that the parents are currently capable of raising their children in a responsible manner. Each stage may involve a mental health evaluation of the child and/or parent. In addition, the MHP may be called to testify as an expert witness (see chapter 4.10, Termination of Parental Rights).

(A) Temporary Custody

The court may take temporary custody of a child, without parental approval, by a law enforcement official or an officer of the court when any of the following conditions exist:[1]

1. there are grounds to believe the child is suffering from illness or injury and is not receiving proper care and removal is necessary to prevent immediate or threatened physical or emotional harm;

2. there are reasonable grounds to believe that the child is in immediate danger from the child's surroundings and removal is necessary to prevent immediate or threatened physical or emotional harm;

---

1. Ohio Rev. Code § 2151.31(A).

3. there are reasonable grounds to believe that another child in the household has been abused or neglected and that this child also is in danger of immediate or threatened physical or emotional harm from the same person;

4. the child has run away from his or her parents;

5. the conduct, conditions, or surroundings are endangering the health, welfare, or safety of the child; or

6. when there is good reason to believe that the child may abscond or be removed from the jurisdiction of the court or will not appear before the court as required.

Taking a child into temporary custody is not considered an arrest, and the child may not be confined in an adult correctional facility.[2] The child cannot be placed in a juvenile detention center (a restricted setting) or shelter care (an unrestricted setting) before implementing the court's final order of disposition, unless the placement is necessary to protect the child or ensure that the child will be available for court appearances.[3]

(B) Adjudication of Alleged Child Abuse or Neglect

In the adjudication of alleged child abuse or neglect, the court may order a social history or physical or psychological examination of the child and/or the parents at any time after the filing of the complaint.[4] Any MHP may perform these evaluations, subject to being accepted by the court as an expert witness.[5]

Within 72 hours after a complaint has been filed, the court must set a date for an adjudicatory hearing, and the hearing must occur within 30 days unless the court establishes that more time is needed for any party to obtain counsel (a 10-day extension) or more time is needed to complete an evaluation (up to a 30-day extension).[6]

At the adjudicatory hearing, the court determines whether the child is abused, neglected, or dependent. The parents have a right to be represented by counsel. If a party appears at the hearing without counsel, the court must ascertain whether the party knows of his or her right to be represented and knows that the

---

2. OHIO REV. CODE § 2151.31(B).
3. OHIO REV. CODE § 2151.31(C).
4. JUV. P. R. 32(A).
5. OHIO R. EVID. 702.
6. OHIO REV. CODE § 2151.28(A).

court will provide counsel if the party is indigent. The court may continue the case to enable a party to obtain counsel. If the interests of the child conflict with those of the parents or guardians, separate counsel must be provided for the child.[7]

The court also determines where the child should live until the dispositional hearing. The court must determine whether any relatives of the child are willing to be temporary custodians of the child and, if there are, the relatives are to be a first choice for placement if the court finds them appropriate. Otherwise, the child may be placed, or remain, in sheltered care.[8]

(C) Dispositional Alternatives

If a child has been adjudicated as abused, neglected, or dependent, the court must hold a separate dispositional hearing no later than 90 days from the time the complaint was filed.[9]

If the court finds a child to be abused, neglected, or dependent, the court may make any of the following dispositions:[10]

1. place the child in protective supervision, in which the child remains in the custody of the parents or guardian and stays in the child's home, subject to conditions and limitations prescribed by the court;

2. commit the child to the temporary custody of a public or private children services agency, or with either parent, a relative residing within or outside the state, or a probation officer for placement in a certified foster home or other home approved by the court;

3. award legal custody of the child to either parent or to any other person who has filed a request for legal custody;

4. commit the child to the permanent custody of a public or private children services agency if the court determines that the child cannot be placed with one of the child's parents within a reasonable time;

5. place the child in a planned permanent living arrangement with a public or private child placing agency; or

6. order removal from the home of the person who committed the abuse or neglect or who is the parent, guardian, or custodian of a child who is adjudicated dependent.

---

7. OHIO REV. CODE § 2151.352.
8. OHIO REV. CODE § 2151.28(B).
9. OHIO REV. CODE § 2151.28(B)(3).
10. OHIO REV. CODE § 2151.353(A).

4.10

Termination of Parental Rights

After child abuse, neglect, or maltreatment has been reported and a finding is made (see chapters 4.8, Reporting of Child Abuse, and 4.9, Abused and Neglected Children), the question sometimes arises as to whether parental rights should be terminated. If a determination is made by the public children services agency to petition for termination of parental rights, the parent is afforded a range of procedural due process rights, which must be strictly satisfied. Because such a decision inevitably involves consideration of the child's emotional well-being and the parent–child relationship, MHPs frequently are called on to undertake individual and family evaluations to assist the court in the decision.

(A) Filing the Termination Petition

A public children services agency or a private child placing agency that has been granted temporary custody of an abused, neglected, or dependent child may file a motion with the court requesting permanent custody of the child. The agency that files such a motion also must present to the court a specific plan to seek an adoptive family for the child and to prepare the child for adoption.[1]

When this motion is filed, the agency also must meet with the parents to review the agency's decision to recommend termination of parental rights.[2]

---

1. OHIO REV. CODE § 2151.413.
2. OHIO ADMIN. CODE § 5101:2-42-95(C).

(B) Grounds for Termination

The primary ground for termination of parental rights is the best interest of the child. In making this determination, the court reviews all relevant evidence about the child, the child's parents, and any other relatives who might be appropriate caretakers. Specifically, the court considers such issues as:[3]

1. whether the child has been abandoned or orphaned and there are no relatives who are able to take permanent custody;

2. whether the child has been in temporary custody for 12 or more months;

3. the nature of the interrelationship of the child with the child's parents, siblings, relatives, foster caregivers, and any others who may affect the child;

4. the wishes of the child, with due regard for the age and maturity of the child;

5. the child's need for a legally secure permanent placement and whether such a placement can be achieved without granting permanent custody to the agency filing the motion;

6. the nature of the parents' ability to improve their child-care skills; in making this determination, the court may rely on medical, psychological, and rehabilitative evaluations and services;

7. whether the parents continued to commit abuse or neglected the child after initial complaints were filed;

8. whether the parent is incarcerated and will not be available to care for the child for at least 18 months; and

9. whether the parent has been convicted of or pleaded guilty to any offenses against the child.

(C) The Termination Hearing and Decision

When a complaint for the allocation of parental rights and responsibilities for the care of a child is made, the court may order investigations into the character, health, family relations, past

---

3. OHIO REV. CODE § 2151.414.

conduct, present living conditions, earning ability, and financial worth of the parties.[4]

The court will schedule a hearing whenever a motion is filed to remove parental rights. Notice must be given to all parties involved, including the child's guardian *ad litem*, who has been assigned to represent the interests of the child. The notice must contain a full explanation that the granting of permanent custody will divest the parents of their parental rights. The parties have the right to legal counsel at the hearing. The court usually holds the hearing within 120 days after the public children services agency or private child placing agency files the motion for permanent custody. The court must make a decision about the matter within 200 days after the agency files the motion. The court may grant permanent custody to the agency if it determines, by clear and convincing evidence, that such a step is in the best interest of the child. If the court assigns permanent custody, it is obligated to file a written opinion that describes its findings of fact and conclusions of law.[5]

(D) Effect of Termination

Termination of parental rights divests the parents of all of their parental rights,[6] including the rights to consent to the child's adoption or marriage, visit the child, and chose the religion of the child, and the responsibility for support of the child.[7]

---

4. Juv. P. R. 32.
5. OHIO REV. CODE § 2151.414(A).
6. OHIO REV. CODE § 2151.353(B).
7. OHIO ADMIN. CODE § 5101:2-1-01.

4.11

Guardianship and Conservatorship for Minors

A guardian may be appointed for a minor in situations in which the custodial parent(s) is unable to care for the child because of death, legal termination of parental rights (see chapter 4.10, Termination of Parental Rights), or other circumstances. In some states, guardians are appointed to undertake parental responsibilities, whereas conservators are appointed to manage the estate (e.g., money, property, and business enterprises). In Ohio, no real distinctions are made between guardians and conservators, and they are covered together in the same set of statutes. Guardianship law provides for appointment of a guardian of the person, guardian of the estate, and guardian of the person and the estate if such powers are given to one individual. MHPs are likely to become involved in a guardian selection process and follow-up treatment, if any, for the children.

(A) Application for Guardianship

The probate court (a division of the court of common pleas that has jurisdiction over these matters) may, on its own initiative or based on the application by an interested party, appoint a guardian or limited guardian of a person, an estate, or both, of a person who is a minor. A person applying for appointment as guardian or limited guardian must file with the probate court an application that contains a statement of the whole estate of the person, its probable value, and the likely value of annual rental of the person's real estate. In addition, the application must include the following information about the applicant: (a) a statement about whether the applicant has ever been charged with or convicted of any crime involving theft, physical violence, or sexual, alcohol, or substance abuse, and, if the applicant has such a history, the date and place of each charge and conviction; (b) a statement of whether a limited guardianship or full guardianship is sought. If limited guardianship is requested, the application must specify the limited powers that are requested and whether the limited guardianship is requested for a definite or indefinite period of time; and (c) a listing of the name, age and residence of the minor; the name and residence of each parent of the minor; the name, age, degree of kinship, and address of next of kin of the minor if no parent is living or cannot be notified; and the name and residence of the person currently holding custody of the minor.[1] A minor over the age of 14 may select a guardian, and the court is likely to appoint this guardian if he or she is a suitable person.[2]

The court may appoint a probate court investigator to investigate the need for the guardianship or to review the functioning of a guardian. The report must contain information about the physical and mental condition of the child and a recommendation regarding the necessity for a guardianship or the functioning of the current guardian.[3]

(B) The Guardianship Hearing

Before appointing a guardian or a limited guardian, the court must conduct a hearing on the matter of appointment. Except in an emergency, the hearing will not be held until at least seven days after the court has notified the minor, each parent, the next of kin of the minor who are known to reside in Ohio, and the person having custody of the minor.[4] Legal counsel is not required[5] but is permitted.

A minor over the age of 14 may select a guardian; the court will appoint this person as guardian if he or she is a suitable person. If a minor over the age of 14 does not select a suitable person, the court may make an appointment without regard to the child's wishes.[6]

When a guardian is appointed for a minor who is under 14 years of age, the guardian continues until the child reaches the

---

1. OHIO REV. CODE § 2111.03.
2. OHIO REV. CODE § 2111.12.
3. OHIO REV. CODE § 2111.042.
4. OHIO REV. CODE § 2111.04(A).
5. OHIO REV. CODE § 2111.02(A).
6. OHIO REV. CODE § 2111.12.

age of majority (age 18), unless the child selects another guardian after the child reaches 14 years of age.[7]

When parents name a person as guardian in a will, that person is given preference in appointment over the person selected by the minor.[8]

The guardianship hearing must consider the following:

1. the proposed guardian or limited guardian must appear at the hearing and swear under oath that he or she will make diligent efforts to file a true inventory of assets in the future and will faithfully and completely fulfill all other duties, including the filing of timely and accurate reports and accountings; and

2. evidence of a less restrictive option to guardianship may be introduced by a relative or legal counsel and, when it is, the court must consider the evidence.[9]

(C) Duties of the Guardian

Guardians for minors have duties similar to those of guardians for incompetent adults (see chapter 4.2, Guardianship for Adults). The court determines whether a guardian is needed and, if so, selects the person to be the guardian. Once appointed, the guardian takes an oath promising to faithfully perform all duties as guardian. The court will specify the duties and power of the guardian; generally the duties are defined so that the minor is permitted to care for him- or herself to the extent possible. In general, the court may assign all powers to the guardian over the person that the person ordinarily would have if he or she were not a minor, except the power to make or revoke a will.[10] Especially relevant for MHPs, a guardian of a minor may authorize the provision of physical and psychological health care to the minor.[11] The court also determines whether to appoint a guardian or a limited guardian. If a limited guardian is appointed, the court will spell out the limited duties in a letter of authority, and the length of time for which limited guardianship is awarded is specified.[12] In the case of a limited guardian, the minor retains all of his or her rights in all areas not affected by the court order appointing the guardian. The guardian is responsible for maintaining

---

7. OHIO REV. CODE § 2111.46.
8. OHIO REV. CODE § 2111.12.
9. OHIO REV. CODE § 2111.02(C).
10. OHIO REV. CODE § 2111.50(B).
11. OHIO REV. CODE § 2111.13(C).
12. OHIO REV. CODE § 2111.02(B).

close contact with the minor so that appropriate decisions can be made.[13]

The guardian or limited guardian is responsible for making timely and accurate reports to the court, at least on a biennial basis. The report must include, among other things, information about the functioning of the person, the approximate number of times the guardian has met with the person and the nature of those contacts, an opinion of the guardian about the necessity for continuing the guardianship, and a statement from a physician or an MHP who has examined the person within three months before the date of the report. On review of the guardian's biennial report, the court may continue the guardian arrangement, direct an investigator to verify aspects of the report, or terminate or modify the guardianship.[14]

(D) Termination of the Guardianship

In general, guardians serve until the child reaches majority age of 18.[15] However, at any time the court may remove the guardian for good cause and the child may request a change in guardian.[16]

If a guardian or limited guardian is temporarily or permanently removed or resigns, and if the circumstances require immediate action, the probate court may appoint, with or without notice to the child or interested parties, an interim guardian for a maximum of 15 days. After a hearing, the court may extend an interim guardianship for up to 30 more days.[17]

If a guardian is terminated before the child reaches age 18 and a new guardian is not appointed but the minor is still in need, the juvenile court may be granted exclusive jurisdiction over the child until the child reaches age 18.[18]

---

13. Ohio Rev. Code § 2111.02(C).
14. Ohio Rev. Code § 2111.49.
15. Ohio Rev. Code § 2111.07.
16. Ohio Rev. Code § 2111.46.
17. Ohio Rev. Code § 2111.02(B).
18. Ohio Rev. Code § 2111.46.

4.12

Conservatorship for Minors

Ohio does not distinguish between guardians and conservators (see chapter 4.11, Guardianship and Conservatorship for Minors).

4.13

Foster Care

Foster care provides residential housing and support, under the supervision of the Department of Social Services or private adoption agencies, for children who are not able to live in their own homes. The person may be placed in a foster home for as little as one night or as long as several years. MHPs may be involved in approving homes and in providing assessment and therapeutic services to those placed in them.

(A) Certification of Foster Parents/ Licensing Requirements

Ohio law provides for regular foster care and for specialized foster care, which includes foster homes that provide specialized medical services and those that incorporate special rehabilitative services, such as for children who are emotionally or behaviorally disturbed.[1]

Foster homes must be certified by the Ohio Department of Job and Family Services to receive children. Public children services agencies, private child placing agencies, and private noncustodial agencies that have been certified to act as representatives of the Ohio Department of Job and Family Services in recommending foster care homes for certification are charged with the responsibility of receiving applications for certification from prospective homes and for conducting home studies. All applications must be made on a specified form that has been prepared by the Depart-

---

1. Ohio Rev. Code § 5103.02.

ment (Form # JFS 01691). Among other things, the application requests information about age, employment, and income of each household member; criminal history of any household members; proposed sleeping quarters of foster children; and types of foster children the applicant will consider. This form and the home study may simultaneously be used for review and approval of an applicant for certification as a foster home and for adoptive placements.[2] In addition to the information obtained from the application form, the agency must conduct a criminal records check and receive a completed medical evaluation form completed by a physician that documents that the caregiver and all members of the foster care household are free from any physical, emotional, or mental conditions that would endanger children or impair the ability of the household to care for a foster child. An agency may require additional examinations by physicians or psychologists in assessing the physical and emotional well-being of the members of the household. Reference checks are also completed on the applicant.[3] Certificates for foster homes are effective for two years.

In addition to regular recertification reviews, which occur every two years, the recommending agency must, within three days, investigate all allegations regarding the unsafe or inappropriate operation of a foster home. The agency may also require corrective action plans for the home. Any act or omission by a foster caregiver or a member of the household that results in death, injury, illness, abuse, or exploitation of a foster child is grounds for the denial of recertification or revocation of the foster home's certificate.[4]

(B) Placement of Children in Foster Homes

A placement in a foster home follows the arrangement by a public children services agency or a private child-placing agency for the out-of-home care of a child of whom the agency has temporary or permanent custody. Foster placement may be for almost any length of time, ranging from a few days in emergency situations to several years. A child may be placed in a foster home for many reasons, including that a court has determined that a child is

---

2. Ohio Admin. Code § 5101:2-5-20(A).
3. Ohio Admin. Code § 5101:2-5-20(G–H).
4. Ohio Admin. Code § 5101:2-5-28.

abused, neglected, and dependent;[5] or delinquent, unruly, or a juvenile traffic offender.[6]

When a child is placed in foster care, the placement agency must provide the foster home with a report of the child's social history, a summary of any delinquent acts of the child, and the conclusions and recommendations of any psychiatric or psychological examinations that have been conducted on the child. In cases in which the court has sealed the records of a child, those records are not available to the foster home. If a psychological examination has not been conducted on the child within the past year, the placement agency must have one completed and must provide the foster home a summary.[7]

The agency that places children into foster care, as well as into any other forms of shelter care, must develop a case plan for each child in placement, unless the parents have voluntarily surrendered custody. The plan must be filed with the juvenile court within 30 days of placement. The foster home is expected to participate in the case plan as needed. The agency that develops the case plan must attempt to obtain agreement on the plan among all parties, including the parents, guardian or custodian, and guardian *ad litem* (person selected by the court to represent the needs of the child). If agreement is not obtained, the court must determine the content of the case plan, and the plan then becomes part of the dispositional order for the child. Changes to the case plan may be requested by the agency of the court at any time, and the agency may make emergency changes when necessary, although the court must approve any continuing changes to the plan.[8]

Each case plan for children in temporary custody must include the following general goals:

1. consistency with the best interests of the child, to achieve an out-of-home placement in the least restrictive, most family-like setting available in close proximity to the child's original home or the home in which the child will be permanently placed;

2. elimination of the need for the out-of-home placement so the child can safely return home.[9]

If a child in temporary custody has been the victim of abuse or neglect, or has witnessed abuse or neglect of a sibling, a parent, or other household member, the case plan must include require-

---

5. Juv. P. R. 34.
6. Ohio Rev. Code § 2151.312.
7. Ohio Rev. Code § 2151.62(A)–(E).
8. Ohio Rev. Code § 2151.412(A)–(E).
9. Ohio Rev. Code § 2151.412(F).

ments that the child's parents, guardian, or custodian participate in mandatory counseling and any other supportive services that are written into the case plan.[10]

(C) Placement Review

Routine court reviews of foster placement are completed one year after the date on which the complaint in the case was filed or the child was first placed into foster care, whichever date comes first. The review considers the success of the child's placement and custody arrangement, the case plan prepared for the child, the plans for the long-term care or placement of the child, and any other relevant aspects of the child's placement. Follow-up review hearings are conducted no later than every 12 months after the initial placement review until the child is adopted, returned to the parents, or the court otherwise terminates the placement. If problems arise with the child's foster placement, the court may conduct a special review at any time.[11]

---

10. Ohio Rev. Code § 2151.412(H).
11. Ohio Rev. Code § 2151.417.

4.14

Adoption

The law provides that a person who wishes to adopt a child must meet certain minimum requirements (described in the following sections). Also, the adopted child and natural parents have rights and responsibilities that must be fulfilled for the adoption to be valid. MHPs may contribute to this process by providing evaluations of prospective adoptive parents and children and treatment to the adopted children, if necessary.

(A) Adoption Requirements

A child may be placed for adoption either by a public or private agency that is certified, licensed, or empowered to do so by law, or by an attorney. An attorney may not represent both the person seeking to adopt and the parent placing a child for adoption.[1]

Any child under the age of 18 may be adopted. In addition, an adult may be adopted under any of the following conditions:

1. the adult is totally and permanently disabled;
2. the adult is mentally retarded; or
3. the adult had been in foster care with the petitioner as a minor and the adult now consents to the adoption.[2]

The following persons may adopt:

1. a husband and wife together, at least one of whom is an adult;
2. an unmarried adult;

---

1. OHIO REV. CODE § 3107.011.
2. OHIO REV. CODE § 3107.02.

3. the unmarried minor parent of the person to be adopted; or

4. a married adult without the spouse joining as a petitioner if any of the following apply:
   a. the other spouse is a parent of the person to be adopted and supports the adoption;
   b. the petitioner and the spouse are legally separated; or
   c. the failure of the spouse to join in the petition or to support the adoption is because the spouse has been absent, unavailable, incapacitated, or otherwise unavailable to grant support or refusal.[3]

An Ohio court may not make parenting determinations unless Ohio is the home state of the child at the time of the proceeding or Ohio has been the child's home state within six months before the start of proceedings and at least one parent continues to live in the state.[4]

(A)(1) Birth Parents

The birth parents must consent to the adoption. To complete the adoption process, the birth parents must personally appear before the court, sign appropriate forms that terminate parental rights and responsibilities, and indicate to the court that they understand the adoption process and that the decision to place the child for adoption was made voluntarily.[5]

Except as noted, a petition to adopt a minor is only granted if written consent has been obtained from all of the following:[6]

1. the mother of the child;

2. the father of the child;

3. the putative father of the child (i.e., a man who may be a child's father but is not married to the mother, has not adopted the child, has not developed a parent–child relationship with the child, and has not acknowledged paternity of the child)[7];

4. any person or agency that has permanent custody of the child;

5. the juvenile court of the jurisdiction if the legal guardian or custodian of the child is not authorized to consent; and

6. the child, if more than 12 years of age, unless the court determines that the child's consent is not required because it is not in the child's best interest.

---

3. Ohio Rev. Code § 3107.03.
4. Ohio Rev. Code § 3107.22.
5. Ohio Rev. Code § 3107.081.
6. Ohio Rev. Code § 3107.06.
7. Ohio Rev. Code § 3107.01(H).

Consent to adoption is not required of any of the following:[8]

1. a parent of a minor, when it is alleged in the petition for adoption and the court agrees that the parent has failed without good cause to communicate with the child or provide support for at least one year immediately preceding either the filing of the adoption petition or the placement of the child in the home of the petitioner;

2. the putative father, if he fails to register as the minor's putative father with the putative father registry not later than 30 days after the child's birth, or if he has willfully abandoned or failed to care for and support the child, or he abandoned the mother during her pregnancy and up to the time of her surrender of the child;

3. a parent who has entered into a voluntary agreement to surrender permanent custody;[9]

4. a parent whose parental rights have been terminated by order of a juvenile court;

5. a parent who is married to the petitioner and supports the adoption;

6. the father, or putative father, if the child is conceived as the result of rape;

7. a legal guardian or guardian *ad litem* (person selected by the court to represent the interests of the child) of a parent judicially declared incompetent;

8. a legal guardian of the child, other than a parent, who has failed to respond in writing to a request for consent within 30 days or who the court concludes is withholding consent unreasonably;

9. the spouse of the person to be adopted, if the failure of the spouse to consent is a result of prolonged unexplained absence, unavailability, incapacity, or other circumstances that make it impossible or unreasonably difficult to obtain the consent;

10. any parent or guardian in a foreign country, if the person to be adopted has been released for adoption pursuant to the laws of the country in which the person resides; or

11. any guardian or other party who has temporary custody of the child.

---

8. Ohio Rev. Code § 3107.07.
9. Ohio Rev. Code § 5103.15.

(A)(2) Adoptive Parents

The person or persons seeking to adopt a minor, or the agency or attorney who is arranging the adoption, must submit a petition for the adoption to the probate court, preferably no later than 90 days after the date the child was placed in the person's home. The petition is not required if the person seeking to adopt is the minor's stepparent, the minor was not originally placed in the person's home with the intent of the person adopting the minor, or the minor is a child with special needs.[10]

(A)(3) Adoptive Child

On finalizing of the adoption, the adopted child becomes the legal child of the adoptive parents. Adoption relieves the biological or other previous legal parents of the adopted child of all parental rights and terminates all legal relationships between the adopted child and his or her relatives, including inheritance. The adoption also creates a relationship between the child and the adoptive parent as if the adopted child were a legitimate blood descendant of the adoptive parent for all purposes, including inheritance.[11]

(B) Petition for Adoption

The petition for adoption is filed in the court in the county in which the person to be adopted was born, the petitioner or the child currently resides, the petitioner is stationed in military service, or in which the agency that has permanent custody of the child is located. The petitioner may ask the court to change the name of the child at this time.[12]

A petition for adoption must include the following information:

1. the date and place of birth of the person to be adopted;

2. the name of the person to be adopted, if known;

3. the name to be used for the person being adopted;

4. the date of placement of a minor in the home of the prospective adoptive parents and the name of the person(s) placing the minor;

5. the name, age, place, and duration of residence of the petitioner;

---

10. OHIO REV. CODE § 3107.051.
11. OHIO REV. CODE § 3107.15.
12. OHIO REV. CODE § 3107.04.

6. the marital status of the petitioner, including the date and place of marriage;

7. the relationship to the petitioner of the person to be adopted;

8. a statement that the petitioner has the resources to provide for the person to be adopted;

9. a description and estimate of value of all property of the person to be adopted;

10. the name and address, if known, of any person whose consent is needed for the adoption but who has not consented and facts that explain the lack of consent; and

11. a certified copy of the birth certificate of the person to be adopted.[13]

A home study is conducted of the prospective adoptive parent to ascertain whether the person seeking to adopt is suitable to adopt.[14] MHPs eligible to conduct the home study include psychologists, social workers, and counselors.[15] A written report of the home study must be filed with the court at least 10 days before the petition for adoption is heard.

Before the court issues a final decree of adoption, an assessor must conduct a prefinalization assessment of the child and prospective adoptive parent.[16] The qualifications of home study assessors are specified in the statute.[17] Professional counselors, social workers, psychologists, and others who are employed by a court or children services agency are identified as fulfilling the requirements for being an assessor. Assessors must complete educational programs on adoption placement practices, federal and state adoption assistance programs, and postadoption support services.[18]

The assessor's report typically must be filed with the court not fewer than 20 days before the date scheduled for the final hearing on the adoption. This assessment is not required if the petitioner for adoption is the child's stepparent, unless the court specifically orders it. The assessment is also not required if the child is to be adopted by the child's foster caregiver if the child has lived in the foster home for at least 12 months before the date of the application for adoption. The assessment must include information about the following:

1. the adjustment of the child to the adoptive placement;

2. the current and anticipated needs of the minor and prospective adoptive parents, as determined by a review of the child's

---

13. Ohio Rev. Code § 3107.05.
14. Ohio Rev. Code § 3107.031.
15. Ohio Rev. Code § 3107.014.
16. Ohio Rev. Code § 3107.12.
17. Ohio Rev. Code § 3107.014.
18. Ohio Rev. Code § 3107.015.

medical and social history and for adoption-related services such as counseling and case management;

3. the physical, mental, and developmental condition of the minor;

4. if known, the child's biological family background, including identifying information about the biological or other legal parents;

5. the reasons for the child's placement with the prospective adoptive parents and their attitude toward the proposed adoption and the circumstances under which the child was placed in their home; and

6. if feasible, the attitude of the child about the adoption.

(C) Adoption From Authorized Agencies

Public or private agencies that seek to place children for adoption must be certified, licensed, or otherwise empowered by law or rule to do so by the Department of Job and Family Services.[19] Authorized agencies and attorneys are permitted in Ohio to conduct the proceedings for adoption. The adoption process includes a petition for adoption (see earlier section in this chapter) that must be filed no later than 90 days after the child is placed in the adoptive home.

A foster caregiver may make application to a public or private adoption agency to adopt a foster child who has lived in the foster home for at least 12 months. In this instance, the foster caregiver does not need to furnish information that already was provided as part of the application to be a certified foster home placement.[20]

(D) Private-Placement Adoptions

Birth parents may voluntarily choose to place their child for adoption. This procedure is referred to as an "open adoption" in Ohio statutory law. An attorney or agency must be involved in the adoption, but an agency or attorney who has been asked to complete the adoption process may refuse. If the attorney or agency refuses to complete the adoption, the attorney or agency must

---

19. Ohio Rev. Code § 3107.01.
20. Ohio Rev. Code § 3107.012.

offer to refer the birth parents to another agency or attorney who will complete the adoption.[21]

An open adoption does not permit the birth parents to share with the adoptive parent any parental control or authority over the child or to limit the adoptive parent's control and authority. The open adoption must still be finalized by the court, but the court is obligated to approve a proposed placement unless the court concludes that the open adoption is not in the best interest of the child or that the terms of the adoption agreement made between the birth parents and the adoptive parents violate the statute.[22]

In an open adoption, the birth parents may request that the agency or attorney arranging the adoption provide the birth parents with profiles of prospective adoptive parents who have been recommended by an assessor. The profile may include identifying information about a prospective adoptive parent if the prospective adoptive parent agrees to include this information. If a birth parent chooses a prospective adoptive parent from a profile, the attorney or agency must give that prospective adoptive parent priority when determining with whom the child will be placed.[23]

(E) Adoption Subsidies

If a public service agency has a child for adoption who has special needs, the agency enters into an agreement with the child's adoptive parent before the child is adopted under which the agency promises to make payments as needed so the child can obtain needed services.[24] Payments may be made for expenses for medical, surgical, psychiatric, psychological, and counseling services. Payments for similar services also may be made to the adoptive parent if the agency determines, postadoption, that the child has serious needs that existed before the adoption was completed or developed later but were due to a preexisting condition. The agency may make these payments if the following criteria are met:

1. the adoptive parent has the ability to provide a permanent family relationship for the child in all areas except financial need to meet the child's special needs;

2. the needs of the child exceed the resources of the adoptive family as determined by the agency; and

---

21. OHIO REV. CODE § 3107.63.
22. OHIO REV. CODE § 3107.65.
23. OHIO REV. CODE § 3107.61.
24. OHIO REV. CODE § 5153.163(B).

3. the agency concludes that the acceptance of the child as a member of the adoptive parent's family would not be in the best interest of the child unless payments are made on the child's behalf.

4.15

Delinquency and Persons in Need of Supervision

The family court has exclusive jurisdiction to hear complaints about juveniles who are alleged to be delinquent or in need of supervision. Children who appear before the court may see an MHP as part of the process. Although this generally occurs during the dispositional phase, MHPs may also contribute at other stages.

(A) Juvenile Delinquency

(A)(1) Terms and Definitions

Delinquent child includes any child, except a juvenile traffic of-fender, who violates any law of the state of Ohio, the United States, or a political subdivision of Ohio that would be an offense if committed by an adult; any child who violates an order of the court; any child who violates the statute making it illegal for a minor to purchase a firearm; or any child who is a habitual or chronic truant. *Juvenile* or *child* is any person less than 18 years of age. However, a minor who is adjudicated a delinquent child or juvenile traffic offender before attaining 18 years of age may be considered a juvenile or child until the person attains 21 years of age. *Status offense* is an act prohibited by law that would not be an offense if committed by an adult. *Juvenile court* means the division of the court of common pleas (a state court found in each county) or a juvenile court, separately and independently created, having jurisdiction over offenses committed by minors. *Detention* means the temporary care of children pending court adjudication or disposition in a public or private facility designed to physically restrict the movement and activities of children. *Permanent custody* is a legal status that vests in a public or private children services agency all parental rights and duties and removes such rights from the parents. *Probation* is a legal status created by court order following an adjudication that a child is a delinquent, a juvenile traffic offender, or an unruly child, whereby the child may remain in the parents' home under their supervision. *Residential care facility* refers to an institution or facility that is licensed by the Department of Mental Health and provides care for children. *Residual parental rights* means those rights that remain with the natural parent after the transfer of legal custody of the child, including such things as the privilege of visitation and the authority to determine the child's religious affiliation, as well as the responsibility for financial support. *Secure correctional facility* refers to a facility under the direction of the Department of Youth Services that is designed to physically restrict the activities of children after adjudication and disposition. *Serious youthful offender* means a person who is eligible for a mandatory or discretionary transfer to adult court but is not transferred to adult court.[1]

(A)(2) Petition

Any individual knowing of a child who appears to be delinquent may file a sworn complaint in the juvenile court of the county in which the child lives or in which the delinquent behavior allegedly occurred. The complaint must describe the particular facts on which the allegation is based.[2]

If a child appears to be a delinquent child who is eligible for a serious youthful offender dispositional sentence and the prosecuting attorney wishes to seek such a sentence, the prosecuting attorney of the county in which the alleged delinquency occurs may initiate a case in the juvenile court by presenting the case to a grand jury for indictment.

(A)(3) Initial Appearance: Detention Hearing

When a child is brought before the court or delivered to a detention center, an authorized officer of the court immediately makes an investigation and must release the child unless it appears that the child's detention or shelter care is warranted. A delinquent child may be held for up to six hours for processing purposes in a county jail or other facilities where adult offenders are held.[3] If the child is not released, a complaint or indictment must be filed by the investigator and an informal hearing must be held to determine if detention or shelter care is needed. This hearing must be held promptly, not later than 72 hours after the child is

---

1. Ohio Rev. Code § 2152.02.
2. Ohio Rev. Code § 2152.021.
3. Ohio Rev. Code § 2151.311.

placed in detention or shelter care. Reasonable oral or written notice of the hearing must be given to the child and the parents, guardian, or custodian. Before the hearing, the court must inform the parties of their right to counsel and of the child's right to remain silent regarding the allegations.[4]

The juvenile court may conduct its hearings in an informal manner and may exclude the general public from its hearings. If it does so, it must first hold a separate hearing to determine if this step is appropriate. If a complaint alleges a child to be delinquent, the parent, guardian, or custodian of the child must attend all proceedings of the court. Failing to attend may lead to a charge of contempt and may result in a fine or placement in jail in an effort to coerce the person to attend the proceedings.

(A)(4) Fact-Finding Hearing

No later than 72 hours after the complaint is filed, the court must schedule a time for an adjudicatory hearing that is held in accordance with Ohio Juvenile Rules. The court then issues a summons to the child, or parent, guardian or custodian if the child is under 14 years of age, and to any adults that the court believes are necessary parties to the proceedings.[5] The summons includes the name and telephone number of a court employee designated by the court to arrange for the prompt appointment of counsel, if needed. If the court concludes that the child may abscond or be removed from the jurisdiction and not attend the hearing, the court may order that the child be taken into immediate custody.[6]

The court may order a social history or physical or mental examination at any time after the filing of the complaint under any of the following circumstances: (a) on the request of the person to be examined; (b) when there is a possibility the child will be transferred for adult prosecution; (c) where the examination may clarify questions about whether neglect, abuse, or dependency has occurred; (d) when legal responsibility or competency on the part of the person to be examined are at issue; and (e) when such an examination is needed to determine whether emergency medical care is needed.[7]

When such examinations are completed before the adjudication step, the results may only be used for the limited purposes noted earlier. The person who prepared the examination report

---

4. OHIO REV. CODE § 2151.314.
5. OHIO REV. CODE § 2151.28.
6. OHIO REV. CODE § 2151.28(G).
7. JUV. P. R. 32(A).

may not testify about the findings, except in a hearing to determine whether the child should be transferred to adult court for criminal prosecution.[8] The court also may order that the contents of the report, in whole or part, not be disclosed to specified persons, although the court must state its reasons to counsel for such denial. The court may also, for good cause shown, deny counsel access to part or all of the report.[9]

The court will appoint a guardian *ad litem* to protect the interests of the child in the proceedings if the child has no parent, guardian, or legal custodian or if the court finds that there is a conflict of interest between the child and the parent, guardian, or legal custodian. Whenever possible, the guardian *ad litem* should be a volunteer who is judged to be qualified by the court. On request from guardians *ad litem*, the Department of Jobs and Family Services will provide for their special training.[10]

If the court at the adjudicatory hearing finds beyond a reasonable doubt that the child is a delinquent, the court proceeds either immediately or at a subsequent postponed hearing to hear the evidence to make a disposition. If the court does not find the child to be delinquent, it dismisses the case and the child is discharged.

The court may confine a child who is alleged to be, or is adjudicated, delinquent in a detention facility for up to 90 days for information to be gathered about the child's family and personal history, school performance, and any other information that will assist the court in its disposition of the charges.[11]

A juvenile court may impose a serious youthful offender dispositional sentence on a child that adds penalties otherwise reserved for adult offenders. Such a sentence may be considered only if the prosecuting attorney of the county in which the delinquent act allegedly occurred initiates the process against the child. If the original complaint did not seek this type of sentence, the prosecuting attorney must file with the juvenile court a written notice of intent to seek this sentence within 20 days of the filing of the original complaint. The court must then serve notice on the child. Depending on the information available to it, the court then may hold a preliminary hearing to determine if there is probable cause that the child committed the act and if the child is eligible for this sentence. Once the court determines that the child is eligible for a serious youthful offender sentence, the child is entitled to an open and speedy trial by jury in juvenile court.[12]

---

8. JUV. P. R. 32(B).
9. JUV. P. R. 32(C).
10. OHIO REV. CODE § 2151.281.
11. OHIO REV. CODE § 2152.04.
12. OHIO REV. CODE § 2152.13.

The child is afforded all rights, including a jury trial, afforded an adult who is prosecuted for committing a crime, including the right to counsel.

(A)(5) Dispositional Hearing

If a child is adjudicated a delinquent child, the court may make any of many orders of disposition, including the following:

1. provide care for the child by the public service children's agency as is available to a child who is considered abused, neglected, or dependent;

2. commit the child to the temporary custody of a school, camp, or other institution that is operated for the care of delinquent children;

3. place the child on community control under any sanctions, services, and conditions that the court prescribes. Community control may include probation supervision, a period of day reporting, community service, a requirement that the child obtain a high school diploma or other educational certificate, a period of drug and alcohol use counseling and/or monitoring, a requirement that the child observe a curfew, a period of time of house arrest and/or electronic monitoring in which the person's movements are monitored electronically, and suspension of a driver's license;

4. commit the child to the custody of the court;

5. require the child not to be absent from school without legitimate excuse for more than prescribed times;

6. if appropriate, require the child—and if necessary the parents— to participate in a truancy prevention mediation program (such programs may include special tutoring and monitoring at the school, counseling, assistance for the parents in assuring that their child attends school, and, if available, assignment of the child to an alternative school);[13]

7. make any other dispositions that the court may find proper, except that there are restrictions regarding placing the child in adult correctional facilities;[14] or

8. impose a fine and a requirement to make restitution to the victim.[15]

---

13. Ohio Rev. Code § 3321.191.
14. Ohio Rev. Code § 2152.19(A), (B).
15. Ohio Rev. Code § 2152.20.

If the delinquent child committed an act that caused, attempted to cause, or created a risk of physical harm to the victim, the court, before issuing an order of disposition, shall order the preparation of a victim impact statement by the probation department. The court considers this information in determining the disposition.[16]

The court may establish a victim–offender mediation program in which victims and their offenders meet to discuss the offense and suggest possible restitution. If the court obtains the assent of the victim, the court may require the delinquent child to participate in the mediation program.[17]

If the court finds from clear and convincing evidence that the child violated Ohio law regarding possessing, using, purchasing, or receiving cigarettes or other tobacco products, the court may require the child to attend a youth smoking education or treatment program and/or impose a fine of not more than $100.[18]

If a child is adjudicated a delinquent child for committing an act that requires a mandatory serious youthful offender dispositional sentence, the juvenile court must impose a sentence as if the child were an adult except that the court may not impose a death penalty or life imprisonment without parole. The juvenile court shall also impose on the child one or more traditional juvenile dispositions. The adult portion of the dispositional sentence must be stayed pending the successful completion of the traditional juvenile dispositions imposed.[19]

If a child is eligible for a discretionary serious youthful offender dispositional sentence, the court may impose either one or more traditional juvenile dispositions or a blended juvenile and adult sentence. The juvenile court makes this decision based on the nature of the violation, the history of the child, and the options available in the juvenile system. Whenever a child is given a serious youthful offender dispositional sentence, the child may appeal the adult portion of the sentence.[20]

The juvenile court may commit a delinquent child to the legal custody of the Department of Youth Services for secure confinement in one of its facilities for various periods, but not beyond the time when the child reaches 21 years of age. During the period of court control, the Department may not move the child to a nonsecure setting without the court's permission.[21]

---

16. OHIO REV. CODE § 2152.19(D).
17. OHIO REV. CODE § 2152.19(C).
18. OHIO REV. CODE § 2151.87(F).
19. OHIO REV. CODE § 2152.13.
20. Id.
21. OHIO REV. CODE § 2152.16(A)(1–2).

Before making a final disposition for a delinquent child, the court considers whether the child has previously been adjudicated a delinquent child. If so, the court considers the previous delinquent adjudication as a conviction (as if it had been committed by an adult) in determining the degree of the current offense.[22]

Certain delinquents are also subject to the law regarding sex offenders and may be required to register as sex offenders (see chapter 7.21, Services for Sex Offenders).

To assist in making decisions, the juvenile court may order that physical and mental examinations be completed on the child by a physician or psychologist. The costs of these examinations are paid by the county.[23]

The court must warn the parent, guardian, or custodian of a delinquent child that any subsequent adjudication of the child as delinquent may result in a criminal charge against the parent, guardian, or custodian.[24]

(B) Persons in Need of Supervision (PINS)

Ohio statutory law defines "unruly" children as those being in need of supervision.

(B)(1) Terms and Definitions

Unruly child includes any of the following:[25]

1. any child who is not under sufficient control of a parent, guardian, or custodian;

2. any child who is persistently truant from home;

3. any child who is a habitual truant from school; if school truancy continues after the child is determined to be an unruly child, the court may then determine that the child is a delinquent child;

4. any child who endangers the health or morals of self or others;

5. any child who attempts to enter a marriage relationship without the consent of a parent, custodian, or guardian;

6. any child who is found in a disreputable place or a place prohibited by law or associates with vagrant, vicious, criminal, notorious, or immoral individuals;

---

22. OHIO REV. CODE § 2152.13(C).
23. OHIO REV. CODE § 2151.53; JUV. P. R. 32.
24. OHIO REV. CODE § 2151.354.
25. OHIO REV. CODE § 2151.022.

7. any child who engages in an occupation prohibited by law or is in a situation that is injurious to the health or morals of the child or others; or

8. any child who violates a law other than those having to do with the purchase of firearms or possession or use of tobacco products.

Chronic truant means any child of compulsory school age who is absent without legitimate excuse for 7 or more consecutive days, 10 or more days in one month, or 15 or more days in a school year.[26] *Habitual truant* means any child of compulsory school age who is absent without legitimate excuse for 5 or more consecutive days, 7 or more days in one month, or 12 or more days in a school year.[27]

(B)(2) Petition

Any individual having knowledge of a child who appears to be unruly may file a sworn complaint in the juvenile court of the county in which the child has residence or in which the unruly behavior occurred. The complaint must include a description of the facts on which the complaint is based. If the complaint alleges misbehavior involving school property or activities held under the auspices of the Board of Education, the court must give written notice of the allegations to the superintendent of schools.[28]

Ohio law[29] requires courts and various state and local agencies that provide services to children and families to coordinate services for alleged unruly children and to develop services that divert unruly children from the juvenile court system. As part of this effort, the court may hold in abeyance a complaint that a child is an unruly child, pending the child's successful completion of a program of activities, such as a school attendance plan or assisting the parents in providing close monitoring of the child's activities, that are designed to divert the child from the juvenile court system.[30]

(B)(3) Hearings

If a complaint alleges that a child is an unruly child, an adjudicatory hearing must be held in accordance with the *Ohio Juvenile*

---

26. OHIO REV. CODE § 2152.02.
27. OHIO REV. CODE § 2151.01(B)(17).
28. OHIO REV. CODE § 2151.27.
29. OHIO REV. CODE § 121.37.
30. OHIO REV. CODE § 2151.27(F).

Rules. The court must issue a summons to the child, the parents, guardian, or custodian and any other individuals that the court considers helpful, requiring them to appear before the court to respond to the allegations. The notice includes the name and telephone number of a court employee designated to arrange for appointment of counsel, if needed. The court may order that the child be placed in custody if the court believes the child will not be brought to court for the hearing or if the child's conduct or surroundings endanger the child or others.[31] The court may appoint a guardian *ad litem* to protect the interests of the child or the interests of the parent if the parent appears to be mentally incompetent or under 18 years of age.[32]

(B)(4) Dispositions

The court may order any of several dispositions for an unruly child, including the following:[33]

1. make any of the dispositions that are authorized for abused, neglected, or dependent children (see earlier section in this chapter);
2. place the child on community control (probation) with restrictions and services as necessary;
3. suspend or revoke the driver's license and vehicle registrations of the child;
4. commit the child to the custody of the court;
5. make any of the dispositions that are authorized for delinquent children, except that the child may not be committed to a secure correctional facility, and commitment to a detention facility typically may not exceed 24 hours;
6. if the child's unruly behavior involved drug or alcohol misuse, require the child to participate in a drug abuse or alcohol abuse counseling program and suspend or revoke the child's driver's license; and
7. if the child is adjudicated an unruly child for being a habitual truant, require the child to participate in relevant educational activities and medical or psychological treatment. The court also may require the parent or guardian to participate in community service programs, preferably a program that requires

---

31. Ohio Rev. Code § 2151.28.
32. Ohio Rev. Code § 2151.281.
33. Ohio Rev. Code § 2151.354.

the involvement of the parent or guardian in the school attended by the child.

The court may order a physical and mental examination by a physician (including a psychiatrist) or psychologist to assist it in making a disposition, as described earlier.[34]

---

34. OHIO REV. CODE § 2151.53; JUV. P. R. 32.

4.16

Competency of Juveniles to Stand Trial

An incapacitated person is a respondent in a juvenile delinquency proceeding who, as a result of mental illness, mental retardation, or developmental disability, lacks the capacity to understand the proceedings or to assist in his or her defense. At any time the court believes that the respondent may be an incapacitated person, it may issue an order that the child be examined.

Although Ohio statutory law governs the issue of competency to stand trial for adults (see chapter 7.5, Competency to Stand Trial), the state does not have comparable statutory provisions for juveniles.

The supreme court of Ohio has not addressed the issue of juvenile competency relative to due process. However, a few Ohio appellate courts[1] have spoken on the issue and have generally agreed that the right not to be tried while incompetent is as applicable in the juvenile system as in the adult system. Most recently, for example, a court of common pleas (a state court found in each county) held that the due process clauses of the United States and Ohio constitutions require a juvenile court to observe procedures that safeguard the child's right not to be adjudicated while incompetent to stand trial.[2] Furthermore, this court also found that it was appropriate for the juvenile court to apply the adult competency statute to juvenile proceedings, provided the court uses juvenile rather than adult norms. It is important to note, however, that "juvenile norms" have not been defined.

---

1. In re Chambers, 116 Ohio App.3d 312, 688 N.E.2d 25 (Ohio App. 3d Dist. 1996); In re D.G., 698 N.E.2d 533 (Ohio Com. Pl. 1998); In re Williams, 116 Ohio App.3d 237, 687 N.E.2d 507 (1997).
2. In re D.G., 698 N.E.2d 533 (Ohio Com. Pl. 1998).

4.17

Nonresponsibility Defense

In most states, most defenses available to an adult charged with a crime are extended by statute to juveniles charged with delinquency. These defenses include mental disease or defect ("insanity"), justification, duress, and entrapment. The legal standard for an insanity defense may be the same for juveniles as for adults in Ohio (see chapter 7.9, Criminal Responsibility), but no Ohio statute or reported case has addressed this issue. MHPs may participate in the process by performing evaluations and providing testimony in court.

Ohio statutory law does not address the juvenile insanity issue, and the Ohio supreme court has not ruled on it. One appellate court has ruled that a juvenile may not assert a defense of insanity in juvenile proceedings but rather that insanity is a factor to be asserted by the defense during the trial court's determination of delinquency.[1] The Ohio supreme court declined a discretionary appeal of that decision.[2]

---

1. In re Chambers, 116 Ohio App.3d 312, 688 N.E.2d 25 (Ohio App. 3d Dist. 1996).
2. In re Chambers, 78 Ohio St. 3d 1464, 678 N.E.2d 221 (1997).

4.18

Transfer of Juveniles to Stand Trial as Adults

Under certain circumstances the law allows a minor to be transferred from juvenile court to adult criminal court. This is likely to occur either when the juvenile has a history of contacts with the juvenile court and further treatment is not likely to be beneficial or when public safety requires continuing incarceration past the 18th birthday (or 21st birthday in instances in which the juvenile is given an adult sentence). The juvenile court may request evaluation by MHPs to provide evidence at the transfer hearing.

(A) Definitions

Category one offense includes aggravated (involving the use of a deadly weapon) murder and murder. *Category two offense* includes voluntary manslaughter (done by design or intention), kidnapping, rape, aggravated arson, aggravated robbery, and aggravated burglary.[1] Refer also to definitions in chapter 4.15 (Delinquency and Persons in Need of Supervision).

(B) Removal Procedures

After a complaint has been filed by any person alleging that a child age 14 or older is a delinquent child for committing an act that would be an offense if committed by an adult, the juvenile

---

1. OHIO REV. CODE § 2152.02.

court may transfer the case for criminal prosecution to the appropriate adult court.[2] On transfer of the case, the juvenile court states the reasons for the transfer and its jurisdiction is ended for the delinquent acts alleged in the complaint.

(C) Factors in a Removal Determination

In considering whether to transfer a case to adult court, the juvenile court considers the following factors:

1. whether there is probable cause to believe that the child committed the act;

2. whether the act charged was a category one offense and either or both of the following apply to the child:
   a. the child was 16 years of age or older at the time of the act;
   b. the child previously was adjudicated a delinquent for an act that is a category one offense or a category two offense and was committed to the legal custody of the Department of Youth Services;

3. whether the act charged was a category two offense, the child was 16 year of age or older when the act was committed and either the child previously had been adjudicated a delinquent for committing a category one offense or a category two offense and was committed to the legal custody of the department of youth services or the child is alleged to have had a firearm while committing the offense and to have displayed or used the firearm to commit the act;[3]

4. whether the court may also order a mental examination by an MHP to determine if the child is amenable to care or rehabilitation and if the safety of the community may require that the child be controlled beyond majority age of 18;

5. whether the victim was a child 5 years of age or younger;

6. whether the victim sustained physical harm;

7. whether the child has a history of failure to benefit from at least one rehabilitation attempt; and

8. whether the victim was 65 years of age or older or was permanently and totally disabled at the time of the act.[4]

---

2. OHIO REV. CODE § 2151.26(A).
3. OHIO REV. CODE § 2151.26.
4. Id.

If a minor allegedly commits an act that would be a felony if committed by an adult but the person is not apprehended for the act until after the person attains 21 years of age, the juvenile court does not have jurisdiction over the case and the case is handled by the appropriate adult criminal court.[5]

---

5. Ohio Rev. Code § 2151.26(G).

4.19

Voluntary Admission and Civil Commitment of Minors

Minors, defined as persons under 18 years old, generally are covered under the same psychiatric hospitalization laws as adults (see chapters 8.3, Voluntary Admission of Mentally Ill Adults, and 8.4, Involuntary Commitment of Mentally Ill Adults), with a few special provisions discussed herein. MHPs may become involved in the process by recommending that a minor be hospitalized, by involvement in the treatment of a hospitalized minor, or by participating in a commitment hearing.

(A) Voluntary Admission of Minors

A parent, guardian, or custodian of a child may make application to a hospital on behalf of the child for voluntary admission. The child then may be admitted to any hospital for observation, diagnosis, care, or treatment, unless the chief clinical officer finds that hospitalization is inappropriate. In the case of a public hospital, no person may be admitted without the authorization of the mental health board of the person's county of residence.[1]

If a minor is admitted on a voluntary basis by a parent, guardian, or custodian, the court must determine if continued hospitalization is warranted if a petition objecting to the commitment is filed with the court by the Legal Rights Service, counsel, a relative, or one acting as a friend.[2] The Legal Rights Service is a state system providing counsel to individuals who are detained or institutionalized.

---

1. OHIO REV. CODE § 5122.02(B).
2. OHIO REV. CODE § 5122.02(C).

The chief clinical officer must discharge any voluntary patient who has recovered or whose hospitalization is no longer advisable. The chief clinical officer also may discharge any voluntary patient who refuses to accept appropriate treatment.[3] When voluntarily admitted patients request release in writing (presumably this would be completed by the parents or guardian in the case of a minor patient), the chief clinical officer, within three days from the receipt of the request, may file with the court in the county where the patient is hospitalized or in the county where the patient is a resident an affidavit stating that the patient is a mentally ill person subject to hospitalization by court order (requiring an involuntary hospitalization; see chapter 8.4, Involuntary Commitment of Mentally Ill Adults.[4]

(B) Involuntary Civil Commitment

The juvenile court has the power to hospitalize a minor by court order, following the procedures that have been established for adult clients (see chapter 8.4, Involuntary Commitment of Mentally Ill Adults).

(C) Notice Requirements

The chief clinical officer of the hospital must inform voluntary patients (parents and guardians in the case of a child) of their rights to release as noted earlier and assist in making and presenting requests for release.[5]

The notice requirements and hearing proceedings for involuntarily committed persons (presumably for minors as well) are described in chapter 8.4 (Involuntary Commitment of Mentally Ill Adults).

(D) Admission to Residential Treatment Facilities

A juvenile court may place a child who has been adjudicated as an abused, neglected, or dependent child[6] or a delinquent child[7]

---

3. OHIO REV. CODE § 5122.02(C).
4. OHIO REV. CODE § 5122.03(B).
5. OHIO REV. CODE § 5122.03(B).
6. OHIO REV. CODE § 2151.353(A)(5).
7. OHIO REV. CODE § 2152.11.

in a residential treatment facility. To do so, the court must notify the parents of this intention and provide the parents with a full explanation of their right to be represented by counsel and to have counsel appointed if they are indigent. When the court places a child in a residential treatment facility, as part of its dispositional order the court must create a written case plan (a treatment plan) for the child.[8] The court retains jurisdiction over the child while the child resides in a residential treatment facility, until the child reaches the age of 18, or age 21 if the child is mentally retarded, developmentally disabled, or physically impaired. Jurisdiction may continue longer for a specified period of time to enable the child to graduate from high school or vocational school.[9]

Any public children services agency, private child placing agency, the Department of Job and Family Services, or any party other than a parent whose parental rights have been terminated may file a motion with the court at any time to request a modification of the disposition. The court then must hold a hearing after giving all the parties notice of the hearing and their right to be represented by counsel. These parties also may request that the placement in the residential treatment facility be terminated. If no parties object to the proposed termination within seven days after notification, the court may terminate the placement without a hearing

---

8. OHIO REV. CODE § 2151.11(D).
9. OHIO REV. CODE § 2151.253(E).

4.20

Education for Gifted and Handicapped Children

The law provides that any person over five and under 21 years old who has not received a high school diploma is entitled to attend public schools without payment of tuition. This includes children who are handicapped who can receive appropriate educational opportunities only from a program of special education. MHPs may become involved in the special education process through evaluations of the children and consultations with special education personnel.

(A) Terms and Definitions

Handicapped child means a person under 21 years of age who is developmentally handicapped, hearing handicapped, speech handicapped, visually disabled, severe behavior handicapped, orthopedically handicapped, specific learning disabled, autistic, or traumatic brain injured and because of the handicap needs special education.[1] *Handicapped preschool child* means a handicapped child who is at least 3 years of age who but is not yet of school age and is not currently enrolled in kindergarten.[2] *Special education* means the required related services and instruction designed to meet the unique needs of a handicapped child, including classroom instruction, home instruction, and instruction in hospitals and other settings.[3] *Gifted child* means students who perform

---

1. OHIO REV. CODE § 3323.01(A).
2. OHIO REV. CODE § 3323.01(K).
3. OHIO REV. CODE § 3323.01(B).

or show promise of performing at remarkably high levels of accomplishment compared with others of their age.[4]

(B) Referral and Special Educational Evaluation

The state Board of Education has established standards and procedures for the identification, location, and evaluation of all handicapped children. No single method or evaluation criterion may be the sole criterion for determining an educational program for a handicapped child. The state board requires each school district, in consultation with the local board of mental retardation and developmental disabilities and the boards of alcohol, drug addiction, and mental health services to identify, locate, and evaluate all handicapped children in the district to determine which ones are not receiving appropriate services.[5]

(C) Placement in a Special Education Program

Each school district must ensure that handicapped children are served by appropriately licensed or certified education personnel and must document annually that it employs the appropriate number of these personnel to serve the children's needs. The law requires school districts to provide school psychological services at a ratio of 1 school psychologist per 2,500 students.[6]

Each school district must consult with the educational service center and the Mental Retardation/Developmental Disability board serving the district.[7]

To the maximum extent appropriate, the state Board of Education must ensure that handicapped children are educated with children who are not handicapped.[8] The law specifies the ratio of children to service providers for speech–language pathology services and school psychological services.[9] School districts must provide speech–language services at a ratio of 1 service provider

---

4. Ohio Rev. Code § 3324.01.
5. Ohio Rev. Code § 3323.03.
6. Ohio Rev. Code § 3317.15(F).
7. Ohio Rev. Code § 3317.15.
8. Ohio Rev. Code § 3323.04.
9. Ohio Rev. Code § 3317.15(F).

per 2,000 students, and it must provide school psychological services at a ratio of 1 school psychologist per 2,500 students.

(D) Parental Rights

The state Board of Education has established procedures to ensure that handicapped children and their parents are guaranteed procedural safeguards regarding the identification, evaluation, and placement of the child. These procedures include (a) the opportunity for parents to examine relevant records and to obtain, at their own expense, an independent evaluation of their child; (b) previous written notice of any proposal or refusal to initiate or change the placement of the child; (c) the right to present complaints about the placement to the superintendent and to have a due process hearing conducted by an impartial hearing officer; and (d) the right to appeal to the state Board of Education.[10]

(E) Preschool Children With Handicapping Conditions

Each school district, educational service center, Mental Retardation/Developmental Disability board, and each institution operating a special education program must maintain a record of all handicapped preschool and school aged children and the services they are receiving. The superintendent of each district must certify these figures to the state Board of Education annually.[11]

(F) Gifted Pupils

Each school district is required to identify gifted students in grades kindergarten through 12th. Four categories of giftedness are specified: superior cognitive ability, specific academic ability, creative thinking ability, and visual or performing arts ability. Broad criteria for each category are specified.[12] Each district must obtain approval from the Ohio Department of Education for its policies and procedures for identifying gifted students.[13] Each

---

10. OHIO REV. CODE § 3323.05.
11. OHIO REV. CODE §§ 3317.032, 3323.02.
12. OHIO REV. CODE § 3324.03.
13. OHIO REV. CODE § 3324.04.

district must inform parents about the criteria and methods that it uses in identifying gifted students, policies and procedures that the district uses to ensure equal access for minority, disadvantaged, and disabled children and for those for whom English is a second language, and provisions to ensure that all students identified as gifted receive services.[14]

14. Ohio Rev. Code § 3324.06.

Consent, Confidentiality, and Services for Minors

Whenever a minor requests or receives services without parental knowledge or consent (see chapter 3.1, Informed Consent for Services), legal issues arise concerning the minor's capacity to give informed consent and the scope of the confidential relations between the minor and the MHP. Because both failure to obtain consent from the appropriate person before providing services and failure to maintain confidential information are grounds for loss of licensure, a malpractice suit, or other types of civil liability for MHPs (see chapters 3.10, Malpractice Liability, and 3.11, Other Forms of Professional Liability), it is important to identify the client from a legal perspective—the minor or the parent. Ohio law does not comprehensively address these issues. This chapter discusses those circumstances that the law does address.

(A) Emergency Treatment

Every hospital in Ohio that provides organized emergency services must provide that a physician is available on call 24 hours each day to examine individuals reported to a law enforcement agency to be victims of sexual offenses. Each victim must be informed of available venereal disease, pregnancy, medical, and psychiatric services. A minor may consent to examination regarding a sexual offense without advance parental consent, although the hospital subsequently must give written notice to the parents that such an examination has taken place. The parents are not liable for payment for these services.[1] The statute does not specify who, if anyone, is responsible for payment.

A minor may give consent, without the involvement of parents, for the diagnosis and treatment of a venereal disease. Parents are not liable for payment for these services.[2] The statute does not specify who, if anyone, is responsible for payment.

(B) Treatment for Alcohol Abuse

A minor may give consent for diagnosis and treatment by a physician of any condition that was caused by use of drugs or alcohol. A physician who provides medical or surgical services to the minor is not subject to civil or criminal liability for assault and/or battery. The parent or guardian of the minor is not responsible for paying for these services unless the parent consents to subsequent treatment.[3]

(C) Consent for Mental Health Treatment of Minors

Ohio law permits minors 14 years of age and older to request and receive outpatient mental health services, excluding medication, without parental knowledge and permission. The MHP may not inform the parent or guardian unless the professional determines that there is a compelling need for disclosure because of potential of harm to the minor or to other persons and the minor has been informed of the professional's intent to inform the parent or guardian. A limit of six sessions or 30 days of service, whichever occurs first, is applied in this context. The child's parents are not liable for the costs of the services.[4] The statute does not specify who, if anyone, is responsible for payment.

---

1. OHIO REV. CODE § 2907.29.
2. OHIO REV. CODE § 3709.241.
3. OHIO REV. CODE § 3719.012.
4. OHIO REV. CODE § 5122.04.

4.22

Consent for Abortion

Although it is constitutionally forbidden for the state to give parents complete veto power over a mature minor woman's informed consent to abortion, state law requires parental notification. MHPs may become involved in this process by evaluating and testifying about whether the minor woman is mature enough to make the decision without parental notification.

(A) Standard for Consent

Ordinarily, parental notification and consent would be required for a minor to obtain an abortion. Ohio law recognizes that, in some instances, parental notification and permission may not be wise.

An unemancipated, unmarried minor who wishes to have an abortion without notification of her parents, guardian, or custodian may file a complaint in juvenile court requesting permission to give consent.[1] The complaint must include all of the following:

1. a statement that she is pregnant;
2. a statement that she is unmarried, under 18 years of age, and unemancipated;
3. a statement that she wishes to have an abortion without notification of her parents, guardian, or custodian;

---

1. OHIO REV. CODE § 2151.85(A).

4. an allegation of one or both of the following:
   a. that she is sufficiently mature to make the decision alone;
   b. that one or both parents, her guardian, or her custodian have been engaged in a pattern of abuse against her, or that notification of her parents, guardian, or custodian is not in her best interest; and
5. a statement about whether she has retained an attorney, and if so, the name, address, and telephone number of her attorney.

(B) Notification Hearing

A hearing on the request must be held by the court at the earliest possible time, but not later than the fifth business day after the request is filed. The court must make its conclusion immediately after the hearing is concluded. If the court does not hear the request within five days, the individual may proceed with the abortion as if the court had granted full permission. If a hearing is held, the court appoints a guardian *ad litem* (a person selected by the court to represent the child's interests) and an attorney, if one has not been retained. Hearings are conducted in a manner that will preserve the confidentiality of the complainant. Records of the hearing are not public records (see chapter 3.6, State Freedom of Information Act). Filing fees and court costs are not assessed to the minor.[2]

---

2. Ohio Rev. Code § 2151.85(H).

4.23

Evaluation and Treatment of Children at the Request of a Noncustodial Parent

MHPs may be asked to provide services to children at the request of noncustodial parents. Some state laws provide that when one parent has custody, that person exercises exclusive authority over the care and upbringing of the child and the noncustodial parent does not have legal authority to give consent to evaluation or treatment of the child. MHPs who provide services at the request of a noncustodial parent without first obtaining the permission of the custodial parent may be vulnerable to a malpractice claim on the basis that consent to the services was not given (see chapter 5.1, Mental Status of Licensed or Certified Professionals) and may not be able to enforce on the custodial parent an obligation to pay for the services provided.

Ohio statutory law defines custody as a legal status that vests in the custodian the right to have physical care and control of the child and to determine where and with whom the child will live and the right and duty to protect, train, and discipline the child and to provide the child with food, shelter, education, and medical care.[1] The noncustodial parent retains residual rights that include such things as reasonable visitation, consent to adoption, the privilege to determine the child's religious affiliation, and the responsibility for support.[2] Obtaining medical or psychological evaluation or treatment is a right and responsibility of the custodial parent but not of the noncustodial parent.

Ohio statutory law provides that, unless specifically denied access by a court order, the noncustodial parent has equal access to records regarding the child as the custodial parent.[3]

---

1. Ohio Rev. Code § 2151.011(B)(11).
2. Ohio Rev. Code § 2151.011(B)(38).
3. Ohio Rev. Code § 3109.051(H).

Other Civil Matters

5.1

Mental Status of Licensed or Certified Professionals

State laws governing the licensure of professionals increasingly include provisions concerning the mental status of these persons. Such provisions generally pertain to disciplinary procedures rather than license application screening. Mental health professionals (MHPs) may be asked to evaluate and testify before the credentialing board or a court concerning a professional's mental status and its effect on job performance.

(A) Licensed Professionals

(A)(1) Attorneys

All disciplinary actions for attorneys are conducted by the Board of Commissioners on Grievances and Discipline.[1] The Board receives evidence, makes findings, and submits recommendations to the Ohio supreme court concerning complaints of misconduct and the mental illness of any attorney or judge. *Mental illness* is defined as "a substantial disorder of thought, mood, perception, orientation, or memory that grossly impairs judgment, behavior, capacity to recognize reality, or ability to meet the ordinary demands of life."[2] The Ohio supreme court may suspend the attorney or judge from the practice of law. To assist in making a decision about the attorney, the Board may order a medical or psychiatric examination by one or more physicians designated by the Board. The report from the examination is made available to both parties and the Board. If the supreme court suspends the

---

1. OHIO GOV'T BAR R. 5.
2. OHIO REV. CODE § 5122.01.

attorney because of mental illness, the attorney's license is shifted to inactive status. The suspension information is not published, but it is a matter of public record. A suspension may be terminated on application from the attorney that demonstrates that the cause of the suspension has been removed. The termination of suspension is certified by the Board to, and affirmed by, the supreme court. A suspended attorney may be employed by another attorney, provided the employment does not involve the practice of law. Both the suspended and employing attorney must register the employment with the Board of Commissioners on Grievances and Discipline.

(A)(2) Dentists

The state Dental Board is empowered to discipline a licensed dentist for inability to practice under accepted standards of the profession because of a physical or mental disability or excessive use of or dependence on alcohol or other drugs.[3] The Board may take one or more of the following disciplinary steps:[4]

1. censure the dentist;
2. place the dentist on probation with requirements to make regular reports to the Board, limit practice to areas specified by the Board, and continue or renew professional education until a satisfactory degree of knowledge or competency has been attained;
3. suspend the license of the dentist for practice; or
4. revoke the license.

If the Board suspends a dentist's license, the Board also must identify the conditions under which the license will be restored. The Board must restore the license unconditionally when these conditions are met.

The Board may order the licensee to submit to examinations by physicians, including psychiatrists, designated or approved by the Board and at the Board's expense.[5]

If the Board has reason to believe that the dentist represents a clear and immediate danger to the public if allowed to practice, or the dentist has failed to comply with an order to obtain an examination, the Board may apply to the court of common pleas (a state court located in each county) for an order temporarily suspending the dentist's license, without a hearing, until the

---

3. OHIO REV. CODE § 4715.30(A)(8).
4. OHIO REV. CODE § 4715.30(C).
5. OHIO REV. CODE § 4715.30(D).

Board is able to conduct an adjudication hearing to determine the dangerousness of the dentist.[6]

(A)(3) Pharmacists

The state Board of Pharmacy, after giving notice to the pharmacist and conducting a hearing in which evidence is heard, may revoke, suspend, limit, place on probation, or refuse to grant or renew a license, or may impose a monetary penalty, if the Board finds that a pharmacist or pharmacy intern is addicted to or abusing drugs or alcohol or is impaired physically or mentally to the extent that the person is unfit to practice pharmacy.

The Board may require the pharmacist or pharmacy intern to submit to a physical or mental evaluation, or both.[7]

(A)(4) Physical Therapists

The Licensing Board for Occupational Therapy, Physical Therapy, and Athletic Trainers may refuse to grant a license to an applicant or may suspend or revoke the license of a physical therapist or physical therapist assistant or reprimand or place a license holder on probation for any of several reasons. Among the reasons are excessive use of controlled substances and alcohol to the extent that the person cannot practice competently and an adjudication by a court that the person is legally incompetent for practice.

When a license is revoked, application for reinstatement may not be made sooner than one year after the date of revocation. If the physical or mental condition of a licensee is at issue in a disciplinary proceeding, the licensing board may require the person to submit to an examination by a physician, including a psychiatrist.[8] If the Board places a license holder on probation, the Board must identify the conditions under which that person may be removed from probation.[9]

(A)(5) Physicians

The state Medical Board may revoke or suspend an individual's license to practice, refuse to reinstate a license, or reprimand or place on probation a physician, including a psychiatrist, for inability to practice according to acceptable standards of care because of mental illness or physical illness, and/or for habitual or excessive use of drugs or alcohol.[10]

---

6. OHIO REV. CODE § 4715.30(E).
7. OHIO REV. CODE § 4729.16.
8. OHIO ADMIN. CODE § 4755-21-03(D).
9. OHIO REV. CODE § 4755.47.
10. OHIO REV. CODE § 4731.22(B)(19).

The Board may require a physician to submit to a mental or physical examination, or both. The physician must bear the cost of the examination. If the Board finds a physician unable to practice, the Board must require the person to submit to treatment, by physicians approved by the Board, as a condition for reinstatement. The relevant statute also states that, by virtue of having been granted the privilege to practice medicine in the state, the physician is deemed to have given consent to submit to a mental or physical examination when directed by the Board to do so and to have waived any claims to privileged communication regarding admissibility of testimony and examination reports.[11]

Before being eligible for reinstatement, the impaired physician must demonstrate to the Board the ability to resume practice. If the license suspension was a result of the physician's excessive use or abuse of drugs, alcohol, or other substances, the demonstration of ability to resume practice must include certification from a treatment provider that the person has successfully completed any required inpatient treatment, evidence of full compliance with an aftercare contract, and two written reports indicating that the person's ability to practice has been assessed and the person has been found capable of practicing. The reports must be made by providers approved by the Board and must describe the basis for their determination.[12] When drug, alcohol, or other substance abuse was a factor in the license suspension and the license subsequently is restored, the physician will continue to be monitored by the Board for at least two years.[13]

(A)(6) Psychiatric Nurses

The Board of Nursing may deny, revoke, suspend, or place restrictions on a nurse's license and may impose a fine of not more than $500 for one or more of many reasons, including both habitual use of drugs or alcohol and mental disability to the extent that the ability to practice is impaired.

The Board may conduct hearings and may require a nurse to submit to a mental or physical examination, or both, at the expense of the individual. Failure to submit to a required mental or physical examination constitutes an admission of the allegations. Reports from examinations are reviewed by the Board. If the Board finds the nurse to be impaired, the Board must require the nurse to submit to treatment approved or designated by the Board as a condition for renewed authority to practice. If the Board suspends a nurse's license, the Board must specify the conditions

---

11. OHIO REV. CODE § 4731.22(B)(19).
12. OHIO REV. CODE § 4731.22(B)(26).
13. *Id.*

under which the person may be reinstated to practice, although the Board has the authority to specify that the suspension is permanent.[14]

(A)(7) Psychologists

The state Board of Psychology may refuse to issue a license to an applicant, issue a reprimand, or suspend or revoke the license of a psychologist or school psychologist if a court has adjudicated that the person is incompetent to hold a license. A previously incompetent person's license may be issued or reinstated only on determination by a court that the person is presently competent to practice and a decision by the Board that the person now is capable of practicing.

The Board may require a physical or mental examination before making its determination that the person is competent to practice.[15]

14. OHIO REV. CODE § 4723.28(B).
15. OHIO REV. CODE § 4732.17.

5.2

Workers' Compensation

Workers' compensation law provides employees with protection against the treatment costs and income losses resulting from work-related accidents or diseases. The employer purchases compensation insurance (or is self-insured) to provide the benefits for its employees. These benefits are awarded regardless of whether the employee or employer, or neither of them, is at fault. In return, the employee relinquishes the right to sue the employer civilly. The employee may elect to forego insurance benefits and retain the right to sue only if worker's compensation coverage is rejected by the employee before an accident. Otherwise, the employee is presumed to have elected the insurance coverage.

This law, as it concerns MHPs, pertains primarily to psychologists and psychiatrists; they may become involved in the workers' compensation process in two ways. An injured employee may consult one of these professionals for diagnosis and treatment, with the costs for these services paid for by workers' compensation insurance. Second, an insurance company may request a psychologist or psychiatrist to conduct an independent evaluation to determine the existence, nature, and extent of an employee's injury, and to testify about the findings at a hearing.

(A) Scope of the Coverage

The Ohio constitution specifies that workers' compensation must be available to workers and their dependents, for death, injuries, and occupational diseases occurring in the course of employment. This form of compensation is in lieu of all other rights to compensation or damages otherwise obtainable through suing the employer civilly[1] (however, see chapter 3.11, Other Forms of Professional Liability). State law specifies many diseases that are compensable,[2] although the law also states that a disease, not listed, that meets the statutory definition of a disease may be compensable.[3] *Injury* is defined as an injury received in the course of, and arising out of, the injured employee's employment. The statute specifically states that *injury* does not include psychiatric conditions, except when the condition has arisen from an injury or occupational disease. That is, a psychiatric condition is compensable only when it is the result of a physical injury or disease. Also not included are self-inflicted injuries, injuries caused by intoxication or drug abuse, and suicide.[4]

State law specifies the formula for calculating the amount of compensation that an employee will receive under total disability. Payment is not made when the employee has returned to work, an employee's treating physician has made a written statement that the employee is capable of carrying out the duties of the previous position, or the employee has reached the maximum medical improvement. If the worker is capable of returning to work but the employer is unable to offer the employee any employment, the employee must register with the Office of Job and Family Services for assistance in obtaining employment. When an employee has received compensation for 200 consecutive weeks for temporary total disability, the Bureau of Workers' Compensation must schedule an examination to determine if the person is permanently disabled.[5]

(B) Workers' Compensation and Mental Stress–Disorder

Mental stress and disorder are not listed in the statute as compensable disorders unless the psychiatric condition has arisen from an injury or occupational disease.[6] The statute is clear that mental–mental claims (psychiatric conditions that arise solely from job-related emotional distress) are not compensable. On the other

---

1. Ohio Const. art. II, § 35.
2. Ohio Rev. Code § 4123.68.
3. Ohio Rev. Code § 4123.01(C)(1).
4. Ohio Rev. Code § 4123.54(A), (B).
5. Ohio Rev. Code § 4123.56.
6. Ohio Rev. Code § 4123.01(C)(1).

hand, mental–physical claims in which emotional distress stems from a physical injury are compensable. The statute is not clear about whether only the employee who was physically injured may be compensated for a psychiatric condition or if a psychiatric condition also is compensable if it develops in another person as a result of that person participating in, or observing, an accident to another employee. The Ohio supreme court has provided partial clarification to this question.[7] It ruled that a psychiatric condition arising from a compensable physical injury or disease suffered by a third party is compensable in Ohio. In this case, a claimant suffered depression as the result of an accident in which he killed a coworker. The claimant was not physically injured in the accident and the Workers' Compensation Board had argued that depression suffered by a worker who was not physically injured was not compensable. The supreme court disagreed.

(C) Processing a Claim

The Industrial Commission of the Bureau of Workers' Compensation is charged with adopting rules as to the conduct of hearings, and it has developed forms for submitting an application for benefits. The rules allow adequate notice to the parties, a public hearing conducted by the Commission or district hearing officers, written decisions by the Commission or district hearing officer, impartial assignment of staff to cases, and the securing of witness attendance and testimony at hearings. All meetings of the Commission and district hearing officers are open to the public, and the Commission compiles a file of all of its memoranda, orders, and decisions about each case and makes these files available to the public.[8]

In addition to medical examinations that the employee or Commission may request, the employer of a claimant may require, without the approval of the Industrial Commission, that the claimant be examined, by a physician of the employer's choice, one time on any issue raised by the claimant. The employer pays the cost of such examinations. If the employee refuses to submit to the examination without good cause, the employee's right to have his or her claim for compensation considered is suspended.[9]

---

7. Bailey v. Republic Engineered Steels, Inc., 91 Ohio St. 3d 38, 741 N.E.2d 121 (2001).
8. Ohio Rev. Code § 4121.36(E–F).
9. Ohio Rev. Code § 4123.651.

(D) Workers' Compensation Benefits

Compensation may be available for claims alleging impairment of earning, permanent partial disability, permanent total disability, or death. The average weekly wage of the disabled or deceased employee is the basis on which the Bureau typically computes benefits.[10] If it is determined that the disabled employee likely would have earned increases in compensation, that fact may be used in determining the employee's compensation.[11]

No compensation is allowed for the first week after an injury or after the onset of an occupational disease and no compensation is available for the first week of total disability, unless and until the employee is totally disabled for a continuous period of two weeks or more. If disability continues for two weeks or more, then compensation is paid for the first week of disability. There is no waiting period for payment of funeral expenses.[12] State law specifies formulae for determining the amounts of compensation that are due to the employee, or to dependents in the case of the employee's death.[13]

If an injury results in the death of the employee and the employee has no dependents, the disbursement is limited to the expenses provided for in the statute.[14] If the employee has wholly dependent persons, then the weekly payment is 66⅔rds of the employee's average weekly wage, subject to additional variables such as the average statewide weekly wage and whether the employee had been receiving benefits before death. Payments to multiple dependents are apportioned. Payments to a dependent spouse continue until the remarriage or death of the spouse. If the dependent spouse remarries, an amount equal to two years of compensation is paid in a one-time lump sum to the spouse. Payments to a dependent minor continue until the minor reaches 18 years of age, or 25 years of age if the dependent is pursuing a full-time educational program, or, if the minor is mentally or physically incapacitated from earning any income, until the person is no longer incapacitated.[15]

---

10. Ohio Rev. Code § 4123.61.
11. Ohio Rev. Code § 4123.62.
12. Ohio Rev. Code § 4123.55.
13. Ohio Rev. Code § 4123.56.
14. Ohio Rev. Code § 4123.66.
15. Ohio Rev. Code § 4123.59.

5.3

Vocational Disability Determinations

The Rehabilitation Services Commission administers a vocational disability program through its Office of Vocation Rehabilitation (OVR). It is funded jointly by the state and federal governments for individuals who have a physical or mental disability that currently prevents them from obtaining employment but who might be able to engage in a gainful occupation if given vocational rehabilitation services. These services include assessment and psychotherapy from licensed physicians (psychiatrists), psychologists, and social workers. Other mental health workers who are directly employed by the OVR as rehabilitation counselors provide nonpsychological and nonpsychiatric services in accordance with OVR policies.

(A) Definitions

Handicapped person means any person with a physical or mental disability that is a substantial handicap to being employed and is of a nature that vocational rehabilitation services may be expected to be beneficial in obtaining employment. *Physical or mental disability* refers to a physical or mental condition that limits a person's activities or functioning. *Vocational rehabilitation* means services calculated to enable a handicapped person to engage in gainful employment.[1]

---

1. OHIO REV. CODE § 3304.11.

(B) Recipient Eligibility Requirements

The Rehabilitation Services Commission is responsible for processing referrals and applications and determining eligibility for services. Eligible individuals include those who have a physical or mental impairment that results in a substantial impediment to employment, can benefit from services in terms of an employment outcome, and require services to prepare for or obtain employment. A person who is receiving Social Security Disability Insurance benefits is eligible for rehabilitation services unless the Rehabilitation Services Commission can demonstrate by clear and convincing evidence that the person is incapable of benefiting from services because of the severity of the disability. The Commission may use other agencies' criteria to establish eligibility, such as those used by Social Security to determine disability insurance benefits.

Eligibility usually must be determined within 60 days after a person has submitted an application. The determination of eligibility cannot be based on the particular service needs or the anticipated costs of services required by an applicant or on the income level of the applicant or the applicant's family.

The Commission usually provides an assessment of the applicant to determine eligibility or whether a period of trial work is needed to make the determination. The assessment may include medical, psychological, educational, and vocational factors.[2]

(C) Psychological and Psychiatric Services

The Commission staff provides counseling and guidance services to assist individuals to make informed choices about services and employment opportunities. The staff also may refer the person to other agencies for services, such as those provided by local community mental health centers, and is obligated to promote coordination of services among community mental health agencies in the area where the person lives.[3]

(C)(1) Service Provider Qualifications for Psychologists

Licensed psychologists are eligible to provide evaluations and treatment. No additional qualifications are required.

---

2. OHIO ADMIN. CODE § 3304-2-54.
3. OHIO ADMIN. CODE § 5122-29-12.

(C)(2) Service Provider Qualifications for Psychiatrists

Licensed physicians are eligible to provide evaluations and treatment. No additional qualifications are required.

(C)(3) Fees

The consumer is expected to pay for services to the extent possible. Services must be provided at the least cost, while still meeting the training needs of the consumer.[4]

The Commission pays fees to professionals in accordance with a fee schedule. If medical or dental services are unavailable for the maximum amount allowed in the fee schedule, the Commission may exceed the maximum on the recommendation of the area manager. The Commission does not pay for missed appointments. If a consumer chooses to receive services from a provider other than the lowest cost provider, the Commission only pays the amount on its fee schedule and the consumer is expected to pay the difference.[5]

(D) Evaluation and Rehabilitation Studies

(D)(1) Evaluations

A comprehensive vocational assessment may be ordered when existing information does not permit the Commission to determine the general health status of the applicant, identify the rehabilitation needs of the person, and develop and determine the likely employment outcome and nature of services that will be needed. The assessment may include gathering information such as the medical, psychiatric, psychological, neuropsychological, vocational, cultural, social, and environmental factors that affect the employment needs of the person. Information also may be gathered regarding the individual's personality, career interests, interpersonal skills, intelligence, and other capacities and the individual's work experience and vocational aptitudes and interests.[6]

(D)(2) Restoration Services

If eligibility criteria are met but it is not clear whether rehabilitation services will be beneficial for the person because of the severity of the disability, the Commission may provide diagnostic

---

4. OHIO ADMIN. CODE § 3304-2-52(B), (C).
5. OHIO ADMIN. CODE § 3304-2-52(C), (D).
6. OHIO ADMIN. CODE § 3304-2-54.

services to allow the person additional opportunities to become capable of benefiting from services or to provide clear evidence that the person is incapable of benefiting from services. The Commission must provide these services until eligibility or ineligibility is determined.[7]

7. *Id.*

5.4

Emotional Distress as a Basis for Civil Liability

Emotional distress, also known as mental suffering or distress, may be the basis for a civil tort suit (i.e., one alleging physical or personal injury) or be part of a larger claim. The cause of the distress, the nature of the injury, and the motivations of the injured person determine whether a suit must be part of a larger claim or can stand by itself. MHPs may be asked to evaluate the person who claims to have suffered the distress and to testify about its existence, etiology, severity, and duration, as well as methods of treating it.

(A) Intentional Infliction of Emotional Distress

As noted in chapter 5.2 (Workers' Compensation), the Ohio workers' compensation plan provides immunity from negligence suits if the employer complies with the plan.[1] However, the Ohio supreme court has ruled that this protection does not extend to intentional tortuous conduct.[2]

In *Van Fossen v. Babcock & Wilcox Co.*,[3] the Ohio supreme court further outlined what an employee must establish in a complaint of an intentional tort. The court stated that, to establish an intentional tort, proof beyond that required to prove negligence or recklessness must be established. The court distinguished be-

---

1. Ohio Rev. Code § 4123.74.
2. Yeager v. Local Union 20, 6 Ohio St. 3d 369; 453 N.E.2d 666 (1983).
3. Van Fossen v. Babcock & Wilcox Co., 36 Ohio St. 3d 100, 522 N.E.2d 489 (1988).

tween (a) negligence, where the employer acts despite knowledge of some risk; (b) recklessness, where the employer acts with knowledge of an increased probability that the consequence will follow; and (c) intention, in which the employer acts knowing that injuries to employees are substantially certain to result.

The tort of intentional infliction of emotional distress has also been applied in a case in which immunity from civil suit was claimed by the defendant. In *Oglesby v. City of Columbus*,[4] an Ohio appellate court concluded that a trial court had erred in dismissing a complaint for intentional infliction of emotional distress in which a Columbus municipal employee alleged that the behavior of his supervisor was sufficiently egregious that she (the supervisor) was not immune from suit. In Ohio, immunity from civil liability is provided to a political subdivision and its employees, except that an employee is personally liable for conduct undertaken with maliciousness, in bad faith, or in a wanton or reckless manner.[5] In this case, the appellate court concluded that the employee plaintiff had presented allegations sufficient to state a claim for intentional infliction of emotional distress against the supervisor.

(B) Negligent Infliction of Emotional Distress

The Ohio supreme court also has defined what is necessary for a claim of negligent infliction of emotional distress. The court has recognized this tort even in the absence of a corresponding physical injury. In such a claim, for negligence to be found the emotional injuries sustained must have been both serious and reasonably foreseeable. Factors to consider include the following:

1. whether the plaintiff was located near the scene of the accident or further away;

2. whether the shock resulted from a direct emotional impact on the plaintiff from direct observance of the accident or, by contrast, from learning about the accident from others; and

3. Whether the plaintiff and victim (if any) were closely or more distantly related.[6]

To constitute serious emotional distress, the injury must "go beyond trifling mental disturbance" or "mere upset or hurt

---

4. Oglesby v. City of Columbus, WL 102257 (Ohio App. 10 Dist., 2001).
5. OHIO REV. CODE § 2744.03(6).
6. Paugh v. Hanks, 6 Ohio St. 3d 72, 451 N.E.2d 759 (1983).

feelings."[7] The standard is whether a reasonable person would be unable to cope adequately with the mental distress triggered by the situation.

(C) Emotional Distress as an Element of Damages

Aside from a separate lawsuit for emotional distress, a person may recover damages for emotional distress suffered as a result of another compensable injury. For example, one appellate court found it appropriate to grant damages for emotional distress to a prison inmate who was imprisoned for several days beyond the limits of his sentence.[8]

---

7. Carney v. Knollwood Cemetery Association, 33 Ohio App.3d 31, 40, 514 N.E.2d 430, 438 (1986).
8. Rainay v. Lorain Correctional Facility, 700 N.E.2d 90 (Ohio App. 10 Dist., 1997).

Insanity of Wrongdoers and Civil Liability

A person's mental status may affect whether he or she is liable under civil law for injurious behavior caused to another, whether the person can sue another for wrongs caused to him or her, or whether any special procedural rights will be provided to ensure a fair trial. Furthermore, and potentially more important, a party's mental status at the time of the conduct may determine whether the person is covered under a liability insurance policy. MHPs, therefore, may be asked to evaluate the person and testify about that person's mental status both when the injuries occurred and at the time of trial.

(A) The Liability of an Insane Person

No Ohio statutes address this issue, but an appellate court[1] has addressed it. The court followed the general rule that insane or otherwise mentally disordered individuals are civilly liable for injuries resulting from their intentional acts (see chapter 3.11, Other Forms of Professional Liability).[2]

(B) Insanity and Liability Insurance

Many insurance policies exclude coverage for acts that were intentional. These exclusionary clauses can be interpreted broadly. The court, in determining intention, may distinguish between a person

---

1. Clark v. Estate of Halloran, 1994 WL 11321 (1994).
2. RESTATEMENT (SECOND) OF TORTS, § 895 (1965).

who is mentally ill but still capable of forming intent and one who is legally insane and thereby incapable of forming intent. For example, in a case involving the shooting of a woman by a man who likely was mentally ill but not legally insane, a homeowners' insurance company was held not liable for damages because the policy excluded intentional acts.[3]

(C) Procedural Rights of Insane Persons

When an incompetent person is subject to civil legal proceedings, Ohio statutes specify that the court must ensure that the person has a guardian who may sue or defend on behalf of the person. When an incompetent person is not represented, the court must appoint a guardian *ad litem* to represent the person's best interests or make other orders that protect the person.[4]

---

3. Western Reserve Mutual Casualty Company v. Eberhart, 610 N.E.2d 481 (Ohio App. 9 Dist., 1991).
4. OHIO CIV. R. 17(B).

Competency to Contract

A person wishing to buy or sell property must have a minimum degree of mental capacity. This is a passive requirement in that every adult is presumed to possess it. It can become an issue if one of the parties to the contract (or that person's legal representative, such as a guardian) wishes to be excused from fulfilling his or her part of the agreement. An MHP may be asked to evaluate the competence of the person and to testify about the mental status either before or at the time the person entered into the contract.

(A) Legal Test of Competency to Contract

It is generally assumed that all adults are competent to enter into a contract, unless it is proven otherwise. In Ohio, the test used to determine mental capacity to enter into a contract is the ability of the person to understand the nature, scope, and extent of the business he or she is about to transact.[1]

(B) Determination of Competency to Contract

Determination of competency to enter into a contract is made on a case by case basis. Evidence can be gained from witnesses to

---

1. Vnerakraft, Inc. v. Arcaro, 110 Ohio App. 62, 168 N.E.2d 623 (1959); Testa, Exr. v. Roberts et al., 44 Ohio App.3d 161; 542 N.E.2d 654 (1988).

the signing of the contract and, in some instances, from others who are well acquainted with the person before and after the signing of the contract. The party seeking to prove mental incapacity must do so by clear and convincing evidence.[2]

---

2. *Testa*, 44 Ohio App.3d 161, 542 N.E.2d 654.

5.7

Competency to
Sign a Will

Individuals who make new wills or amend existing ones (referred to as *testators*) must meet minimum mental status requirements. If it is later shown that the person did not have the requisite testamentary capacity, the testator's estate will be distributed according to the terms of a previous valid will, if any, or by the state's intestacy (i.e., without a will) statutes. Mental health consultation or testimony may be used when an MHP treated or evaluated the testator (but see chapters 3.3, Confidential Relations and Communications, and 3.4, Privileged Communications, for limitations on the use of such information). Alternatively, an MHP may be asked to provide an opinion of the person's mental status at the time the will was signed, based on reports of other witnesses and any other relevant information.

(A) Legal Test of Testamentary Capacity

Unless a person has been adjudicated incompetent, there is a presumption of testamentary capacity. The standard for testamentary capacity was established by the Ohio supreme court.[1] Testamentary capacity exists when the testator has sufficient mind and memory to (a) understand the nature of the business in which he or she is engaged; (b) comprehend generally the nature and extent of his or her property; (c) hold in his or her mind the names and identity of those who have a natural claim to the property; and

---

1. Niemes v. Niemes, 97 Ohio St. 145, 119 N.E. 503 (1917).

(d) be able to appreciate his or her relation to the members of the family.[2]

(B) Proving Testamentary Incapacity

The burden of proof for incapacity is on the contestant of the will. The contestants must produce evidence that provides a reasonable basis for sustaining their claim.[3] Evidence may be introduced regarding the testator's mood, ability to care for self, and ability to make other decisions. The testimony of the testator's physician[4] and others who knew the testator well may be introduced to show lack of capacity.

(C) Undue Influence

The elements of undue influence are (a) a susceptible party; (b) another's opportunity to exert influence; (c) improper influence exerted or attempted; and (d) a result showing the effect of such improper influence.[5] Undue influence is found when the wishes of another person substitute for those of the testator in the making of the will. The influence must be such as to control the mental operations of the testator, overcome his or her power of resistance, and oblige him or her to make a disposition of property that would not otherwise have been made. The mere presence of influence, however strong, is not undue unless brought to bear directly on the act of making the will. Contestants to a will must show by clear and convincing evidence that a person exerted improper influence over the testator.[6]

---

2. Niemes v. Niemes, 97 Ohio St. 145, 119 N.E. 503 (1917).
3. Gannett et al. v. Booher et al., 12 O.B.R. 190, 465 N.E.2d 1326 (1983).
4. Gilbert v. Durlist, Ohio App 6th Dist 293, 1 Ohio Laws Abs. 507 (1923).
5. Poythress et al. v. Clark et al., 2001 WL 276896 (Ohio App. 11 Dist., 2001).
6. West v. Henry, 173 Ohio St. 498, 184 N.E.2d 200 (1962).

5.8

Competency to Vote

The right to vote can be denied or revoked on the basis of a person's mental status. MHPs may be asked to evaluate a person in this regard.

(A) Legal Test of Competency to Register

Every citizen of the United States 18 years of age and older who has been a resident of the state, county, or other political subdivision for at least 30 days,[1] and has been registered to vote for 30 days, is entitled to vote in all elections.[2] However, persons who have been found by the court to be incompetent are not entitled to register to vote, nor to vote if already registered.[3]

(B) Cancellation of Registration

Each county probate court (a court that has jurisdiction over wills, guardianship, and individuals found to be incompetent) files monthly reports with its respective Board of Elections listing persons who are no longer eligible to vote, including those who have been adjudicated incompetent. Ohio law requires the Board of Elections to cancel the voter registration of such individuals.[4]

---

1. Ohio Rev. Code § 3505.20.
2. Ohio Const. art. V, § 1.
3. Ohio Rev. Code § 5122.301.
4. Ohio Rev. Code § 3503.18.

Competency to Obtain a Driver's License

The registrar of motor vehicles includes as part of the application for an original operator's license and for renewal applications questions about the existence of a physical or mental condition that might impair the applicant's ability to operate a motor vehicle safely. If the presence of such conditions is acknowledged, the registrar may require an examination of the applicant by a physician, including a psychiatrist (the only MHP specifically identified) as a prerequisite to issuing a license. The applicant pays for the examination.

Similarly, when in the course of a routine driver license examination the examiner has reason to believe the applicant has a physical or mental condition that might impair the ability of the applicant to drive safely, the registrar must instruct the applicant to obtain a medical evaluation, signed by a physician, including a psychiatrist. The driver's license is not issued before a favorable report is received from the physician.[1]

Driver's licenses are removed from individuals whose driving is impaired because of excessive use of alcohol or controlled substances. Driving privileges are not restored until the registrar receives information from a physician, psychologist, or certified alcohol counselor stating that the person has successfully completed treatment and has maintained sobriety for a continuous six-month period. If the person receives a subsequent conviction of alcohol or drug abuse within one year of restoration of driving privileges, the registrar must again suspend the license.[2]

---

1. Ohio Admin. Code § 4501:1-1-18(A–B).
2. Ohio Admin. Code § 4501:1-1-18(C–D).

The law provides that a person who has been adjudged to be incapacitated and placed under guardianship (see chapter 4.2, Guardianship for Adults) cannot be issued a driver's license if, at the time of the application, the incapacity (need for guardianship) has not been removed.

5.10

Product Liability

Product liability is a legal term that describes a theory (claim) for personal injuries or property damages arising from the use of a product. Although a product liability claim may be based on principles of negligence or warranty, this chapter is limited to a third basis: strict tort liability. The central element of this claim is that the product was unreasonably dangerous to the user. MHPs who have special expertise in human factors may be asked to evaluate the safety of a product and testify in court about the results.

(A) Elements of a Product Liability Claim

Ohio law provides for claims of product liability against either the manufacturer or supplier of products.

A person making a claim of product liability against a manufacturer must prove two elements by a preponderance of the evidence: (a) The product was defective in manufacture or construction, in design, in providing adequate warnings or instructions, or in conforming to its representations and (b) the defect was the proximate cause of harm.[1]

A supplier is subject to liability for compensatory damages based on a product liability claim only if the claimant establishes, by a preponderance of the evidence, that either of the following applies: (a) The supplier was negligent and the negligence was

---

1. Ohio Rev. Code § 2307.73.

a proximate cause of the harm or (b) the product did not conform to a representation made by the supplier and this failure was a proximate cause of the harm. A supplier of a product is subject to product liability if the manufacturer would be liable, but for various reasons the manufacturer is not subject to judicial process in Ohio.[2]

In addition to compensatory damages, the court may award additional damages against a manufacturer or supplier if the claimant establishes, by clear and convincing evidence, that the harm was the result of misconduct of the manufacturer or supplier demonstrating a flagrant disregard for the safety of the user of the product.[3] Such awards are called punitive or exemplary damages and often are assessed as a means of punishing the offender or making an example of the offender.

(B) Defenses to a Product Liability Claim

There are two defenses to product liability claims. One defense is "assumption of risk," which applies when the user knew about the risks of using the product but used it anyway. In such a case, the assumption of risk defense bars the user from later suing for damages. Contributory negligence (carelessness in the use of the product) may also be asserted as a defense. Under the theory of contributory negligence, the inappropriate behavior of the product user contributed to the harm. That is, the person may have used the product for a purpose not intended by the manufacturer or handled the product in a careless manner. Contributory negligence does not create a complete bar to the plaintiff's recovery in Ohio. Instead, under the newer doctrine of comparative negligence, damages are diminished by an amount that is proportionately equal to the percentage of negligent conduct of the user.[4]

---

2. Ohio Rev. Code § 2307.78.
3. Ohio Rev. Code § 2307.801.
4. Ohio Rev. Code § 2315.20.

5.11

Unfair Competition

Business competitors may engage in fierce battles to win a share of the market. They cannot, however, use tactics that do not serve the public interest or have been judicially or legislatively declared to be "unfair," such as defaming competitors or their goods, stealing trade secrets, or starting a business with a former employer's customer lists. A large area of unfair competition of interest to MHPs, particularly psychologists, is a type of marketing that attempts to confuse the consumer into believing that one business's products or services were produced by another business. MHPs may be asked to conduct consumer surveys to determine whether the defendant's business practices resulted in such confusion and to testify in court about their findings.

(A) Legal Test of Unfair Competition

Unfair competition refers to the use by two or more persons, corporations, or associations of tactics that are dishonest or fraudulent or are not in the public interest. Examples of unfair competition include

1. agreeing to limit production of a commodity or to increase or decrease the price of a commodity;

2. agreeing to prevent competition in the manufacturing, transportation, sale, or purchase of a commodity;

3. agreeing to fix the price of a commodity; or

4. agreeing not to buy or sell a specific product.[1]

---

1. Ohio Rev. Code § 1331.01.

Each day's violation of the unfair competition statute is a separate offense.[2] Anyone who engages in unfair competition may be fined $500 by the state of Ohio for each day that the violation continues after due notice is given by the Ohio attorney general or a county prosecuting attorney.[3] In addition, the person or business injured by unfair competition may sue the competitor and recover triple the actual amount of damages sustained.[4]

Any contract or agreement in violation of unfair competition statutes is void.[5]

(B) Trademark Confusion

A trademark is a mark or symbol used by a person or company to identify goods and services and to distinguish them from the goods and services of others.[6] It is a form of unfair competition when a seller uses a trademark that so closely resembles that of a competitor that an ordinary citizen is likely to confuse them.

(C) Product Confusion

Product confusion is similar to trademark confusion, except that in product confusion a manufacturer, supplier, or seller creates goods that are easily confused with those created by a competitor. It is unfair competition to sell one's goods as so similar to those of another that purchasers are deceived.[7] The following are examples of deceptive trade practices involving product confusion:

1. passing off goods or services as those of a competitor;

2. causing confusion as to the source, sponsorship, or certification of goods and services;

3. misleading customers about the geographic origin of goods and services;

4. misrepresenting that goods or services have certain sponsorship, approval, or benefits;

5. misrepresenting that goods or services are of a particular standard or quality;

---

2. OHIO REV. CODE § 1331.04.
3. OHIO REV. CODE § 1331.03.
4. OHIO REV. CODE § 1331.08.
5. OHIO REV. CODE § 1331.06.
6. OHIO REV. CODE § 4165.01.
7. OHIO REV. CODE § 4165.02.

6. disparaging the goods or services of another by false representations of fact;

7. advertising goods or services with intent not to sell or provide them as advertised; and

8. making false statements about the reasons for price reductions.

Not included under these restrictions are (a) conduct that is in compliance with the orders or rules of a governmental agency; and (b) publishers, broadcasters, printers, and others who disseminate information without knowledge of its deceptive nature.[8]

A person or company who is likely to be damaged by deceptive trade practices may initiate civil action to stop the deceptive practice. A person who suffers financial losses because of deceptive trade practices also may initiate a civil action to recover financial damages.[9] Other civil and criminal remedies also may be available to the injured party, such as litigation for copyright or trademark infringements.[10]

---

8. Ohio Rev. Code § 4165.04(A).
9. Id.
10. Ohio Rev. Code § 4165.03.

5.12

Employment Discrimination

The law prohibits employers from engaging in discriminatory employment practices. This applies to professionals who have employees, as well as to management consultants who advise employers concerning personnel selection, discharge, and promotion. MHPs should be aware of this law as it pertains to industrial consulting, test construction, and product marketing and in the management of their own businesses.

Individuals who believe they have been subject to illegal employment (or housing) discrimination may pursue solutions either through private civil litigation or through a complaint with the Ohio Civil Rights Commission. The Civil Rights Commission was created by the Ohio legislature, in part to receive, investigate, and rule on written charges of unlawful discriminatory practices as an alternative to the court system.[1] The Commission attempts to induce compliance with the law by informal methods such as conferencing, conciliation, and persuasion, but it also is empowered to (a) order respondents to stop unlawful practices; (b) require respondents to take affirmative actions to get into compliance with the law, such as hiring, reinstating, or upgrading employees, providing back pay, or granting admission to union membership; and (c) require respondents to report to the Commission on steps taken to come into compliance.[2]

Charges of unlawful discrimination may be filed with either a civil court or the Civil Rights Commission but not with both,[3] except when state remedies are mixed with federal remedies. This would occur, for example, when a federal statute requires that,

---

1. Ohio Rev. Code § 4112.03 and 4112.04.
2. Ohio Rev. Code § 4112.05.
3. Ohio Rev. Code § 4112.08.

before a claim may be brought under it, the aggrieved party must first resort to the state's administrative remedies.[4] Ohio courts have enforced this requirement.[5]

Ohio law identifies the following categories or features of individuals that may not be used to discriminate for employment purposes unless legitimate occupational qualifications have been established: race, color, religion, sex, national origin, disability, age, or ancestry. As used here, *disability* refers to a physical or mental impairment that substantially limits one or more major life activities.[6] The category of disability as used does not include any physiological disorder or condition, mental or psychological disorder, or disease caused by an illegal use of any controlled substance by an employee or applicant.[7]

(A) Who Is Affected by Employment Discrimination Law

The following are among those affected by Ohio's employment discrimination law:

1. any employer with four or more employees, in its hiring, refusing to hire, and discharging of employees. Part-time employees are counted toward the minimum of four needed to qualify as an employer;[8]

2. employment agencies or personnel placement services;

3. labor organizations in classifying members or limiting job opportunities;

4. employers, labor organizations, and joint labor–management committees who operate apprentice training programs;

5. except when based on bona fide occupational qualifications, employers, employment agencies, placement services, or labor organizations eliciting information, keeping records, advertising positions, or using a quota system based on discriminatory categories;

---

4. 29 U.S.C. § 621.
5. Fowler v. Hudson Foods, 96 Ohio Misc.2d 19, 708 N.E.2d 792 (Ohio Com. Pl. 1998).
6. Ohio Rev. Code § 4112.01(A)(13).
7. Ohio Rev. Code § 4112.02(Q).
8. In re Mantell, CRC 4022 (6-19-85).

6. any person seeking employment who advertises his or her race, color, religion, sex, national origin, disability, age, or ancestry or preference of a prospective employer as to these categories;

7. any person who sells, rents, leases, or finances housing accommodations;

8. any person discriminating against another who has opposed unlawful discriminatory employment practices; and

9. any person aiding, abetting, or compelling someone to engage in an unlawful discriminatory practice, or obstructing a person who is trying to avoid discriminatory practices.

The law provides for some exceptions regarding, among other things, limits of accommodations for handicapped individuals and for the establishment of bona fide employment qualifications, seniority systems, pension plans, and a maximum age for employment in certain sectors such as law enforcement.[9]

Also specifically affected by employment discrimination law in Ohio are all contracting agencies for or on behalf of the state or its political subdivisions. Discrimination is prohibited in the hiring of employees by any contractor or subcontractor. All contractors from whom the state or its political subdivisions make purchases must have a written affirmative action program for the employment and use of economically disadvantaged individuals.[10]

Individual employees, not deemed by the statute to be an "employer," may be individually liable for violations of employment discrimination provisions.[11]

Individuals who work as independent contractors are not considered employees under the provisions of this statute if their work is not controlled by the employer.[12]

Finally, county boards for alcohol, drug addiction, and mental health services and agencies and companies under contract with these boards may not discriminate in the provision of services, in employment, or in development of contracts on the basis of race, color, sex, creed, physical and mental disability, national origin, or the inability to pay for the services. In addition, each community mental health and drug and alcohol program must have a written affirmative action program that includes goals for employment and use of services with members of economically

---

9. Ohio Rev. Code § 4112.02.
10. Ohio Rev. Code § 125.111.
11. Cheek v. Industrial Powder Coatings, Inc., 84 Ohio St. 3d 534, 706 N.E.2d 323 (Ohio, 1999).
12. Eyerman v. Mary Kay Cosmetics, Inc., 967 F.2d 213 (C.A. 6 (Ohio) 1992).

disadvantaged groups roughly in proportion to the population that is served.[13]

(B) Unlawful Employment Practices

Ohio law identifies many employment practices as unlawful when based on race, color, religion, sex, national origin, disability, age, or ancestry.[14] Several examples are listed:

1. employers discriminating against a person with respect to hiring, tenure, terms and conditions of employment, or any other matter directly or indirectly related to a person's employment;

2. employment agencies or personnel placement services refusing or failing to accept, classify, or refer applicants for employment or to comply with a request from an employer for referral of applicants when it is apparent the employer wishes to discriminate against certain applicants;

3. labor organizations limiting or classifying their membership according to the protected categories of persons;

4. employers or others controlling apprentice training programs to discriminate against trainees;

5. except when based on legitimate occupational qualifications certified in advance, employers, employment agencies, placement services, or labor organizations eliciting protected information about applicants, making or keeping a record of the protected information on applicants, using an application blank that elicits protected information, publishing advertisements related to employment indicating a preference based on protected information, employing a quota system, or using recruitment companies known to discriminate;

6. individuals seeking employment publishing protected information on themselves or expressing a preference of working for or with protected classes of employees;

7. places of public accommodation denying any person access to and full use of the facilities;

8. any person refusing to rent, sell, lease, or finance housing based on protected information;

---

13. Ohio Rev. Code § 340.12.
14. Ohio Rev. Code § 4112.02.

9. any person discriminating in any way against another person because she or he has opposed an unlawful discriminative practice; and

10. any person aiding, encouraging, or compelling someone to engage in an unlawful discriminative activity.[15]

The law recognizes several exceptions to these general rules. For example, religious organizations are not barred from limiting sales, rentals, or occupancy of housing accommodations that it owns or operates for individuals of the same religion, except that they may not discriminate on the basis of race, color, or national origin. Private or fraternal organizations may limit rentals or occupancy to their members. Property owners are not required to rent or lease to tenants who constitute a direct health or safety threat. Employers are not required to employ or train handicapped individuals under circumstances that would significantly increase the occupational hazards affecting either the handicapped employee, other employees, or the general public.[16]

Individuals who violate Ohio employment discrimination law are subject to a civil action for damages, injunctive relief (ordering the discriminatory practices to stop), or other forms of relief as provided by the courts.[17]

---

15. OHIO REV. CODE § 4112.02(A–J).
16. OHIO REV. CODE § 4112.02(K–L).
17. OHIO REV. CODE § 4112.99.

Civil and Criminal Trial Matters

6.1

Jury Selection

Jury selection is an area of importance to attorneys because the process allows them, to a degree, to "select a jury." In actuality, potential jurors are rejected from serving rather than selected. Mental health professionals (MHPs) may be involved in this process by conducting pretrial surveys, constructing questions to ask potential jurors, and evaluating jurors on the basis of the results of pretrial surveys or in-court observations of them.

(A) Juror Qualifications

A juror must be 18 years of age or older, a resident of the county, eligible to be a voter (even if not currently registered to vote), and have a valid current driver's license.

In addition, a juror may be challenged on the suspicion of prejudice for either party, for lack of competent knowledge of the English language, or for other reasons that may render the person an unsuitable juror.[1]

Individuals selected as jurors also may be excused from duty for any of the following:

1. the juror is physically absent and will not return in time to serve;

2. the public interest will be injured by the person's participation;

3. the person is physically unable to serve;

---

1. Ohio R. Crim. P. 24.

4. the juror's spouse or near relative has recently died or is seriously ill; or

5. the juror is a cloistered member of a religious organization.[2]

Ohio law also specifies that race and color may not be used to exclude a citizen as a juror.[3]

(B) Criminal Trials

(B)(1) When a Jury Is Allowed

The Ohio constitution provides that the right of criminal trial by jury is inviolate.[4] Ohio law further provides that a jury is allowed at any trial, in any court, for the violation of any statute of the state or any ordinance of municipal corporations, except when the maximum potential penalty involved does not exceed a fine of $100.[5]

(B)(2) Jury Size

In felony cases, juries consist of 12 members. In misdemeanor cases, juries consist of 8 members. If a defendant is charged with a felony and a misdemeanor, or if a felony and a misdemeanor involving different defendants are joined for trial, then the jury consists of 12 members.[6]

If the trial is likely to be protracted, the judge may permit the selection of alternate jurors who participate in the same manner as the regular jurors, except that they are dismissed on final submission of the case to the jury.[7] Alternate jurors are selected to replace jurors who may become ill or for other reasons are not able to continue to participate in the trial.

(B)(3) Unanimity Requirement

In criminal trials, the verdict must be unanimous.[8]

(B)(4) Change of Venue

The location of a trial may be changed if it appears that a fair and impartial trial cannot be held in the jurisdiction or when it appears that the trial should be moved for the convenience of the

---

2. OHIO REV. CODE § 2313.16.
3. OHIO REV. CODE § 2313.47.
4. OHIO CONST. art. I, § 5.
5. OHIO REV. CODE § 2945.17.
6. OHIO R. CRIM. P. 23.
7. OHIO REV. CODE § 2313.37.
8. OHIO R. CRIM. P. 31.

parties and in the interests of justice.[9] MHPs may assist attorneys who seek a change in venue by, for example, conducting survey research directed at determining the effects of pretrial publicity on the pool of potential jurors.

(B)(5) *Voir Dire*

Voir dire refers to the phase of a trial in which the attorneys question prospective jurors to determine potential biases that might influence their judgments about the case. Attorneys develop strategies for the trial and may question jurors to determine which ones will be most receptive to their strategies. After the prospective jurors are sworn in, the attorneys follow a set of guidelines that determine how the challenging of jurors is accomplished. Each party may exercise peremptory challenges—that is, may reject particular juror candidates without having to specify any reasons for the rejections. In criminal cases, the number of peremptory challenges may not exceed six for each side when a death sentence may be involved, four when a sentence of imprisonment may be imposed, or three in all other prosecutions. One additional peremptory challenge may be allowed for each defendant in a multidefendant criminal proceeding.[10] Additional peremptory challenges are allowed against alternate jurors. One additional challenge is allowed if one or two alternate jurors are impaneled, two challenges if three or four alternates are impaneled, and three peremptory challenges are allowed if five or six alternates are impaneled.[11]

The law provides for unlimited challenges for cause to any person called as a juror who, among other things:

1. has been convicted of a crime that renders him or her disqualified to serve on a jury;

2. has an interest in the cause before the court;

3. has an action pending against either party;

4. was formerly a juror in the same cause;

5. has an important relationship with either party, such as employer, employee, spouse, or counselor;

6. is subpoenaed as a witness in the case;

7. is a party to another action in which an attorney in the present case is an attorney, either for or against him or her;

8. has served as a juror in any cause within the previous 12 months; or

---

9. Ohio Rev. Code § 2901.12.
10. Ohio Trial Court Jury Use and Management Standard 9(D).
11. Ohio Trial Court Jury Use and Management Standard 9(E).

9. discloses that he or she cannot be a fair and impartial juror or will not follow the law as given by the court.[12]

(C) Civil Trials

(C)(1) When a Jury Is Allowed

Any party to a civil trial may demand a trial by jury.[13] However, the parties or their attorneys may consent to a trial without a jury and the court may on its own initiative conclude that a right of trial by jury does not exist.[14] The U.S. Constitution, Seventh Amendment, requires a jury trial in a civil case based on common law involving a dispute of more than $20. Thus, a judge could find either (a) that the controversy involves less than $20 or (b) that the basis for the lawsuit does not exist at common law (e.g., the case is based on a right created by a statute that does not explicitly provide for a jury trial).

(C)(2) Jury Size

In most civil actions, the jury is composed of 8 members or fewer, although as many as 12 members may be used in cases involving the appropriation of a right of way brought by a corporation.[15]

For the sake of economy, the court also may direct that no more than four additional jurors be selected as alternate jurors. Alternate jurors participate in the proceedings in the same manner as do regular jurors, except that alternate jurors are dismissed when the jury retires to consider its verdict.[16]

(C)(3) Unanimity Requirement

In general, a verdict requires the concurrence of three fourths or more of the jurors. Whenever three fourths of the jury does not consist of an integral number, the next higher number of votes is required. For juries with fewer than four members, the verdict must be unanimous.[17]

(C)(4) Change of Venue

Either party in the case may request a change of venue, or the court on its own initiative may transfer any civil action to an

---

12. Ohio Rev. Code § 2313.42.
13. Ohio R. Civ. P. 38.
14. Ohio R. Civ. P. 39.
15. Ohio R. Civ. P. 38.
16. Ohio R. Civ. P. 47.
17. Ohio R. Civ. P. 48.

adjoining county when it appears that a fair and impartial trial cannot be conducted in the county where the suit is pending.[18]

(C)(5) *Voir Dire*

Attorneys are permitted to interview potential jurors to determine which ones may be most receptive to their strategies. In civil cases, the number of peremptory challenges may not exceed three for each side.[19] If alternate jurors are impaneled, up to three additional peremptory challenges are allowed for each side. One peremptory challenge is permitted if one or two alternate jurors are impaneled, two challenges are allowed if three or four alternates are impaneled, and three challenges are allowed if five or six alternates are impaneled.[20] Unlimited challenges are permitted for cause in civil cases, as is the case for criminal cases (see earlier in this chapter).[21]

---

18. Ohio R. Civ. P. 3.
19. Ohio Trial Court Jury Use and Management Standard 9(C).
20. Ohio Trial Court Jury Use and Management Standard 9(E).
21. Ohio Rev. Code § 2313.42.

6.2

Expert Witnesses

MHPs may testify as expert witnesses if they can provide testimony on a topic that is beyond the trier's competence and this information will permit the trier to rationally decide the case before it. MHPs frequently are called to testify as expert witnesses on a wide variety of issues.

(A) Qualifying as an Expert Witness

An expert witness generally is defined as one who possesses special skill, knowledge, or experience and can assist the court in drawing correct conclusions about matters that are beyond the everyday experience of laypersons.[1] In addition, the Ohio supreme court has stated that expert testimony is admissible in all proceedings involving matters of a scientific and professional nature that are not within the common knowledge of laypersons.[2]

To testify about liability for physicians, podiatrists, or hospitals, prospective expert witnesses must devote at least one half of their professional time to active clinical practice or its instruction.[3]

---

1. OHIO R. EVID. 702.
2. Ragone v. Vitali & Beltrami, Jr., Inc., 42 Ohio St. 2d 161, 327 N.E.2d 645 (1975).
3. OHIO R. EVID. 601.

(B) When an Expert Witness May Be Called to Testify

Before 1994, the standard for admission of expert testimony in Ohio was stated in a variety of ways. In 1994, Rule of Evidence 702 was amended by clarifying that the information forming the basis of expert testimony must be "reliable." The 1994 amended standard is as follows:

1. the witness's testimony either relates to matters that an average layperson would not understand or it dispels a common misperception;

2. the witness is qualified because of specialized knowledge, skill, experience, training, or education; and

3. the witness's testimony is based on reliable scientific, technical, or other specialized information. If the expert reports on the results of a procedure or test, the testimony is considered to be reliable only if the following apply:
   a. the theory on which the procedure or test is based is objectively verifiable or is validly derived from widely accepted knowledge or principles;
   b. the design of the procedure reliably implements the theory; and
   c. the procedure was conducted in a way that will yield accurate results.[4]

Since 1994, the Ohio supreme court has decided only a few cases concerned with this standard. In *State v. Stowers*[5] the court ruled that psychological testimony (described as "specialized knowledge") was admissible even though it was not presented as "scientific or technical knowledge" as outlined in the 1994 standard, because the testimony would assist the trier of fact in understanding the evidence at issue. In *State v. Nemeth*,[6] the court concluded that expert testimony on battered child syndrome is admissible in Ohio when it is relevant to the case, even though the battered child syndrome is not recognized as an independent defense in Ohio.

In *Miller v. Bike Athletic Co.*,[7] the court designated four factors to be considered in evaluating the reliability of scientific evidence. The four factors are whether (a) the theory or technique has been tested, (b) it has been subjected to peer review, (c) there is a known

---

4. OHIO R. EVID. 702.
5. State v. Stowers, 81 Ohio St. 3d 260, 690 N.E.2d 881 (1998).
6. 82 Ohio St. 3d 202, 694 N.E.2d 1332 (1998).
7. 80 Ohio St. 3d 607, 687 N.E.2d 735 (1998).

or potential rate of error, and (d) the methodology has gained general acceptance. These factors were adopted from *Daubert v. Merrell Dow Pharmaceuticals, Inc.*[8] The *Miller* court emphasized that these factors should not be used to exclude all evidence of questionable reliability. Rather, the test of reliability should be more a matter of whether the evidence is helpful to the jury in reaching a decision.

(C) Form and Content of Testimony

There are two categories of facts or data on which an expert may base an opinion. The first includes facts or data perceived by the expert in the process of collecting information by examination or testing. The second category includes the facts and data presented to the expert at the hearing.[9]

Some states prohibit testimony about the ultimate issue in a case. The Ohio supreme court has ruled[10] that expert witnesses may testify about their opinions on the ultimate issue. In this ruling, the court concluded that it was permissible for an expert witness to convey her belief to the jury that the behavior of children who had changed their stories about having been sexually abused between the time of investigation and trial is consistent with the behavior of children who have been abused. The court interpreted Ohio Rule of Evidence 704 as meaning that opinion evidence is not objectionable solely because it embraces an ultimate issue of fact. Thus, testimony on an ultimate issue is not per se inadmissible in Ohio.

---

8. 509 U.S. 579 (1993).
9. OHIO R. EVID. 703.
10. State v. Stowers, 81 Ohio St. 3d 260, 690 N.E.2d 881 (1998).

6.3

Polygraph Evidence

Polygraph examinations are governed by laws regulating the licensure of polygraph examiners and the submission of test results at trial. These laws apply to all MHPs.

(A) Polygraph Examination Definition

Ohio law does not provide a definition of *polygraph examination* but, as noted later in this chapter, the courts admit evidence from polygraph examinations. A polygraph examination refers to a test using a polygraph machine or device that is operated for the purpose of assisting in the detection of deception.

(B) Licensure of Polygraph Examiners

Polygraph examiners are not licensed in Ohio as a separate profession. Rather, such examinations are conducted by individuals licensed as "private investigators" and "security guards."[1] Individuals who are licensed as private investigators may, among other things, conduct investigations relevant to any crime and may obtain information on the identity, habits, conduct, whereabouts, character, and other aspects of any person, and may secure evidence for use in any legislative, administrative, or judicial proceeding.[2] Individuals licensed as security guards serve as watchpersons, guards, and private patrol officers, and generally

---

1. OHIO REV. CODE § 5739.01(EE).
2. OHIO REV. CODE § 4749.01(B).

serve to protect persons or property.[3] Private investigators and security guards are not considered law enforcement officers.[4]

MHPs are not eligible by virtue of their licenses for professional practice to conduct polygraph examinations.

(C) Admissibility of Polygraph Examinations

The Ohio supreme court has ruled that information from polygraph examinations is admissible in criminal trials when specific conditions have been met:

1. both parties sign a stipulation agreeing to the examination and to the subsequent admission at trial of the results and the examiner's opinions;

2. the judge makes the final determination about the admissibility of the evidence—that is, the evidence may be barred if the judge is not convinced that the examiner was qualified or the test was conducted under improper conditions;

3. if the results are offered into evidence, the opposing party has the right to cross-examine the examiner; and

4. the judge instructs the jury that the examiner's testimony does not tend to prove or disprove any element of the crime and that the jury must determine what weight and effect the testimony should be given.[5]

---

3. Ohio Rev. Code § 4749.01(D).
4. Ohio Rev. Code § 4749.08.
5. State v. Souel, 53 Ohio St. 3d 123, 372 N.E.2d 1318 (1978).

6.4

Competency to Testify

A witness in a civil or criminal trial must have the mental capacity to testify accurately and reliably in court; any other rule would open the fairness of the trial to question. Thus, whenever there is a reasonable doubt concerning the competency of a witness, the opposing counsel or the court should raise the issue. Child witnesses may be questioned by the court to determine their ability to relate facts accurately and to testify in a truthful manner. To ensure justice, MHPs have been asked to aid in this assessment and to testify about their findings. In this chapter, the mental status evaluation of rape victims is also discussed.

(A) Legal Test of Competency to Testify

Ohio law considers all individuals to be competent witnesses, except those of "unsound mind" and children under age 10 who appear unable to understand the issues and report them accurately.[1] Persons are not disqualified as witnesses in a criminal prosecution because of their personal interest in the case or because the person has been convicted of a crime. Husband and wife may also testify on behalf of, and against, each other.[2]

---

1. OHIO REV. CODE § 2317.01.
2. OHIO REV. CODE § 2945.42.

(B) Determination of Witness Competency

The judge determines whether a witness is competent to testify.[3] The judge may ask MHPs to assist in making that determination. To testify regarding competency, the expert would first have to quality as an expert witness (see chapter 6.2, Expert Witnesses). An MHP then would testify about the individual's mental ability to observe, recall, and relate events.

Children are not deemed incompetent solely because of age. The court may find a person incompetent to testify if he or she is under 10 years of age and appears incapable of perceiving the facts or events about which he or she is questioned or of relating these facts and events accurately.

In hearings regarding abuse, neglect, or dependency, examinations of a child witness by the judge must be conducted outside of the courtroom and in the presence of only those individuals who are considered necessary to the examination or well-being of the child. The statute is silent about whether MHPs might be considered necessary. A court reporter must be present. The judge may order the attorneys for any party and the guardian *ad litem*, who is appointed by the court to represent the client's best interests, to submit questions for the judge's use in the examination.[4]

Under certain circumstances, the court may admit as evidence videotaped preliminary hearing testimony of a child victim under 13 years of age in lieu of the child victim appearing in person at trial. For such testimony to be admitted into evidence at trial, all of the following conditions must apply:

1. the videotape was made at the preliminary hearing at which probable cause of the violation was found;

2. the videotape was made in accordance with guidelines established by statute;[5] and

3. the testimony in the videotape is not excluded by the hearsay rule and otherwise is admissible under the *Ohio Rules of Evidence.*

If the defendant objects to the use of videotaped testimony, the court must hold a hearing to determine whether the videotaped testimony should be admitted. The child victim is not required to testify at this hearing. After the hearing, the court will not require the child victim to testify in person unless the testimony

---

3. Оню R. Evid. 104(A).
4. Оню Rev. Code § 2317.01.
5. Оню Rev. Code § 2937.11.

is necessary because new evidence has been discovered, the circumstances of the case have changed significantly, or the testimony of the child victim is necessary to protect the right of the defendant to a fair trial.[6]

(C) Competency of Rape Victims to Testify

In some states, specific competency issues are raised when the witness is a rape victim. Other than as noted earlier in this chapter, Ohio has no such conditions, and rape victims are treated the same as all other witnesses for the purpose of determining competency.

---

6. OHIO REV. CODE §2945.49(B).

6.5

Psychological Autopsy

The motivations and mental state of a person before death frequently are critical issues in litigation. For instance, whether a gift was made by a person "in contemplation of death" has significant tax consequences. Similarly, a finding that a person committed suicide rather than died accidently may determine whether there is insurance coverage. MHPs may contribute in this area by providing a retrospective psychological profile of the decedent.

(A) Admissibility of Psychological Autopsies

Ohio statutory law does not address the admissibility of psychological autopsies. The Ohio supreme court has not addressed this issue, but one lower court[1] has ruled that psychological autopsy evidence was inadmissible in that particular case during the trial phase. However, it left open the option that such information might be admissible during the sentencing phase. Lacking direction from the legislature and the Ohio supreme court, lower courts may determine admissibility on a case by case basis.

---

1. State v. Huber, Hamilton County Court of Common Pleas, 62 Ohio Misc.2d 237, 597 N.E.2d 570 (1992).

6.6

Battered Woman's Syndrome

The battered woman's syndrome pertains to a woman who has been physically abused by her husband or paramour on a regular basis over a period of time. In some states, the law recognizes a defense to criminal charges of serious physical injury to a husband, on the basis of the battered woman's syndrome. MHPs may provide testimony on the defendant's subjective state of mind.

(A) Legal Test of Battered Woman's Syndrome

An Ohio statute[1] recognizes the battered woman's syndrome. The statute declares that the nature of the syndrome is not within the general knowledge of average individuals and that expert witnesses (see chapter 6.2, Expert Witnesses) are required when the syndrome is raised as a defense to criminal charges.

(B) Raising the Battered Woman's Syndrome

Testimony about the syndrome and that the woman suffered from the syndrome may be introduced when the defendant uses the

---

1. OHIO REV. CODE § 2901.06.

defense of self-defense in a case involving the use of force against another person.[2]

Defendants also may introduce expert testimony about the syndrome when a defense of not guilty by reason of insanity is presented (see chapter 7.9, Criminal Responsibility).[3]

(C) Standard of Proof

The syndrome is not intended to be an independent affirmative defense. Rather, the evidence of the syndrome is only one factor for the trier of fact to consider in determining whether the defense of self-defense applies—that is, whether the defendant acted out of a reasonable belief that she was in imminent danger of death or great bodily harm and the use of force was her only means of escaping.[4] The defendant has the burden of proof, by a preponderance of the evidence, on the issue of self-defense.[5]

2. Ohio Rev. Code § 2901.05.
3. Ohio Rev. Code § 2945.392.
4. State v. Daws, 104 Ohio App.3d 448, 662 N.E.2d 805 (1994).
5. State v. Martin, 21 Ohio St. 3d 91, 488 N.E.2d 166 (1986).

Rape Trauma Syndrome

Rape trauma syndrome describes behavioral, somatic, and psychological sequelae of an attempted or successful forcible rape. In some states, the law allows a party to introduce evidence from MHPs that a rape victim is suffering from rape trauma syndrome to assist in a prosecution when the defendant acknowledges that sexual intercourse occurred but claims that it was consensual. The presence of rape trauma syndrome tends to disprove that the victim consented. It also has been used as a defense when the raped individual attempts to murder the rapist. In this situation, the rape victim attempts to argue "diminished capacity" (see chapter 7.8, Diminished Capacity) because she was unable to form the necessary intent to commit that crime as a result of the syndrome.

Ohio does not have a statute on this subject, so courts may consider this issue on a case by case basis. One appellate court[1] has permitted testimony on this syndrome. In that case, the rape trauma syndrome testimony was admitted into evidence by the court under the rubric of child sexual abuse syndrome, which has been recognized explicitly by the Ohio supreme court.[2] In the latter case, the supreme court held that an expert witness's testimony that the behavior of an alleged child victim of sexual abuse was consistent with behavior observed in sexually abused children is admissible under the *Ohio Rules of Evidence*.

---

1. State v. Rowe, 1999 WL 668573.
2. State v. Stowers, 81 Ohio St.3d 260, 690 N.E.2d 881 (1998).

Hypnosis of Witnesses

A person who experiences stress or trauma while witnessing a legally important event may be unable to recount the event in sufficient detail to allow the police or attorneys to reconstruct the exact circumstances. Hypnosis induced by MHPs may be used to alleviate the stress or other condition to allow for better recall. A legal issue arises regarding the reliability of the hypnotic memory when it is used for a legal purpose, such as in forming the basis for a search warrant or as evidence at a trial.

(A) Hypnotically Induced Information in a Police Investigation

The police may use information gained through hypnosis of a victim or witness.[1] For example, the police may rely on such information to obtain a search or arrest warrant as long as the judge who authorizes the warrant is told that the information is based, at least in part, on hypnosis.

---

1. State v. Sneed, WL 1476140 (2000).

(B) Hypnotically Induced Courtroom Testimony

An Ohio appellate court[2] has ruled that hypnotically refreshed testimony may be admissible if it is determined that use of hypnosis is appropriate for the kind of memory loss encountered, the witness has no apparent motivation for remembering or not remembering certain events, and appropriate safeguards are applied. The safeguards suggested, but not required, by the court include the following:

1. a psychiatrist or psychologist experienced in the use of hypnosis must conduct the session;

2. the professional conducting the session should be independent of and not regularly employed by the prosecution, defense, or investigators in the case;

3. information given to the professional must be recorded in some form;

4. the hypnotist should obtain a statement of facts from the subject before the session;

5. all contacts between the hypnotist and subject must be recorded; and

6. only the hypnotist and subject should be present during all phases of the session, including during pre- and posthypnotic interviews.

The court concluded that testimony that substantially complies with these safeguards does not violate the accused's right to confront witnesses.

---

2. State v. Weston, 16 Ohio App.3d 279, 475 N.E.2d 805 (1984).

6.9

Eyewitness Identification

The role of the eyewitness to any event is critical in many trials. Such individuals may be parties to the action, victims, or bystanders. Their testimony raises the issue of whether their identification at the time of the event, at a subsequent lineup (or other identifying procedure), or during the trial was valid. MHPs can contribute experimental and clinical expertise to aid the jury or court in evaluating the testimony of eyewitnesses.

(A) Admissibility of Expert Testimony on Eyewitness Identification

The Ohio supreme court has concluded that expert testimony on eyewitness identification is admissible under narrow conditions.[1] It ruled that expert testimony concerning the variables or factors that may impair the accuracy of a typical eyewitness identification is admissible. However, such testimony is not permitted regarding the credibility of a particular witness unless there is a special factor, such as a physical or mental impairment, which might affect the witness's ability to observe or recall details.

---

1. State v. Buell, 22 Ohio St. 3d 124, 489 N.E.2d 795 (1986).

Criminal Matters

7.1

Screening of
Police Officers

Applicants to police departments must satisfy training or selection criteria. In some states, mental fitness is one of the specific qualifications governing recruitment, appointment, and retention of those personnel. Ohio does not have such a requirement for qualification as a police officer as a matter of state law.

Competency to Waive the Rights to Silence, Counsel, and a Jury

Individuals taken into custody by police for a criminal offense have the option of waiving the rights to silence and counsel, which are guaranteed under the U.S. and Ohio constitutions. Criminal defendants may also waive these rights and the right to a jury trial at the time of trial. Mental health professionals (MHPs) may be asked to examine criminal defendants and testify as to whether they were competent to waive these rights at the arrest and investigation stages or at the trial.

(A) Right to Silence

The Fifth Amendment to the U.S. Constitution gives the accused the right to remain silent. The accused may waive that right by signing a waiver, orally acknowledging the waiver, or just continuing to talk with investigators after being advised of the right to silence. If the accused waives the right and gives a statement, the burden is on the state to show that the waiver was voluntary, knowing, and intelligent.[1] The determination that the waiver was voluntary, knowing, and intelligent is to be based on the totality of the circumstances surrounding the interrogation.[2] To determine if the waiver was involuntary, the court should consider such variables as the age, mentality, and previous criminal experience of the accused; the length, frequency, and intensity of the interrogation; the existence of physical deprivation or mistreatment; and the existence of threats or inducements.[3]

---

1. State v. Eley, 77 Ohio St. 3d 174, 672 N.E.2d 640 (1996).
2. State v.Tibbetts, 2001 WL 303234 (Ohio App. 1 Dist. 2001).
3. State v. Edwards, 49 Ohio St. 2d 31, 358 N.E.2d 1051 (1976).

(B) Right to Counsel

The Sixth Amendment of the U.S. Constitution guarantees the accused the right to legal counsel. But the accused can waive that right as long as the waiver is voluntary, knowing, and intelligent.[4] The state has the burden of showing that the waiver was valid. It is not sufficient for the state to accept the waiver based just on the defendant's statement that counsel is not desired. Rather, the court must ascertain whether the defendant understands the implications of the waiver of the right to counsel.

In felony cases in which the defendant is not represented by legal counsel and enters a plea of guilty or no contest, the court may not accept the plea without first readvising the defendant that he or she has the right to be represented and that the plea waives this right.[5]

(C) Right to Waive a Jury Trial

In any case with a potential for incarceration, the accused has the right to a trial by jury. However, the accused may waive this right before the trial begins. The waiver may also be made during trial with the approval of the court and the consent of the prosecution. The court must ensure that the waiver is knowing, intelligent, and voluntary.

In petty offense cases in which the accused has the right to a trial by jury, the defendant is tried by the court unless the defendant demands a jury trial. Failure to demand a jury trial constitutes a complete waiver of the right.[6]

In felony cases in which the defendant enters a plea of not guilty or no contest, the court may not accept the plea without first addressing the defendant personally and, among other things, determining that the defendant understands that the plea waives the right to a jury trial.[7]

---

4. In re Smith, 753 N.E.2d 930 (Ohio App. 8 Dist. 2001).
5. OHIO R. CRIM. P. 11.
6. OHIO R. CRIM. P. 23.
7. OHIO R. CRIM. P. 11.

Precharging and Pretrial Evaluations

In some states, the prosecutor may request a mental health evaluation to determine whether to charge a person with a criminal offense or to divert him or her to the mental health system. Ohio has such a statutory provision. In addition, there are a number of agencies that provide such evaluation services on the consent of the prosecutor and defendant.

Ohio provides for pretrial diversion programs for certain offenders. The programs are created by the prosecuting attorney's office in each county and are used for adults who are accused of committing criminal offenses and whom the prosecuting attorney believes will not likely offend again.[1] Diversion programs are operated according to written standards approved by the presiding judge.[2] Examples of activities that have been accepted for diversion programs include making restitution to a victim,[3] participating in a batterers' intervention program,[4] and attending Alcoholics Anonymous meetings. If the accused successfully completes a diversion program, the prosecuting attorney must recommend to the trial court that the charges be dismissed. If the accused does not successfully complete the diversion program, he or she may be brought to trial on the original charges.[5]

In addition, the criminal court may order a mentally ill defendant who is probably dangerous to self or others to be evaluated at a hospital for possible civil commitment. In such cases, the

---

1. Ohio Rev. Code § 2935.36.
2. Ohio Rev. Code § 2935.36(A).
3. State v. Curry, 134 Ohio App.3d 113, 730 N.E.2d 435 (1999).
4. State v. Monk, 64 Ohio Misc.2d 1, 639 N.E.2d 518 (1994).
5. Ohio Rev. Code § 2935.36(D).

charges may be dropped if there is sufficient cause to believe that the person is not guilty. Courts may also order presentence investigations, the results of which may be used for pretrial diversion (see chapter 7.11, Sentencing).

Ohio law also specifically provides for treatment in lieu of conviction of some offenders for whom drug dependence was a factor leading to the crime and for whom rehabilitation would substantially reduce the likelihood of additional criminal activity. The offender and the offense also must meet several criteria, such as the offender being accepted into an approved treatment program and the offense with which the person is charged not involving physical harm to another person. To determine if the offender meets criteria for this diversion program, the court may refer the offender for medical and psychiatric examination.[6] If the offender successfully completes the treatment program, the court may dismiss the charge against the offender. If the offender fails to successfully complete the program, the court may enter an adjudication of guilty and impose a jail term.

Ohio law provides for precharging and pretrial mental health evaluations under certain conditions. For example, the court may order an evaluation if a defendant is charged with a violation of a protection order and the defendant has caused harm, or a threat of harm, to the person or property of a family or household member covered by the order or agreement. In such an order, the court may require the defendant to be evaluated by a forensic center or other facility that is designated by the Department of Mental Health to conduct such evaluations or by any other program or facility or examiners of the court's choosing. Examinations may be completed by psychiatrists, psychologists, licensed independent social workers, and licensed professional clinical counselors.[7] Such an evaluation must be completed within 30 days of the court order for the evaluation.

The court may order up to two additional mental health evaluations, with the prosecutor and defendant being invited to make recommendations as to the examiner. These evaluations must be completed within 30 days of the court order for the evaluations.

The statute also specifies some of the issues that the examination report must address. These issues include the findings of the examiner, the facts on which the findings are based, the opinion of the examiner about the mental condition of the defendant, the

---

6. Ohio Rev. Code § 2951.041(B), (C).
7. Ohio Rev. Code § 2919.271(G).

opinion of the examiner of whether the defendant represents a substantial risk of physical harm to other persons, and the examiner's opinion about the types of treatment that the defendant needs.[8]

---

8. Ohio Rev. Code § 2919.271.

7.4

Bail Determinations

Most people charged with a crime have the right to post bail to secure their release from jail pending trial. The court cannot set excessive bail, however. The sole purpose of the amount imposed and any other attendant conditions is to ensure that the defendant returns to court when required. MHPs may contribute to the bail determination through consultation with the court or with other personnel advising the court, such as probation officers, regarding the person's mental health and community stability. However, the law does not require mental health evaluation or consultation in this context.

(A) Determining Whether Bail Is Appropriate

An accused may not be denied bail unless the judge finds by clear and convincing evidence that the accused poses a substantial risk of harm to a person or to the community at large and that no release conditions will ensure the safety of the endangered person or community.

On the initiative of the prosecution or the judge, the court will hold a hearing to determine if bail should be denied. Typically the hearing will be held within three days of the request to hold a hearing about bail. At the hearing, the defendant has the right to be represented by counsel, to testify, and to present witnesses and other evidence to the court. In making the determination about bail, the judge will consider all available evidence, including the following:

1. the nature and circumstances of the offense, including whether the offense involved violence or alcohol or drug abuse;
2. the weight of the evidence against the accused;
3. the history and characteristics of the accused, including the person's character and mental condition, family ties, employment, and length of residence in the community; and
4. the nature and seriousness of danger to any person or the community that the person poses.[1]

In instances in which the defendant is charged with violent crimes, such as homicide, assault, stalking, and domestic violence, the court will also consider whether the defendant has a history of violence toward the complainant or any other individuals, and whether setting bail at a high level will interfere with any treatment or counseling that the person is undergoing.[2]

(B) Determining the Amount and Conditions of Bail

In determining the conditions and amount of bail, the court will consider all relevant information, including but not limited to the nature of the crime, the weight of evidence against the defendant, the defendant's family ties, employment, mental condition, and record of convictions and appearances at court.[3]

The court may impose any of the following conditions of bail:

1. place the person in the custody of another person or organization;
2. place restrictions on the person's travel, association, or living arrangements;
3. place the person under house arrest;
4. regulate or prohibit the person's contact with the victim;
5. regulate the person's contact with witnesses or others;
6. require the person to attend treatment if the offense was alcohol or drug related; and

---

1. Ohio Rev. Code § 2937.222.
2. Ohio Rev. Code §§ 2903.212 and 2919.251.
3. Ohio R. Crim. P. 46.

7. any other reasonable condition considered necessary to ensure appearance and public safety.[4]

In allegations of domestic violence and stalking, the court must determine whether it will order an evaluation of the mental condition of the defendant before it sets bail.[5]

---

4. *Id.*
5. Ohio Rev. Code § 2937.23.

7.5

Competency to Stand Trial

Justice requires not only that a criminal defendant be "sane" at the time of the offense (see chapter 7.9, Criminal Responsibility), but that the defendant be aware of and able to participate in any criminal proceedings against him or her. This right, originating in common law (case law), is guaranteed under the U.S. Constitution.[1] Psychiatrists and psychologists may be appointed to conduct competency evaluations in Ohio.

(A) Legal Determination of Competency to Stand Trial

The judge determines whether the accused is competent to stand trial.

(A)(1) Test of Competency

Competency at the time of trial is presumed, and the party claiming incompetency has the burden of proof.[2] A defendant may be determined to be incompetent to stand trial if the defendant is found to be incapable of understanding the nature and objective of the proceedings against the defendant or of assisting in the defense.[3]

---

1. Dusky v. U.S., 362 U.S. 402 (1960).
2. OHIO REV. CODE § 2945.37(G).
3. OHIO REV. CODE § 2945.371.

(A)(2) Raising the Competency Issue

The court, the prosecutor, or the defense may raise the issue of the defendant's competency to stand trial. If the question is raised before the beginning of the trial, the court holds a hearing on the issue. If the issue is raised after the trial has begun, the court holds a hearing on the issue only for good cause or on the court's own motion.[4] For example, once the trial has begun the court may consider such things as doubts expressed by counsel about competency, evidence of the defendant's irrational behavior and demeanor during the trial, and previous medical opinions regarding the person's competency.[5]

(B) Competency Evaluation

If the issue of a defendant's competency to stand trial is raised, the court may order one or more evaluations of the defendant's present mental state. The examiner must file a report with the court within 30 days of the court order for the evaluation. The court then supplies copies to both attorneys.

The report must include all of the following:

1. the examiner's findings;
2. the facts on which the findings are based;
3. whether the defendant is capable of understanding the nature and objective of the proceedings and of assisting in the defense;
4. if the examiner's opinion is that the defendant is not competent to stand trial, whether the defendant presently is mentally ill or mentally retarded and, if so, subject to institutionalization by court order;
5. if the examiner's opinion is that the person is not competent to stand trial, what is the least restrictive treatment alternative that might restore or produce competency; and
6. if the examiner's opinion is that the person is not competent to stand trial, the examiner must predict the likelihood of the person becoming competent within one year if treatment is provided.[6]

If the court orders an evaluation and the defendant who has been released on bail or recognizance refuses to submit to a complete evaluation, the court may amend its conditions of bail

---

4. Ohio Rev. Code § 2945.37(B).
5. State v. Draughn, 76 Ohio App.3d 664, 602 N.E.2d 790 (1992).
6. Ohio Rev. Code § 2945.371.

or recognizance and order the sheriff to take the defendant into custody and to deliver the defendant to an appropriate facility for evaluation for a period of up to 20 days.[7]

A defendant in a criminal case does not have an absolute right to independent psychiatric evaluations,[8] but the court may order one or more evaluations to determine competency to stand trial. If the court orders more than one evaluation, both parties may recommend to the court an examiner whom each prefers to conduct the evaluation.

If it is the examiner's opinion that the defendant is not competent to stand trial and the defendant appears to be mentally retarded subject to institutionalization by court order, the court must order the defendant to participate in a separate mental retardation evaluation conducted by a psychologist selected by the director of the Department of Mental Retardation and Developmental Disabilities. The second evaluation must be completed within 30 days of the order for evaluation.

(C) Competency Hearing

If the issue of competency is raised before the beginning of the trial, the court must conduct a hearing within 30 days after the issue is raised. If the court has ordered an evaluation of the defendant, then the hearing must be held within 10 days of receipt of the report.

At the hearing, the defendant is represented by counsel. Both parties may submit evidence regarding the defendant's competency to stand trial. The court will not find a defendant incompetent to stand trial just because the person is receiving or has received treatment as a voluntary or involuntary mentally ill patient or mentally retarded resident of an institution. Neither is the court to find the person incompetent just because he or she takes psychotropic medications, even if the person might become incompetent to stand trial if the medication were terminated. Being mentally ill does not necessarily equate with the definition of legal incompetence to stand trial.[9] The judge makes the decision regarding competency to stand trial based on the preponderance of the evidence.[10]

---

7. Ohio Rev. Code § 2945.371(C).
8. State v. Marshall, 15 Ohio App.3d 105, 472 N.E.2d 1139 (1984).
9. State v. Berry, 72 Ohio St. 3d 354, 650 N.E.2d 433 (1995).
10. Ohio Rev. Code § 2945.37.

(D) Confidentiality and Privileged Communications

A defendant who is referred for a competency evaluation must participate in the examination; the defendant may not refuse to participate. The court may order a defendant who has been released on bail to submit to an evaluation and may modify the bail as necessary to enforce its order for an evaluation.[11]

Defendants are encouraged to be candid with their mental health examiners because the law restricts the use of information that examiners obtain from a defendant about the offense. No information related to guilt or innocence obtained in a mental health examination may be used in evidence against the defendant on the issue of guilt.[12]

(E) Disposition of Defendants Found Incompetent to Stand Trial

Revisions to Ohio statutes regarding treatment for individuals found incompetent to stand trial and not guilty by reason of insanity were enacted in 1997. The new law provided greater emphasis on compliance with mental health treatment and public safety. However, in 2001 the Ohio supreme court[13] ruled that one provision of the statute[14] was unconstitutional and repealed the entire section. The court ordered that the previous version of the statute be reinstated. Senate Bill 122, effective February 20, 2002, corrected the constitutional defect identified in the *Sullivan* case, reinstated the remaining provisions of the 1997 statute,[15] and added several new provisions.

Under the current statute, if the judge determines that the person is restorable if provided with treatment, the judge must order treatment in the least restrictive environment, but with an emphasis on public safety. If medication is determined to be necessary to restore the defendant's competency and the patient lacks capacity to give informed consent or refuses medication,

---

11. Ohio Rev. Code § 2919.271(C).
12. State v. Cooey, 46 Ohio St. 3d 20, 544 N.E.2d 895 (1989).
13. State v. Sullivan, 90 Ohio St. 3d 502, 739 N.E.2d 788 (2001).
14. Ohio Rev. Code § 2945.38.
15. *Id.*

the treatment program may petition the court for authorization for involuntary administration of medication.[16]

If the judge cannot determine whether the defendant has a substantial probability of being restored to competency if provided treatment, the judge may commit the defendant to a treatment facility for up to four months for continuing evaluation and treatment to determine restorability. If at any time the supervisor of the treatment concludes that the defendant is either competent or unrestorable, the supervisor must report this finding to the court.[17] If the defendant continues in treatment for four months, the court must make a determination of whether the person is restorable.[18]

If, following a course of treatment, the court finds the defendant competent to stand trial, the case proceeds to trial. The court may authorize continuing medication or other treatment to maintain the defendant's competency.[19]

The maximum treatment time that the court will wait for restoration to competency varies according to the charges filed. The maximum required treatment time is one year for murder and violent first- and second-degree felony charges. It is six months for all other felony charges, 60 days for first- and second-degree misdemeanor charges, and 30 days for all other misdemeanor charges.[20] Defendants may not voluntarily admit themselves to a hospital until after the applicable initial involuntary commitment is completed, and they are not permitted supervised off-grounds movement or unsupervised on- or off-grounds movement.[21]

If the court determines that competency is not likely to be achieved with treatment, it may dismiss the charges or order the person to be hospitalized. The court also may retain jurisdiction over the person if the person is charged with aggravated murder (showing extreme indifference to human life or using a deadly weapon), murder, or a violent first- or second-degree felony, is found to have committed the criminal act by clear and convincing evidence, and is subject to hospitalization by court order.[22]

---

16. Ohio Rev. Code § 2945.38(C).
17. Ohio Rev. Code § 2945.38(F).
18. Ohio Rev. Code § 2945.38(B).
19. Ohio Rev. Code § 2945.38(G).
20. Ohio Rev. Code § 2945.38(D).
21. Ohio Rev. Code § 2945.38(E).
22. Ohio Rev. Code § 2945.38(A).

7.6

Provocation

The law provides that individuals who have been charged with second-degree murder (without deliberation or premeditation) may offer an affirmative defense of "provocation."[1] An affirmative defense means that the person offers an excuse or justification for the offense, which the defendant may be asked to support with evidence.[2] Such a defense will be a bar to a conviction on second-degree murder charges, but the offense still may be grounds for a conviction on charges of first-degree, or voluntary manslaughter (murder without deliberate intent). Voluntary manslaughter is a felony of the first degree[3] and is punishable by a prison term of 3 to 10 years and a fine of not more than $20,000.[4] MHPs may provide testimony on the issue of provocation.

To mitigate the conviction, the defendant accused of murder or aggravated murder (showing extreme indifference to human life or using a deadly weapon) must persuade the finder of fact that he or she acted under the influence of sudden passion or in a sudden fit of rage, brought about by serious provocation by the victim that was sufficient to incite the defendant into using deadly force. Ohio courts have accepted self-defense, extreme emotional disturbance, insanity,[5] and intoxication[6] as affirmative defenses.

---

1. Ohio Rev. Code § 2903.03.
2. Ohio Rev. Code § 2901.05(C).
3. Ohio Rev. Code § 2903.03(B).
4. Ohio Rev. Code § 2929.14.
5. Krzeminski v. Perini, 614 F.2d 121, 16 Ohio Op.3d 306 (1980).
6. Mann v. Gray, 622 F. Supp. 1225 (N.D. 1985).

If the finder of fact is persuaded of the affirmative defense, then it may find the defendant guilty of voluntary manslaughter rather than murder or aggravated murder. The mitigating circumstances must be established by the defendant by a preponderance of the evidence.[7]

---

7. State v. Rhodes, 63 Ohio St. 3d 316, 590 N.E.2d 261 (1992).

7.7

Mens Rea

The criminal code prescribes that the minimum requirement for criminal liability is a voluntary act (or omission to perform a duty) that caused the criminal result, plus the necessary "culpable mental state," formerly referred to as *mens rea.* The purpose of determining a mental state is to distinguish between inadvertent or accidental acts and those that are performed with a "guilty mind." MHPs are legally qualified to testify as experts on this issue (see chapter 6.2, Expert Witnesses). They most frequently do so when a defendant argues that, because of mental illness or defect, he or she lacked the culpable mental state required as an element of a crime (see chapter 7.8, Diminished Capacity).

(A) Culpable Mental States

Ohio law[1] specifies that a person is not guilty of an offense unless both of the following apply:

1. the person engaged in voluntary conduct or there was an omission to perform an act or duty that the person was capable of performing; and

2. the person operated with the necessary culpable mental state ("guilty mind").

In the law, *culpability* refers to any of four different mental states: purpose, knowledge, recklessness, and negligence on the part of the offender. The law also provides general definitions of the four states. A person acts with purpose when it is the person's

---

1. Ohio Rev. Code § 2901.21.

intent to cause a specific result or to engage in specific conduct without regard to the likely outcome. Individuals act knowingly when they are aware that their conduct will likely cause a certain result. Individuals act recklessly when, with indifference to the likely outcome, they perversely disregard a known risk. Persons act negligently when, because of a substantial departure from due care, they fail to perceive or avoid a risk.[2]

---

2. Ohio Rev. Code § 2901.22.

7.8

Diminished Capacity

There are two primary versions of diminished capacity law in the United States. In some jurisdictions, the diminished capacity defense reduces the degree of crime for which the defendant may be convicted, even if the defendant's conduct satisfied the formal elements of a higher offense, including the requisite mental state. However, in most states, but not including Ohio, the diminished capacity concept allows a criminal defendant to introduce evidence through MHPs of mental abnormality at trial to negate a mental element of the crime charged (see chapter 7.7, *Mens Rea*), thereby completely exonerating the defendant of that charge.

Ohio law does not permit a defense of diminished capacity or irresistible impulse as a means of completely exonerating the defendant of a charge. On the other hand, Ohio law does permit the option of an affirmative defense of provocation as a means of reducing the degree of crime for which the defendant may be convicted (see chapter 7.6, Provocation). The Ohio supreme court has ruled that defendants may not offer expert psychiatric testimony, unrelated to the insanity defense, to show that, because of mental illness, intoxication, or other factors, the defendant lacked the mental capacity to form the mental state required for conviction of a crime.[1]

---

1. State v. Mitts, 81 Ohio St. 3d 223, 690 N.E.2d 522 (1998).

(A) Intoxication and Diminished Capacity

Voluntary intoxication may not be considered to negate the mental element of the crime charged and may not be used to prove a defense of not guilty by reason of insanity (NGRI; see chapter 7.9, Criminal Responsibility). Intoxication, along with mental illness and other matters, may be admitted as evidence in considering mitigating or extenuating factors. Evidence of intoxication may be admissible to show whether or not the person was physically able to perform the act with which the person is charged.[2]

---

2. Ohio Rev. Code § 2901.21(C).

7.9

Criminal Responsibility

An early yet still controversial contribution of MHP expertise in the courtroom has been the evaluation of criminal defendants who plead not guilty by reason of insanity because of their mental state at the time of the offense. MHPs may evaluate a defendant and testify about his or her psychological functioning at the time the criminal behavior occurred. The issue is raised by the defendant, who requests the court to appoint an expert or privately arranges for an MHP to conduct the evaluation. Once the issue is raised, the prosecution has the right to retain its own expert to perform a separate evaluation.

(A) Legal Determination of Insanity

A person is found "not guilty by reason of insanity" only if the person proves that, at the time of the crime, the person did not know, as a result of a severe mental disease or defect, the wrongfulness of the act.[1] In contrast, *mental illness* refers to a substantial disorder of thought, mood, perception, orientation, or memory that grossly impairs judgment, behavior, capacity to recognize reality, or ability to meet the demands of everyday life.[2] Every person is presumed to be sane, so an allegation of insanity must be proven by the defendant.[3]

---

1. Ohio Rev. Code § 2901.01(A)(14).
2. Ohio Rev. Code § 5122.01.
3. Ohio Rev. Code § 2901.05.

(A)(1) Burden of Proof

The burden of proof to establish a defense of not guilty by reason of insanity is on the accused, by a preponderance of the evidence.[4] To establish a defense of not guilty by reason of insanity, it must be proven that, at the time of the offense, the defendant did not know, as a result of a severe mental disease or defect, the wrongfulness of the act.[5] Proof that a person's reason at the time of the offense was so impaired that the person did not have the ability to refrain from the act does not constitute a defense.[6] Evidence of diminished capacity (see chapter 7.8, Diminished Capacity) does not establish insanity.[7] Insanity may be a defense to any crime.[8]

The insanity defense is usually pled at the time of arraignment (when the accused is brought before the court to plead to the criminal charges), but the court will permit the plea any time before the trial begins if good cause is shown.[9]

(B) Mental Examination

If the defendant enters a plea of not guilty by reason of insanity, the court may order one or more evaluations of the defendant's mental condition at the time of the crime. If more than one evaluation is ordered, each party may recommend to the court an examiner whom it prefers. If the court does not select an examiner recommended by the defendant, the court must inform the defendant that he or she may have an independent expert evaluation and that, if necessary, it will be obtained at public expense.[10] Current law does not define which MHPs may conduct the examinations, although a previous version of the statute identified psychiatrists and psychologists as qualified to do so.

The examiner must consider all relevant evidence. If the defendant is a woman and she has been charged with an offense that included the use of force against another person, the examiner must consider evidence related to the "battered woman syndrome" (see chapter 6.6, Battered Woman's Syndrome).[11] The examiner must file a report with the court within 30 days of the court order for the evaluation, and the court then supplies copies

---

4. Ohio Rev. Code § 2901.05(A).
5. Ohio Rev. Code § 2901.01(14).
6. Ohio Rev. Code § 2945.391.
7. State v. Wong, 95 Ohio App.3d 39, 641 N.E.2d 1137 (1994).
8. State v. Curry, 45 Ohio St. 3d 109, 543 N.E.2d 1228 (1989).
9. Ohio R. Crim. P. 11.
10. Ohio Rev. Code § 2945.371(A)–(H).
11. Ohio Rev. Code § 2945.371(F).

to both parties. The examiner's report must include all of following information:[12]

1. the examiner's findings;
2. the facts on which the findings are based; and
3. the examiner's findings about whether the defendant, at the time of the crime, did not know, as a result of a severe mental disease or defect, the wrongfulness of the acts that are charged.

(C) Confidentiality and Privileged Communications

Defendants are encouraged to be candid with their mental health examiners because statements about guilt or innocence made by the defendant during the examination may not be used against the defendant on the issue of guilt.[13]

(D) Commitment of Defendants Found Not Guilty by Reason of Insanity

When a defendant is found not guilty by reason of insanity, the trial court must conduct a full hearing to determine whether the person is mentally ill or mentally retarded and subject to hospitalization by court order. The trial judge may issue a temporary order of detention for the person for up to 10 days or until the commitment hearing.[14]

The person has a right to attend all hearings and must be informed by the court that he or she has the following rights:[15]

1. the right to be represented by counsel and to have counsel provided at public expense if necessary;
2. the right to have an independent psychiatric evaluation, at public expense if necessary;
3. the right to subpoena witnesses and documents, to present evidence, and to cross-examine witnesses;

---

12. OHIO REV. CODE § 2945.371(G).
13. OHIO REV. CODE § 2945.371(J).
14. OHIO REV. CODE § 2945.40(A).
15. OHIO REV. CODE § 2945.40(C).

4. the right to testify on his or her own behalf and to not be compelled to testify; and

5. the right to have copies of any relevant medical or mental health documents that the state possesses unless the court concludes that possession of a document would crate a substantial risk of harm to any person.

The hearing is open to the public and is conducted according to the *Ohio Rules of Civil Procedure*. The court may consider all relevant evidence, including relevant psychological and medical testimony and reports.[16]

If the court determines that there is not clear and convincing evidence that the person is mentally ill or mentally retarded and subject to institutionalization by court order, the court will discharge the person, unless the Department of Rehabilitation and Correction has requested that the person be kept in its custody.[17]

If the court determines that there is clear and convincing evidence that the person is subject to institutionalization by court order, it will commit the person to an appropriate facility. The court must order the least restrictive commitment alternative available, taking into account the welfare of the person and public safety. Public safety is more important than the welfare of the person in this determination.[18]

When the court orders a person to be committed to an institution, the prosecutor sends to the place of commitment all relevant reports of the person's mental condition. On admission, the agency must send to the Board of Alcohol, Drug Addiction, and Mental Health Services or the Community Mental Health Board serving the county in which the charges were filed a copy of all reports of the person's current mental condition.[19] Such patients may not be voluntarily admitted until after the termination of the involuntary commitment[20] (see chapter 8.4, Involuntary Commitment of Mentally Ill Adults).

Individuals committed by the court to an institution remain under the jurisdiction of the trial court until the termination of the commitment.[21] Termination of commitment occurs when the earlier of one of the following occurs:

1. the person no longer is mentally ill or mentally retarded;

2. expiration of the maximum prison term that the person could have received if the person had been convicted of the most

---

16. OHIO REV. CODE § 2945.40(D).
17. OHIO REV. CODE § 2945.40(E).
18. OHIO REV. CODE § 2945.40(F).
19. OHIO REV. CODE § 2945.40(G).
20. OHIO REV. CODE § 5122.02(D).
21. OHIO REV. CODE § 2945.401.

serious offense that had been charged or to which the person was found not guilty by reason of insanity; or

3. the trial court enters an order terminating the commitment based on its determination that the person is no longer a mentally ill or mentally retarded person subject to court ordered hospitalization or institutionalization.

The treatment facility to which the defendant has been committed must provide written updates on the person's status, commencing six months after first arrival and then at least every two years after the initial report is made. Within 30 days of receiving each report, the trial court must hold a hearing on the continued commitment of the person.[22]

---

22. OHIO REV. CODE § 2945.401(C).

Competency to Be Sentenced

If at any time before the imposition of the sentence the court believes a defendant may be an incompetent person, a mental status evaluation for fitness to proceed must be ordered (see chapter 7.5, Competency to Stand Trial). All judicial proceedings begin again after the defendant regains competency.

Ohio law addresses the issue of a person who is incompetent to be sentenced in the same manner as it handles the matter of a person who is incompetent to be tried. A person must be competent to participate in the proceedings against him or her throughout the entire trial, including through the sentencing phase. That is, if a question is raised about whether a person is incompetent to stand trial before the beginning of the trial or has become incompetent during the course of the trial, the court follows the steps outlined in chapter 7.5 (Competency to Stand Trial).[1] If the court completes the trial phase but then a question is raised about whether the person has become incompetent before the sentencing phase is completed, the court again follows the procedures described in chapter 7.5, including ordering an evaluation of the person[2] and holding a hearing.[3] If the court finds the person to be not competent for sentencing, it may order the person into inpatient or outpatient treatment.[4] If the person is not restored to competency to be sentenced at the end of the longest time that the law permits for treatment for individuals who are not compe-

---

1. Ohio Rev. Code § 2945.371.
2. Id.
3. Ohio Rev. Code § 2945.37.
4. Ohio Rev. Code § 2945.38(B).

tent, the court must dismiss the charge and discharge the perso from treatment unless the court or prosecutor files for a civil commitment (see chapter 8.4, Involuntary Commitment of Mentally Ill Adults).[5]

---

5. OHIO REV. CODE §§ 2945.39, 2945.401.

7.11

Sentencing

After a finding of guilt, many states, including Ohio, permit the court to request a mental health evaluation before reaching a sentencing decision. This information functions as a supplement to the presentence report by a probation officer. This chapter discusses the rules authorizing a mental health evaluation.

(A) Presentence Mental Health Examination

If the court considers placing a person found guilty of a felony into a community control sanction program (such as probation), it must first complete a presentence investigation. The officer conducting the investigation must inquire into the circumstances of the offense and the criminal record, social history, and present condition of the defendant. The officer may also, but is not required to, request a physical and mental examination of the defendant. The examination may include drug testing. If the victim of the offense wishes to make a statement regarding the impact of the offense for the officer's use in completing the presentence report, the officer must receive the statement.[1]

The defendant may review the presentence report, with the exception that neither the defendant nor the defendant's attorney may read about any recommendations about sentence, any diagnostic opinions that the court believes might seriously disrupt the defendant's rehabilitation, sources of information that were

---

1. Ohio Rev. Code § 2951.03(A).

promised confidentiality, and any information that, if disclosed, might result in harm to the defendant or other persons. Before sentencing, the court must permit the defendant to comment on the sections of the report that were made available and may permit the defendant to introduce testimony or other information that relates to the factual accuracy of the report. All information that is made available to the defendant is also made available to the prosecutor.[2]

The contents of the presentence report are confidential and are not a public record. All individuals who receive copies of the report must return them to the court when the sentencing has been completed.[3]

---

2. OHIO REV. CODE § 2951.01(B).
3. OHIO REV. CODE § 2951.01(D).

7.12

Probation

A sentencing court may place a defendant on probation or conditional discharge following conviction. When imposing such a sentence, the court may require that the defendant, among other conditions, undergo available medical or psychological treatment, remain in a specified institution, participate in an alcohol or substance abuse program, and satisfy any other stipulations reasonably related to rehabilitation. If the defendant fails to meet the conditions of probation, the conditions may be modified and probation may be revoked.[1]

The court will consider several factors when it determines whether to place an offender on probation, including the risk that the person will commit another offense; the need to protect the public; the nature and circumstances of the offense; and the history, character, and condition of the offender. Probation is not an option if the person is a repeat or dangerous offender, the offense involved the use of a firearm, or the person was found guilty of aggravated murder (with extreme indifference to human life), murder, or rape. Other factors the court may consider include whether the offense caused or threatened harm to persons or property, the offender acted under strong provocation, and the offender is likely to respond favorably to probation or other treatment.[2] If the offender is in need of rehabilitative services that can best be provided in an inpatient setting, the court is more likely to commit the person to such a facility than to provide probation.[3]

In addition to placing the person on probation, the court may add requirements that will serve justice and rehabilitate the

---

1. Ohio Rev. Code § 2951.02(C).
2. Ohio Rev. Code § 2951.02(B).
3. Ohio Rev. Code § 2951.02(D).

offender. These additional requirements may include making restitution to the victim, obtaining counseling, being subject to random drug testing and being free of drug abuse, and participating in supervised community service work.

If drug or alcohol use or abuse[4] appears to have been a factor leading to a person's offense, the court may accept the person's request for intervention in lieu of conviction. If the court elects to consider the offender's request, it will conduct a hearing and stay all criminal proceedings pending the outcome of the hearing. At the hearing, the court will consider several factors, including the severity of the offense and the recommendations of a drug and alcohol professional regarding the person's eligibility for an intervention and treatment plan. If the court accepts the offender's request for intervention rather than conviction, the court will accept the offender's plea of guilty and waive the defendant's right to trial and other proceedings. If the court does not accept the offender's request for intervention, the court will then proceed as if the request had not been made. If the court accepts the request, then one of the conditions is that the person must abstain from the use of illegal drugs and alcohol and must submit to regular random drug tests. The court may also require any other treatment terms that it believes will rehabilitate the person. If the person successfully completes the conditions imposed by the court, the court will dismiss the proceedings and may seal the records related to the offense. If the court accepts the request for intervention but the person fails to meet the conditions of the intervention plan, the probation officer must advise the court of the failure and the court will hold a hearing to determine if the offender has failed to comply. If the court concludes that the person did fail to comply, it will enter a finding of guilty and impose an appropriate sanction.

As a condition of probation, the court may place individuals who have violated Ohio's statutes regarding endangering children or domestic violence in a program that provides psychiatric or psychological treatment.[5]

---

4. Ohio Rev. Code § 2951.041.
5. Ohio Rev. Code § 2933.16.

7.13

Dangerous Offenders

In some states, the criminal sentencing law has provisions for increasing the term of imprisonment of defendants who pose special risks or who are determined to be "dangerous offenders" because of a propensity for future criminal activity. The legal determination of whether a defendant fits within this category may depend on psychological characteristics that could be assessed by an MHP.

Ohio law defines a "dangerous offender" as one who has committed an offense, whose history and character reveal a substantial risk that the person will continue to be a danger to others, and whose behavior has been characterized by a pattern of repetitive or aggressive behavior with heedless indifference to the outcomes.[1]

In Ohio, minimum sentences are favored for first-time imprisonment whereas maximum sentences are generally disfavored. The law[2] specifies that, if a court does not impose the minimum sentence for first-time imprisonment, it must indicate on the record that the minimum sentence will demean the seriousness of the conduct or will not adequately protect the public from future crimes by the offender. Similarly, Ohio law[3] prevents a court from imposing a maximum sentence for a single offense unless the court specifies on the record its reasons for selecting the maximum. The Ohio supreme court has ruled that these statutes require courts to make it clear on the record that they engaged in an analysis and, depending on the severity of the offense, to also specify the reasons for its conclusion. Defining an offender as a

---

1. Ohio Rev. Code § 2951.01(A).
2. Ohio Rev. Code § 2929.14(B).
3. Ohio Rev. Code §§ 2929.14(C) and 2929.19(B)(2)(d).

dangerous offender would constitute a reason for impo⌐
than the minimum sentence.[4]

Moreover, courts must consider all of the evidence re⌐
a defendant when determining a sentence. When an o⌐ ⌐uer
meets the criteria for a dangerous offender, the court may impose
the maximum sentence that is available for the offense. To assist
in making a decision, the court may appoint up to two psychologists or psychiatrists to examine the defendant and make a report.[5]

Ohio law does not permit individuals who are identified as
dangerous offenders to be eligible for pretrial diversion programs
(see chapter 7.3, Precharging and Pretrial Evaluations)[6] or probation (see chapter 7.12, Probation).[7]

---

4. State v. Edmonson, 86 Ohio St. 3d 324, 715 N.E.2d 131 (1999).
5. OHIO REV. CODE § 2947.06(B).
6. OHIO REV. CODE § 2935.36(A).
7. Id.

7.14

Habitual Offenders

In some states, the criminal sentencing law has provisions for increasing the term of imprisonment of defendants who have a history of criminal offenses. The determination of whether a person is likely to commit additional offenses in the future may depend on psychological characteristics that could be assessed by an MHP.

Habitual offenders are called "repeat offenders" in Ohio law. A repeat offender is a person who has a history of persistent criminal activity and whose character suggests a substantial risk of continued offenses. Repeat offenders are defined as those who have been convicted of one or more offenses such as crimes of violence, sexually oriented offenses, theft, or drug abuse and, having been imprisoned for the offense, commit another crime in the same category.

Courts are expected to exercise judgment in imposing sentences, within the parameters established by law. Typically, courts will impose lesser sentences for first-time offenders, when harm to victims has been minimal, and when the character of the offender suggests that he or she is unlikely to commit such a crime again. The court may impose up to the maximum sentence for an offense when the offender is a repeat offender.[1] The court may appoint up to two psychologists or psychiatrists to examine the offender and report to the court.[2]

Ohio law specifically bars repeat offenders from eligibility for probation (see chapter 7.12, Probation), suspended sentences

---

1. OHIO REV. CODE §§ 2929.12(D)(2), 2929.22(B)(1).
2. OHIO REV. CODE § 2947.06(B).

(in which the court releases the offender from serving the s
usually contingent on the person completing some other 1
ment such as restitution),[3] or pretrial diversion program.
chapter 7.3, Precharging and Pretrial Evaluations).[4]

---

3. Ohio Rev. Code § 2951.02.
4. Ohio Rev. Code § 2935.36.

7.15

Competency to Serve a Sentence

The law in several states provides that a criminal defendant must be competent to serve a sentence. Ohio does not have such a statute. If an inmate suffers from mental illness, the inmate will be transferred to a residential treatment unit within certain prisons, and, if needing hospital level care, to the single prison psychiatric hospital (Oakwood Forensic; see also chapters 7.16, Mental Health Services in Jails and Prisons, and 7.17, Transfer From Penal to Mental Health Facilities).

7.16

Mental Health Services in Jails and Prisons

Mental health services in prisons and jails are a vital part of an overall health care program for incarcerated people. MHPs may provide services as employees of these institutions or in a consulting capacity.

If individuals confined to jail or prison have medical and mental health care insurance coverage, then the person, municipal corporation, or provider of the health care plan will submit claims for payment for these services.[1]

(A) Prisons

A prison is a residential facility operated by the Department of Rehabilitation and Correction used for the confinement of convicted felons.[2]

The Department of Rehabilitation and Correction provides mental health services to its inmates in several ways, with some services provided in each institution and other, more specialized services offered within residential treatment units in certain prisons. The Department also operates one psychiatric hospital for prison inmates (Oakwood Forensic).

If the warden of a correctional facility believes an inmate should be transferred to one of its psychiatric units, the Department holds a hearing to determine whether the inmate is a mentally ill person subject to hospitalization. A mentally ill inmate

---

1. OHIO REV. CODE § 753.021.
2. OHIO REV. CODE § 2929.01(BB).

subject to hospitalization is a person who is mentally ill and for whom any one of the following applies:

1. the person poses a substantial risk of physical harm to him- or herself as demonstrated by threats of, or attempts at, suicide;

2. the person poses a substantial risk of physical harm to others as demonstrated by violent behavior or recent threats;

3. the person represents a substantial and immediate risk of serious physical impairment or injury because of inability to provide for basic physical needs because of the mental illness, and appropriate care is not available in the prison community; or

4. the person is in need of, and would benefit from, treatment in a hospital as manifested by behavior that creates a grave and imminent risk to substantial rights of others or the person.[3]

The hearing is held at the facility in which the inmate is being held, and the Department must provide independent assistance (by someone not employed by the Department) to the inmate for the hearing. An independent decision maker provided by the Department presides at the hearing and determines whether the inmate qualifies for hospitalization. If the decision maker finds clear and convincing evidence that the inmate is a mentally ill person subject to hospitalization, the decision maker must order that the inmate be transferred to a psychiatric unit for observation and treatment for up to 30 days.[4] The staff must examine the inmate within 24 hours of arriving at the unit and then develop a treatment plan for the inmate's care.[5] The Department will hold additional hearings before the end of the 30-day observation and treatment period and, as necessary, at 90-day intervals after the first hearing to determine the need for continued psychiatric care.[6] If an inmate completes his or her term of confinement while in the psychiatric unit, the warden of the prison that houses the psychiatric unit, at least 14 days before the expiration of the sentence, may notify the court that it believes the inmate is a mentally ill or mentally retarded person subject to hospitalization by court order[7] (see chapter 8.4, Involuntary Commitment of Mentally Ill Adults).

Hospitals and other facilities within the Department of Rehabilitation and Correction may share with each other medical and psychological records and other pertinent information. Nonetheless, the information that may be shared about an inmate is limited

---

3. Ohio Rev. Code § 5120.17(A).
4. Ohio Rev. Code § 5120.17(B).
5. Ohio Rev. Code § 5120.17(C).
6. Ohio Rev. Code § 5120.17(E).
7. Ohio Rev. Code § 5120.17(H).

to medication history, medical history, summary of treatment in the hospital, summary of treatment needs, and a discharge summary.[8] The Department may also exchange similar mental health records of inmates with county and other local facilities as long as the inmate consents to the disclosure, or against the inmate's objection if the office or agency that wishes to receive the information documents its attempts to obtain the inmate's consent, the reasons why the consent has not been granted, and why the agency needs the information.[9]

Ohio does not have separate provisions for the care of mentally retarded inmates who become mentally ill. Services are available to them as outlined in this section.

(B) Jails

A jail is a residential facility that is operated by one or more political subdivisions of the state used for the confinement of alleged or convicted offenders. The terms *jail*, *workhouse*, and *minimum security jail* all refer to such a residential facility operated by a local subdivision.[10]

Each minimum security and full service jail must employ or contract with a physician to supervise the implementation of a health care plan that outlines policies and procedures regulating all aspects of medical and mental health treatment to prisoners.[11] A preliminary health evaluation is completed on each new admission that must include behavioral observations and mental status and assessment of suicide risk.[12] Prisoners held in full service jails who evidence signs of serious mental disorder must be referred to the jail physician or other qualified mental health professional or agency for psychological services.[13] Inmates held in minimum security jails who show signs of serious mental disorder or substance abuse withdrawal are transferred to a qualified agency for psychiatric or psychological services.[14]

---

8. Ohio Rev. Code § 5120.17(J).
9. Ohio Rev. Code § 5120.17(J)(6).
10. Ohio Rev. Code § 2929.01(U).
11. Ohio Admin. Code § 5120:1-8-09(A).
12. Ohio Admin. Code §§ 5120:1-8-09(C), 5120:1-9-09(C).
13. Ohio Admin. Code § 5120:1-8-09(S).
14. Ohio Admin. Code § 5120:1-9-09(Q).

Transfer From Penal to Mental Health Facilities

In some states an inmate of a state-operated penal institution who becomes mentally disordered may be eligible for mental health treatment at another facility (see chapter 8.4, Involuntary Commitment of Mentally Ill Adults). However, in Ohio, such inmates are transferred to specialized psychiatric units in certain prisons or to the Oakwood Forensic Hospital, which is operated by the Department of Rehabilitation and Correction (see chapter 7.16, Mental Health Services in Jails and Prisons).

7.18

Parole Determinations

Parole is a conditional release from imprisonment that entitles the parolee to serve the remainder of the term outside of the confines of the prison. It differs from probation in that the convicted person must first serve a period of time in one of Ohio's Department of Rehabilitation and Correction institutions. Although a parole determination is made by the Adult Parole Authority, MHPs in or out of the system may provide information for the parole hearing.

(A) Eligibility for Parole

Except for prisoners who are serving a prison term without an option of parole, prisoners become eligible for consideration for parole at various times, depending on the offense and the nature of the sentence. For example, prisoners who have been sentenced to prison for life for murder become eligible when they have served the minimum term. In other cases, the sentence of imprisonment specifies when the offender becomes eligible for parole.[1]

Each sentence to a prison term for a felony of the first, second, and third degree and for felony sex offenses in Ohio must include a requirement that the offender participate in a period of postrelease control imposed by the Parole Authority after the prisoner is released from prison. The length of this control program is specified by statute and depends on the nature of the offense and the length of the sentence.[2] The Parole Authority may include

---

1. Ohio Rev. Code § 2967.13.
2. Ohio Rev. Code § 2967.28(B).

sanctions as part of the postrelease control program, including a sanction that the offender must participate in approved rehabilitation programs.[3]

(A)(1) Transitional Control Program

The Department of Rehabilitation and Correction may place prisoners in supervised settings outside of the prison that are designed to assist the prisoner in adjusting to parole. This program closely monitors a prisoner's adjustment to community supervision during the final 180 days of the prisoner's confinement. Prisoners selected for this program are placed in community facilities that are approved by the Adult Parole Authority.[4]

At least three weeks before transferring a prisoner to transitional control, the Adult Parole Authority must give notice of its intention to the court in which the indictment was made. The court may disapprove of the request and thereby block the transfer. As part of the request to the court, the Parole Authority may also request that the head of the correctional institution submit a report that describes the prisoner's participation in school, mental health or drug and alcohol treatment, vocational training, and other rehabilitative activities. Victims of the offense may also submit a statement to the Parole Authority regarding the impact of the transfer.

(B) Board of Parole

The Adult Parole Authority is a unit within the Department of Rehabilitation and Correction.[5] When prisoners become eligible for parole, the head of the correctional facility notifies the Parole Authority, which may investigate and examine the prisoners with respect to their conduct in prison, mental and moral qualities, their family relationships, and any other matters relevant to their fitness to be released without being a threat to society.

The Parole Authority may recommend to the governor that prisoners be pardoned, sentences be shortened, or prisoners be granted a parole. The overriding concern of the Parole Authority is that its recommendations further the interests of justice and the welfare and security of society.

---

3. OHIO REV. CODE § 2967.28(E).
4. OHIO REV. CODE § 2967.26.
5. OHIO REV. CODE § 5149.02.

(C) Parole Criteria

Regardless of the offense, each prisoner placed on parole, transition control, or other form of authorized release from prison will be required during the period of control to observe specific sanctions, namely to obtain permission to leave the state and to abide by the law. The Department of Rehabilitation and Correction may also require that the individual not abuse drugs and be subject to random drug testing.[6]

During the period of control, authorized officers of the Parole Authority may search, with or without a warrant, the person, the place of residence, and the person's property if the officers have reasonable grounds to believe that the person is not complying with the sanctions or conditions that were established.[7]

---

6. OHIO REV. CODE § 2967.131(A), (B).
7. OHIO REV. CODE § 2967.131(C).

7.19

Competency to Be Executed

A person who has been convicted of first-degree murder and sentenced to death must be legally sane at the time of execution. The rationale for this law is that the convict must understand the nature of the death penalty and why it was imposed.[1] MHPs may be involved in evaluations of these individuals.

(A) Legal Determination of Competency to Be Executed

Prisoners are assumed to be competent to be executed, so individuals who believe that the prisoner is not competent to be executed must come forward and give notice of the apparent lack of competency.

(A)(1) Test of Competency

As used in this context, *insane* means that the convict does not have the mental capacity to understand the nature of the death penalty and why it was imposed on him or her.[2] Insanity can be distinguished from mental illness, which refers to a serious disruption in mood, thinking, memory, and perception that grossly impairs judgment, behavior, and capacity to recognize reality, or substantially interferes with everyday functioning.[3] A prisoner may be mentally ill but competent to be executed. For

---

1. Ohio Rev. Code § 2949.28(A).
2. Id.
3. Ohio Rev. Code § 5122.01(A).

example, one Ohio court found a prisoner to be competent to be executed even though he suffered from chronic undifferentiated schizophrenia.[4]

(A)(2) Raising the Competency Issue

The warden or the sheriff having custody of the convict, the convict's counsel, or a psychiatrist or psychologist who has examined the convict shall give notice of the apparent insanity to the judge who imposed the sentence, or if that judge is unavailable, to another judge of the same court. If the convict was tried by a three-judge panel, then notice of the apparent insanity is made to any of the three judges. The sentence of execution may be suspended only on an order of the state supreme court.[5]

(B) Competency Evaluation

If the judge determines that probable cause exists that the convict is insane, the judge must hold a hearing to make a final determination. The court may appoint one or more psychiatrists or psychologists, not employed by the Department of Rehabilitation and Correction, to examine the convict. The examiner has access to psychiatric or psychological reports previously submitted to the court regarding the convict and to any current mental health and medical records of the convict. Examiners must submit their reports to the court within 30 days of their appointment. The report must contain the examiner's findings about whether the convict is able to understand the nature of the death penalty and why it was imposed and the facts on which the findings are based.[6]

(C) Competency Hearing

The convict, the prosecuting attorney, and the convict's attorney attend the hearing. Both parties may produce, examine, and cross-examine witnesses.[7] Throughout the proceedings, the convict is presumed to be sane, and the court will find the convict is sane unless the preponderance of the evidence indicates that the convict is insane.[8]

---

4. State v. Scott, 92 Ohio St. 3d 1, 748 N.E.2d 11, *cert. denied*, 532 U.S. 1034 (2001).
5. OHIO REV. CODE § 2949.28(B).
6. OHIO REV. CODE § 2949.28(B), (C).
7. OHIO REV. CODE § 2949.29(A).
8. OHIO REV. CODE § 2949.29(C).

Confidentiality and Privileged Communication

Ohio law does not specifically address confidentiality and privileged communication for convicts in this context. As a general principle, there is no reasonable expectation of privacy.

(E) Disposition of Defendants Found Incompetent to Be Executed

If the court finds the convict to be incompetent to be executed, and if authorized by the Ohio supreme court, the court must continue any stay of execution and order continued confinement for the convict. The court also orders the convict into treatment. Thereafter, the court may conduct additional hearings at any time, and must do so on a motion of the prosecuting attorney to continue its inquiry into the competence of the convict. The court may appoint one or more psychiatrists or psychologists to make additional examinations of the convict and to make reports to the court. If, at a hearing, the court finds the convict is not insane, then the plans for execution move forward. If the court finds the convict is still insane, then the convict continues with the treatment program, indefinitely if necessary.[9] No rules regarding mentally ill or mentally retarded persons other than those written specifically for competency for execution may be applied to the convict.[10]

---

9. Ohio Rev. Code § 2949.29(B).
10. Ohio Rev. Code § 2949.29(D).

7.2

Pornography

The law prohibits promoting, or possessing with intent to promote, any obscene material; or producing, directing, presenting, or participating in an obscene performance. MHPs may be asked to evaluate and testify whether the dominant theme of a work taken as a whole appeals to a prurient interest in sex, whether a work is patently offensive because it affronts contemporary community standards regarding sexual matters, or whether a work is utterly without redeeming social value. However, expert testimony is not necessary for a conviction on any obscenity charge, and a conviction cannot be based on such testimony alone.

Ohio law defines material or a performance as "obscene" when considered as a whole and judged with reference to ordinary adults if it meets any of the criteria listed. A material or performance also is defined as obscene if it was created for sexual deviates or other susceptible groups such as juveniles and, when judged with reference to that group, any of the criteria listed are met:[1]

1. the dominant appeal is to prurient interests;

2. the material or performance contains displays, descriptions, or representations of sexual activity, excitement, or nudity;

3. it displays, describes, or represents bestiality or extreme or bizarre violence, cruelty, or brutality;

4. it displays, describes, or represents human bodily functions of elimination;

5. it makes repeated use of foul language;

---

1. Ohio Rev. Code § 2907.01(F).

6. it displays lurid details of violent physical torture or death of a human being; or

7. it displays criminal activity that tends to glorify or glamorize that activity and, with respect to juveniles, has a dominant tendency to corrupt.

It is illegal to create, reproduce, publish, buy, sell, or distribute obscene materials. To do so is to be guilty of pandering obscenity,[2] which is a second-degree felony, punishable by a prison term of two to eight years and a fine of up to $15,000. It is also illegal for suppliers or distributors to refuse to furnish a customer with items that are desired unless he or she also accepts materials that are obscene.[3]

---

2. OHIO REV. CODE § 2907.32.
3. OHIO REV. CODE § 2907.34.

7.

Services for
Sex Offenders

In some states, the law provides specialized services for sex offenders through commitment or sentencing to a treatment program. MHPs are involved in evaluating the individual, testifying in court, and providing treatment. Ohio law has special provisions for individuals who commit sexually oriented offenses. Depending on the nature of the offense, a person may be categorized as a sexual predator, habitual sexual offender, or as a person convicted of a sexually oriented offense.

(A) Definitions[1]

Sexually oriented offense means any of the following offenses:

1. regardless of the age of the victim of the offense, rape, sexual battery, and gross sexual imposition;

2. regardless of the age of the victim, aggravated murder (with gross indifference to human life or using a deadly weapon), murder, felonious assault (knowingly or recklessly causing injury), kidnapping, or felony-based involuntary manslaughter (wanton or reckless conduct), when the offense was committed with a purpose to gratify the sexual needs or desires of the offender; or

3. any of several offenses involving a minor such as compelling prostitution, certain use of a minor in nudity oriented material, and corruption of a minor.

---

1. Ohio Rev. Code § 2950.01.

Violent sex offense refers to rape, sexual battery, or the former offense of felonious sexual penetration, or gross sexual imposition when the victim is younger than 13; or a felony violation of a former law of Ohio, or another state, or of the United States that is substantially equivalent; or an attempt to commit or complicity in committing one of these offenses. *Sexually violent offense* means a violent sex offense or a designated homicide, assault, or kidnapping offense for which the offender also was convicted of or pleaded guilty to a sexual motivation specification. *Habitual sexual offender* refers to a person who has been convicted of engaging in two or more sexual offenses but does not meet the criteria for a sexual predator. *Sexual predator* refers to a person who has been convicted of or pleaded guilty to committing a sexually oriented offense and is likely to engage in the future in one or more sexually oriented offenses. *Sexually violent predator* means a person who has been convicted of or pleaded guilty to a sexually violent offense and is likely to engage in the future in additional sexually violent offenses.[2]

(B) Legal Test for Sex Offenders

The law specifies two ways in which a person convicted of a sexually oriented offense may be classified as a sexual predator. First, a person may be automatically classified as a sexual predator if (a) the person is convicted of or pleads guilty to committing, on or after January 1, 1997, a sexually violent offense and also is convicted of or pleads guilty to a charge of being a sexually violent predator, or (b) the person is convicted of or pleads guilty to a sexually oriented offense in a state other than Ohio, in a federal court, military court, or an Indian tribal court, and is required under the law of that other jurisdiction, to register as a sex offender until the person's death.[3]

In all other cases in which a person is to be sentenced on or after January 1, 1997, the classification of sexual predator may be made only following a hearing on this matter.[4] The law also contains provisions under which a person who was convicted of or pleaded guilty to a sexually oriented offense before January 1, 1997, and who is serving a prison term may be adjudicated a sexual predator.[5] At the hearing to determine whether the offender should be classified as a sexual predator, the offender and the

---

2. OHIO REV. CODE § 1971.01(H).
3. OHIO REV. CODE § 2950.09(A).
4. *Id.*
5. OHIO REV. CODE § 2950.09(C).

prosecution have an opportunity to testify, present evidence, call and examine witnesses and expert witnesses, and cross-examine witnesses regarding the sexual predator determination. In making a determination about whether a person is a sexual predator, the judge will consider all relevant information about the person, including the following:

1. the age of the offender;

2. the offender's previous criminal record;

3. the age and number of the offender's victims;

4. whether the offender used drugs or alcohol to impair the victim;

5. whether the person has been convicted before of a sex offense and, if so, whether the person participated in available treatment programs for sex offenders;

6. any mental illness or mental disability of the offender;

7. the nature of the sexual activity that made up the offense;

8. whether the offender displayed cruelty or made threats of cruelty; and

9. any other behavioral characteristics that contribute to the offender's conduct.

If the judge determines that the offender is not a sexual predator, the judge must specify this in the offender's sentence and judgment of conviction. If the judge determines by clear and convincing evidence that the offender is a sexual predator, the judge must make this finding clear in the offender's sentence and judgment of conviction and must specify that the determination was pursuant to the law's hearing mechanism.[6]

A person may be designated as a habitual sex offender if he or she has engaged in two or more sexual offenses but does not meet the criteria for a sexual predator.[7]

MHPs may participate in examinations of offenders during presentencing proceedings as described in chapter 7.11 (Sentencing).[8] The judge makes the determination by clear and convincing evidence of whether the offender is a sexual predator.

Ohio law also has provisions for juvenile court judges to classify certain delinquent children as sex offenders and to require them to register as sex offenders[9] (see chapter 4.15, Delinquency and Persons in Need of Supervision, for discussion of juvenile

---

6. OHIO REV. CODE § 2950.09(B).
7. OHIO REV. CODE § 2950.09(C).
8. OHIO REV. CODE § 2950.19(B).
9. OHIO REV. CODE § 2152.82(A).

delinquency). The classification may be applied to children who meet the following criteria:

1. the child was adjudicated delinquent for committing
   a. aggravated murder, murder, felonious assault, kidnapping, abduction, or involuntary manslaughter in the commission of a felony, or for an attempt to commit those offenses, when the crime was committed or attempted for the purpose of sexually gratifying the child;
   b. certain pandering offenses if the child is four or more years older than the minor who is the victim;
   c. other sexually oriented offenses that, if committed by an adult, would be a felony of the first, second, third, or fourth degree.
2. children who are 14 years of age or older at the time of committing the offense; and
3. children who are classified by a juvenile court judge as a "juvenile sex offender registrant." Courts classify juveniles as juvenile sex offender registrants when they have committed a sexually oriented offense and have previously been adjudicated a delinquent child for committing a sexually oriented offense, regardless of the juvenile's age at the time of the earlier offense.[10]

(C) Disposition

Designation as a sexually violent predator leads to enhancement of the incarceration sentence, whereas designation as a sexual predator, habitual sexual offender, or as a person convicted of a sexually oriented offense leads to differential registration and community notification provisions (Ohio's Megan's Law).[11]

Offenders convicted of a sexually oriented offense may be required to register as sex offenders with a sheriff.[12] The duration of registration varies from 10 years to life, depending on the classification as a sexual predator, habitual sexual offender, or conviction of a sexually oriented offense.[13] The law contains provisions that permit the victim of a sexual predator, or of a habitual sex offender in certain circumstances, to receive written notice when the offender registers with a sheriff or notifies the sheriff of a change of residence address.[14] Sheriffs must provide written

---

10. OHIO REV. CODE § 2152.82(A).
11. OHIO REV. CODE § 2950.09.
12. OHIO REV. CODE § 2950.04(A).
13. OHIO REV. CODE § 2950.07(A).
14. OHIO REV. CODE § 2950.10.

notice containing specified information about sexual predators to certain specified persons and entities in the community.[15]

The Department of Rehabilitation and Correction provides special educational and intensive counseling and therapy residential programs within prisons to sexual offenders. These special programs are not required by law, but because judges may inquire about whether offenders have participated in treatment programs for sex offenders when the determination is made to designate them as a sexual predator,[16] several prisons provide such specialized treatment programs. MHPs are involved in assessing offenders and in developing and providing the specialized services.

15. Ohio Rev. Code § 2950.11.
16. Ohio Rev. Code § 2950.09(B)(f).

Services for Victims of Crimes

Some states, including Ohio, have enacted laws that provide services from MHPs and others for victims of crimes.

(A) Board

In Ohio, assistance for crime victims is available through county governmental agencies and approved nonprofit corporations. A statewide advisory committee provides guidance and recommendations regarding funding.

The state Victims Assistance Advisory Committee is appointed by the state attorney general and includes a chairperson, four ex-officio members, and 15 members who represent various constituencies, such as the Ohio victim-witness association, local victim assistance programs, elderly individuals, domestic violence victims, and others. The ex-officio members include the chief justice of the Ohio supreme court, the state attorney general, one member of the state senate designated by the president of the senate, and one member of the state house of representatives designated by the speaker of the house.[1]

The purpose of the Advisory Committee is to advise the attorney general's office in determining crime and delinquency victim service needs, determine state policies for victim services, exercise leadership in the quality of victim programs in the state, and recommend to the attorney general's office which victim assistance programs should receive state financial assistance. Priorities for funding of local programs include those that were in existence

---

1. OHIO REV. CODE § 109.91(A), (B).

before 1985 and programs that offer the broadest range of services and referrals, including medical, psychological, and legal.[2] Local programs may also receive funding from local agencies.

Victim assistance programs include those that provide at least one of the following:

1. services to victims of any offense of violence or delinquency;
2. financial assistance or property repair services;
3. assistance to victims in judicial proceedings; or
4. technical assistance to individuals or organizations that provide services to victims.[3]

(B) Eligibility and Awards

Victims and members of their families are eligible for assistance. Members of victims' families include the spouse, children, stepchildren, siblings, parents, stepparents, grandparents, or other relatives of a victim, excluding the person who is charged with the crime (if that person is a family member).[4]

Services provided to victims include crisis intervention services (including short-term counseling and therapy), emergency services, support services including follow-up counseling and assistance in obtaining services from social service agencies, court-related services such as assisting victims to participate in court proceedings, crime prevention services, and victim–offender mediation services.[5]

(C) Services by MHPs

Victims services programs may provide short-term emotional and psychological services, follow-up counseling and referral services, and victim–offender mediation services.[6]

(D) Other Victim Services

Additional services to victims may be obtained from the Office of Victims' Services in the Department of Rehabilitation and

---

2. OHIO REV. CODE § 109.91(C).
3. OHIO REV. CODE § 109.91(D).
4. OHIO REV. CODE § 2930.01.
5. OHIO REV. CODE § 307.62.
6. Id.

Correction. This Office is located in the Division of Parole and Community Services of the Department.

This Office provides assistance to victims of crime, victims' representatives, and members of victim's families. The assistance includes providing information about the policies and procedures of the Department and the status of offenders. The Office also provides publications that assist victims in contacting staff of the Department about problems with offenders, and it assists the parole board hearing officers in identifying victims' issues.[7]

---

7. OHIO REV. CODE § 5120.60.

Voluntary or Involuntary Receipt of State Services

Medicaid

Medicaid is the federally supported state program through which the states provide direct payments to suppliers of medical care and services (including MHPs) for individuals receiving cash payments in programs such as old-age assistance, aid to needy families with dependent children, aid to blind individuals, and aid to disabled individuals. In Ohio, the program is administered primarily by the Department of Job and Family Services, through 88 local county human services departments.

In Ohio, physicians (including psychiatrists), psychologists, and advanced practice nurses are eligible to become individual providers for Medicaid. Other mental health professionals (MHPs) may be reimbursed by Medicaid for their services if they are employed by an agency or project that is approved by the local county Alcohol, Drug Abuse, and Mental Health Services Board.

A patient's eligibility for Medicaid services is dependent on a number of factors such as income, age, and disability. The director of the Department establishes standards, procedures, and other requirements regarding the provision of medical assistance.[1]

To qualify for Medicaid, a person must be a U.S. citizen and an Ohio resident, have a Social Security number, and meet certain financial requirements demonstrating need. The financial requirements include levels of annual income, resources owned by the person or family, and size of family. Maximum income levels are related to the criteria used to establish the federal poverty level. For example, families who request services may meet the income level criterion if their annual income is less than 100% of the

---

1. OHIO REV. CODE § 5111.01.

federal poverty level, and individuals with disabilities may qualify if their income reaches only 64% of the federal poverty level.

Ohio Medicaid provides payment for a variety of services relevant to MHPs, including medical services to children (up to age 19), pregnant women, families with children under age 18, adults age 65 and over, individuals who are legally blind, and individuals with disabilities.

8.2

Health Care Cost Containment System

Some states have health care cost containment systems that administer payment for medical and other services to indigent persons. In Ohio, several cost containment mechanisms are in place, including for Medicaid programs (see chapter 8.1, Medicaid) and victim assistance programs (see chapter 7.22, Services for Victims of Crimes).

One general cost containment measure entails the setting of reimbursement caps for Medicaid reimbursement for all providers, including MHPs, that are typically lower than the amount the providers charge patients in a fee-for-service arrangement. In addition, to qualify as a provider for Medicaid, the provider must agree to accept the Medicaid reimbursement amount as payment in full; the provider may not bill the patient for any amounts not covered by Medicaid.

The Department of Job and Family Services has implemented, as one of its efforts to control costs, an option for Medicaid enrollees to participate in a managed care plan for health care. The programs are called managed health care programs.[1] Each such program must engage in various cost containment activities, including such things as establishing a utilization management system to ensure appropriateness of patient use of services and engaging in discharge planning and case management,[2] establishing provider reimbursement rates,[3] conducting audits of providers to determine compliance with Medicaid rules and guidelines such as record keeping and billing,[4] and participating in the activities

---

1. Ohio Admin. Code § 5101:3-26-01.
2. Ohio Admin. Code § 5101:3-26-07.
3. Ohio Admin. Code § 5101:3-26-09.
4. Ohio Admin. Code § 5101:3-26-06.

of the Medicaid fraud control unit.[5] These managed health care programs are reimbursed by the Department of Jobs and Family Services through a capitation system in which the program is paid, on a monthly basis, a specified amount for each enrollee for the duration of the agreement regardless of the amount of service the enrollee uses.

The Ohio attorney general's office periodically audits the bill payments and provider reimbursements of the victim assistance program (see chapter 7.22, Services for Victims of Crimes).[6] The attorney general follows cost containment and reimbursement guidelines adopted by the workers' compensation program.[7] Providers who accept payment for services under the victim assistance program may not seek additional reimbursement from the victim.[8]

---

5. *Id.*
6. OHIO REV. CODE § 2743.521(A).
7. OHIO REV. CODE § 4121.44.
8. OHIO REV. CODE § 2743.521(B).

Voluntary Admission of Mentally Ill Adults

The law provides for the voluntary admission of mentally ill persons to state-operated facilities. MHPs are involved in this process both in evaluating the person for admission and in providing services within the facility.

(A) Differences Between Voluntary and Involuntary Admission

The major differences between voluntary and involuntary admissions have to do with how individuals are admitted and how they are discharged. Basically, voluntarily admitted persons can be admitted at their own request and can leave the care of the facility on their own initiative, subject to certain constraints and, to some degree, the willingness of the facility to provide the care. The admission and discharge processes for voluntary patients are discussed next. Involuntarily committed patients are placed in a treatment facility at the initiative of other people or the court, and their continuing commitment is subject to judicial review. Admission and discharge procedures for involuntary patients are discussed in chapter 8.4 (Involuntary Commitment of Mentally Ill Adults).

(B) Evaluation and Admission

Any adult who believes he or she is mentally ill may make written application for voluntary admission to the chief medical officer of a hospital, who makes the decision of whether to admit the person. An application may also be made on behalf of a minor by a parent or guardian or by a person with custody of the child, and on behalf of an adult by the guardian or person with custody of the adult if the adult previously has been adjudicated incompetent.[1] The application, and the specific information that is requested, for voluntary admission is developed by each mental health facility (the state of Ohio does not specify what information must be contained in the application) but generally the application asks for information about the person's mental health problems, what types of care the person is currently receiving, and an acknowledgement that the person understands that she or he is requesting a voluntary admission.

Voluntarily admitted individuals receive observation, diagnosis, care, or treatment unless the chief clinical officer finds that hospitalization is inappropriate. No person may be admitted to a public hospital without the authorization of the mental health board of the patient's county of residence.[2]

(C) Discharge

The chief clinical officer of the hospital must discharge a voluntary patient who has recovered or whose hospitalization is no longer advisable and may discharge a voluntary patient who refuses to comply with a treatment plan.[3] If a minor or incompetent adult is admitted, a court must determine whether the admission or continued hospitalization is in the best interest of the patient.

Voluntarily admitted patients who request their release in writing or whose release is sought by another person such as counsel, parent, legal guardian, spouse, or next of kin must be released immediately unless the patient has not consented to the release or unless the chief clinical officer of the hospital, within three court days from the receipt of the request for release, files with the court a legal statement called an affidavit that states that the person should remain hospitalized.[4] The affidavit may be accompanied by a report from a psychiatrist or a psychologist attesting to the patient's mental condition and need for continued hospitalization.[5] If such an affidavit is submitted, the court must hold a hearing.[6] The hearing must be held within five court days

---

1. OHIO REV. CODE § 5122.02(A), (B).
2. OHIO REV. CODE § 5122.02(B).
3. OHIO REV. CODE § 5122.02(C).
4. OHIO REV. CODE § 5122.11.
5. OHIO REV. CODE § 5122.15(H).
6. OHIO REV. CODE § 5122.141.

from the day on which the patient is detained or the affidavit is filed, whichever occurs first, although the court may delay the hearing for up to 10 more days to allow the participants to fully prepare for the hearing. The patient has the right to attend the hearing and to be represented by counsel and to have access to all documents that will be used in the hearing.[7] If the court finds the patient is a mentally ill person who is subject to court-ordered hospitalization, all provisions for involuntarily committed patients then apply (see chapter 8.4, Involuntary Commitment of Mentally Ill Adults). Before a patient is released from a public hospital, the hospital must notify the mental health board of the patient's county of residence of the pending release.[8]

---

7. OHIO REV. CODE § 5122.15(A).
8. OHIO REV. CODE § 5122.03.

Involuntary Commitment of Mentally Ill Adults

The law pertaining to involuntary civil commitment concerns mentally ill adults as well as minors (see chapter 4.19, Voluntary Admission and Civil Commitment of Minors). MHPs are involved in this process in evaluating the person for admission, testifying in court about their findings, and providing services within the facility to which the person is committed. Physicians must be involved in the evaluation process, although other MHPs may assist.

(A) Definitions

Mental illness refers to a substantial disorder of thought, mood, perception, orientation, or memory that grossly impairs judgment, behavior, capacity to recognize reality, or ability to meet the ordinary demands of life. *Mentally ill person subject to hospitalization by court order* refers to a mentally ill person who, because of the illness:

1. represents substantial risk of harm to self as demonstrated by evidence of threats or attempts at suicide;

2. represents a substantial risk of harm to others as manifested by evidence of recent violent behavior or other evidence of present dangerousness;

3. represents a substantial and immediate risk of serious physical impairment or injury to self as demonstrated by the person's inability to provide for his or her basic physical needs and these needs cannot be met in the community; or

4. would benefit from inpatient treatment and is in need of treatment as manifested by evidence of behavior that creates a grave and imminent risk to substantial rights of others or self.

Hospital means a hospital or inpatient unit that is licensed, established, controlled, or supervised by the Department of Mental Health. *Public hospital* refers to a facility that is tax-supported and under the jurisdiction of the Department of Mental Health. *Community mental health agency* means any agency, program, or facility with which a Board of Alcohol, Drug Addiction, and Mental Health Services contracts to provide mental health services. *Chief clinical officer* means the medical director of a hospital or mental health board. Within community mental health agencies, the chief clinical officer is designated by the governing body of the agency and must be a licensed physician or licensed clinical psychologist. *Independent expert evaluation* means an evaluation conducted by a licensed psychologist or physician, including a psychiatrist, who has been selected by the patient and who agrees to conduct the examination.[1]

(B) Admission

The chief clinical officer of a hospital may, and the chief clinical officer of a public hospital in all cases of psychiatric medical emergencies must, receive for observation, diagnosis, care, and treatment any person whose admission is applied for under either emergency procedures or judicial procedures. On application, the chief clinical officer must notify the Mental Health Board of the patient's county of residence. The Board or an agency designated by the Board must promptly assess the patient, if this has not already been done, to assist the hospital in determining whether the patient meets the criteria for a "mentally ill person subject to hospitalization by court order" (see earlier in this chapter) and whether alternative, less restrictive, services are available. Individuals who are involuntarily detained in a hospital must immediately be provided with a written statement of specific rights, including the right to make a reasonable number of telephone calls to an attorney, physician, psychologist, or others, a right to counsel and an independent expert evaluation of their mental condition, and a right to a hearing to determine if they are subject to hospitalization by court order.[2]

---

1. OHIO REV. CODE § 5122.01.
2. OHIO REV. CODE § 5122.05.

(C) Commitment Proceedings

A court-ordered commitment begins with the filing of a document (affidavit) by any person who provides information that indicates probable cause to believe that the person is mentally ill and subject to a court-ordered commitment. The affidavit may be accompanied by a certificate from a psychiatrist, or from a psychologist and a physician who is not a psychiatrist, that states that the person who issued the certificate has examined the person and believes that the person meets the criteria for commitment. The certificate may also specify that the person has refused to submit to an examination, if that is the case.

If the judge or referee (an attorney who has been selected by the court to hear these cases) who receives the affidavit believes that the evidence supports the request, the judge or referee may issue a temporary detention order to take the person into custody and transport the person to a hospital or other facility or may set the matter for further hearing. The person may be observed and treated until the hearing.[3] Every person who is transported to a facility under these conditions must be examined within 24 hours and, if the chief clinical officer fails to then certify that the person meets criteria for commitment, the person must immediately be released.[4]

Immediately after acceptance of an affidavit for commitment, the court may appoint a psychiatrist, or a psychologist and a physician who is not a psychiatrist, to examine the person. The examiners will report the findings from the evaluation at the first hearing.[5] In addition to requesting the examination, the court also refers the affidavit to the Alcohol, Drug Addiction, and Mental Health Services Board or an agency designated by the Board to assist the court in making the determination of whether the person meets the criteria for involuntary commitment.[6] Before a hearing, the court must give written notice to the patient, the patient's legal guardian, spouse, or parent (if the patient is a minor), the person who filed the affidavit, one other person designated by the patient, the patient's counsel, the facility where the patient is held and to the Board of Alcohol, Drug Addiction, and Mental Health Services serving the patient's county of residence.[7]

The hearing must be conducted within five court days from the day when the person was detained or the affidavit was filed, whichever occurs first, but may be continued for 10 more days

---

3. Ohio Rev. Code § 5122.11.
4. Ohio Rev. Code § 5122.19.
5. Ohio Rev. Code § 5122.14.
6. Ohio Rev. Code § 5122.13.
7. Ohio Rev. Code § 5122.12.

with good cause such as to allow time for the participants to prepare for the hearing. The hearing may be conducted in a hospital in or outside of the county of residence. The person may waive the initial hearing, and then, if the person is still detained, a mandatory full hearing must be conducted within 30 days. If the court finds the person is subject to involuntary commitment, it may issue an interim order of detention to take the person into custody and transport the person to a hospital or other appropriate facility, if the person is not already in such a facility.[8]

Individuals who are involuntarily committed are subject to periodic full hearings. In full hearings, the court may consider the person's entire medical record with all relevant documents, including reports from MHPs. The person has a right to attend the hearing and be represented by counsel. The person also has the right, but may not be compelled, to testify. If, at the completion of the hearing, the court finds by clear and convincing evidence that the person is subject to involuntary commitment, the court must order the person to undergo treatment in an appropriate facility for a period not to exceed 90 days. This order is subject to the consent of the facility to accept the person as a patient. If, during the 90 days, the facility determines that the person can be well cared for in a less restrictive setting, the court may make a new order. The patient may also request to be shifted to a voluntary admission status during the 90-day period and, if the hospital accepts the application based on its judgment that the patient meets the criteria for a voluntary admission (see chapter 8.3, Voluntary Admission of Mentally Ill Adults), the court will dismiss the application for involuntary commitment.

At the end of the 90-day treatment period or any subsequent period of continued commitment, the facility must dismiss the patient or file an application for continued commitment. The court must hold a full hearing on applications for continued commitment at the expiration of the first 90-day period and at least every two years after the expiration of the first 90-day period. During confinement the patient may request another full hearing and may accompany the request with an affidavit of a psychiatrist or psychologist alleging that he or she no longer requires commitment.[9]

(D) Emergency Admissions

In an emergency, any physician (including a psychiatrist), licensed psychologist, health officer, parole officer, police officer, or sheriff

---

8. Ohio Rev. Code § 5122.141.
9. Ohio Rev. Code § 5122.15.

may take a person into custody and transport the person to a general hospital not licensed by the Department of Mental Health where the person may be held if the professional believes that the person is subject to hospitalization by court order. The professional must provide the hospital with a written statement describing the circumstances under which the person was taken into custody and the reasons for the professional's belief that the person should be hospitalized. The professional taking the person into custody also must explain to the person that he or she is being taken to a hospital for examination by mental health professionals.[10]

A general hospital may admit the person. If it does, it must provide an examination within 24 hours. If, after examination, the hospital believes the person is subject to hospitalization by court order, the chief clinical officer may detain the person for not more than three court days following the examination and during this period admit the person as a voluntary patient or file for an involuntary hospitalization.[11]

(E) Discharge

A person who is involuntarily placed in a hospital must be afforded a hearing within five court days to determine whether or not he or she is a mentally ill person subject to hospitalization by court order. If the court finds the person does not qualify for a court-ordered commitment, the court must immediately discharge the person and expunge all record of the proceedings.[12] At any subsequent hearings, the court will discharge the patient if it finds by clear and convincing evidence that the respondent no longer qualifies for involuntary commitment.[13] At the end of the first 90-day period or any subsequent period of continued commitment, the patient must be dismissed unless the facility or other person files with the court an application for continued commitment at least 10 days before the end of the commitment period. The court must hold a hearing on applications for continued commitment at the expiration of the first 90-day period and at least every two years after the expiration of the first 90-day period. During extended periods of confinement, the patient, the person's counsel, or a psychiatrist or psychologist may request a new hearing, alleging that the person is eligible for discharge.

10. OHIO REV. CODE § 5122.10.
11. *Id.*
12. OHIO REV. CODE § 5122.141.
13. OHIO REV. CODE § 5122.15.

The court will discharge the patient unless it finds by clear and convincing evidence that the patient is subject to continued involuntary commitment.[14]

When a patient is admitted as an emergency admission, the hospital may discharge the patient immediately if it determines that the patient does not qualify for involuntary hospitalization, unless a court has issued a temporary order of detention.[15]

The chief clinical officer of a facility may permit the patient to leave the hospital on trial visits for periods of up to 90 days. If the patient successfully completes one year of continuous trial visits, the chief clinical officer must discharge the patient. However, if the patient has been charged with an offense, has been sentenced to imprisonment, or is on probation (see chapter 7.12, Probation) or parole (see chapter 7.18, Parole Determinations), the chief clinical officer must give notice to the court having criminal jurisdiction over the patient of the intention to discharge the patient. Except when the patient has been found not guilty by reason of insanity, the chief clinical officer has final authority to discharge all patients.[16]

At least once every 30 days, the facility must examine every patient, including those involuntarily committed. Whenever the chief clinical officer determines that the conditions justifying commitment no longer apply, he or she must discharge the patient unless the patient has been charged with an offense or has been sentenced for a crime. The officer must immediately inform the Department of Mental Health of the discharge. The officer may also discharge patients who have been charged with a crime, sentenced to imprisonment, or are on probation (see chapter 7.12, Probation) or parole (see chapter 7.18, Parole Determinations), after giving the court 10 days written notice.[17]

(F) Patient Rights

All patients hospitalized or committed must be accorded treatment consistent with a professional standard of care,[18] including the following:

1. sufficient professional care to ensure that the facility can conduct an evaluation of current status, diagnosis, and treatment plan within 20 days from the start of hospitalization;

---

14. Ohio Rev. Code § 5122.15(H).
15. Ohio Rev. Code § 5122.10.
16. Ohio Rev. Code § 5122.22.
17. Ohio Rev. Code § 5122.21.
18. Ohio Rev. Code § 5122.27.

2. a written treatment plan;
3. treatment consistent with the treatment plan;
4. periodic reevaluations of the treatment plan by the facility no less than once every 90 days;
5. adequate medical care for physical disease or injury;
6. humane care in the least restrictive environment consistent with the treatment plan, with the necessary facilities and personnel, and in a humane psychological and physical environment;
7. freedom from unnecessary or excessive medication;
8. freedom from restraints or isolation unless ordered by the chief clinical officer or the patient's individual physician or psychologist in a private or general hospital; or
9. notification of their rights under the law within 24 hours of admission.

In addition, all patients hospitalized or committed have the following rights:[19]

1. the right to a written list of all rights;
2. the right to be treated with consideration and respect for privacy and dignity;
3. the right to communicate freely with and be visited at reasonable times by counsel and to communicate freely with and be visited at reasonable times by a personal physician or psychologist;
4. the right to communicate freely with others unless specifically restricted;
5. the right to have access to writing materials and stamps without cost, to mail and receive unopened mail, and have assistance in writing if requested and needed;
6. the right to personal privileges such as to wear one's own clothes; to be provided with an allotment of neat, clean, and seasonably appropriate clothing if needed; to keep and use personal possessions; to keep and spend a reasonable amount of money for expenses; and to receive reading materials without censorship;
7. the right to free exercise of religion; and
8. the right to social interaction with members of either sex, subject to supervision, unless specifically restricted in the treatment plan.

---

19. OHIO REV. CODE § 5122.29.

The Ohio supreme court[20] has ruled that antipsychotic medication may be administered without the patient's informed consent when the patient poses an imminent threat of harm to self or others. In addition, the court may issue an order permitting the administration of antipsychotic medication against a patient's wishes without a finding of dangerousness when the court finds by clear and convincing evidence that the patient lacks the capacity to give or withhold informed consent regarding treatment, the medication is in the patient's best interest, and no less intrusive treatment will be as effective in treating the mental illness.

Patients may not be compelled to perform labor that involves the operation or maintenance of the facility. Patients may be required to perform therapeutic tasks that do not involve the operation of the facility if those tasks are an integrated part of the treatment plan and supervised by a qualified person. The patient may also be required to perform tasks of a personal housekeeping nature.[21]

Any person detained for commitment is entitled to a writ of habeas corpus on a proper petition, which is a legal process to test the legality of continued commitment.[22]

It is illegal to deprive a former patient of employment solely because of having been admitted to a hospital or for receiving services for a mental illness. Individuals admitted to a hospital, voluntarily or involuntarily, retain all civil rights unless specifically denied or removed by an adjudication of incompetence following a judicial proceeding.[23]

(G) Civil Liability

Ohio law provides immunity for all individuals who act in good faith in assisting in the hospitalization or discharge of patients. The immunity also extends to expert witnesses who testify at commitment hearings.[24]

Ohio law also provides guidance and immunity for MHPs when working with patients who present an imminent threat of harm to third parties when the MHPs take one or more of several specific steps.[25] The statute provides that an MHP provider or organization may be held liable only if the patient or a person

---

20. Steele v. Hamilton County Community Mental Health Board, 90 Ohio St. 3d 176, 736 N.E.2d 10 (2000).
21. OHIO REV. CODE § 5122.28.
22. OHIO REV. CODE § 5122.30.
23. OHIO REV. CODE § 5122.301.
24. OHIO REV. CODE § 5122.34.
25. OHIO REV. CODE § 2305.51.

who is knowledgeable about the patient has communicated to the professional or organization an explicit threat of inflicting imminent and serious physical harm to a clearly identifiable potential victim, the professional or organization believes that the patient has the intent and ability to carry out the threat, and the professional or organization fails to take one or more of the following steps:

1. attempts to hospitalize the patient on an emergency basis;
2. attempts to have the patient voluntarily or involuntarily hospitalized;
3. develops and implements a treatment plan that is reasonably calculated to eliminate the possibility of harm, and simultaneously initiates a second opinion risk assessment with either the clinical director of the organization or, in the case of a professional who is not part of an organization, any licensed independent mental health professional; or
4. notifies an appropriate law enforcement agency in the area where the potential victim resides, where a structure threatened by the patient is located, or where the patient resides, and if possible notifies each potential victim or victim's guardian or parent. When notification is made, the information must include the nature of the threat, the identity of the patient, and the identity of the potential victim.

When faced with a potentially dangerous patient, the professional or organization must consider each of the four alternatives and document the reasons for choosing or not choosing each option. When professionals or organizations follow these guidelines, they are immune from civil liability. Immunity is also provided from actions by licensing boards and other regulatory authorities for the release of confidential information in the course of carrying out these steps.[26]

---

26. Ohio Rev. Code § 2305.51.

8.5

Voluntary Admission and Involuntary Commitment of Alcoholics

The law provides for voluntary as well as involuntary treatment of those individuals who are seriously disabled by alcoholism and alters the focus of the legal intervention from a criminal to a treatment model. MHPs may be part of a multidisciplinary evaluation and treatment team under this law.

(A) Definitions

Alcoholism means the chronic and habitual use of alcohol to the extent that the person can no longer control the use of alcohol or endangers the health, safety, or welfare of self or others.[1] *Acute alcohol intoxication* refers to heavy consumption of alcohol over a relatively short period of time, resulting in brain dysfunction controlling behavior, speech, and memory, and causing characteristic withdrawal symptoms.[2] *Alcoholic* means a person suffering from alcoholism.[3]

(B) Admission and Commitment

If a person is taken before a judge for a misdemeanor charge, the judge may place the person in a drug and alcohol treatment program if it appears to the judge that the person is an alcoholic or is suffering from acute alcohol intoxication and would benefit

---

1. OHIO REV. CODE § 3793.01(A)(1).
2. OHIO REV. CODE § 2935.33(D)(2).
3. OHIO REV. CODE § 3793.01(A)(2).

from treatment. The placement may not exceed five days. The judge may dismiss a charge of disorderly conduct or of a similar municipal ordinance if the person complies with all conditions of treatment ordered by the court.[4]

At the time of sentencing for a variety of misdemeanor charges, such as for disorderly conduct, drunk driving, some charges regarding domestic violence, and violations of protection orders, the judge may commit the person to close supervision in an appropriate drug and alcohol treatment facility if the person appears to the judge to be an alcoholic or suffering from acute alcohol intoxication. The commitment may include outpatient services and part-time release. The commitment may not exceed the maximum term for which the person could have been imprisoned for the offense.[5] Confinement in a treatment facility is not available to multiple offenders.[6]

(C) Emergency Admission

A law enforcement officer who finds a person subject to prosecution for violation of disorderly conduct or a similar municipal ordinance and who has reasonable cause to believe that the person is an alcoholic or is suffering from acute alcohol intoxication and would benefit from immediate treatment may place the person in an alcohol and drug addiction program for emergency treatment. The placement in a treatment facility is in lieu of other arrest procedures and may extend for a maximum of 48 hours. The person may, however, leave the custody of the treatment facility at any time.[7] No formal charges are filed in these instances.

(D) Confidentiality and Patients' Rights

Ohio law provides no additional protections of confidentiality and patients' rights other than those provided for mentally ill patients who are involuntarily committed (see chapter 8.4, Involuntary Commitment of Mentally Ill Adults).

---

4. Ohio Rev. Code § 2935.33(A).
5. Ohio Rev. Code § 2935.33(B).
6. State v. Johnson, 23 Ohio St. 3d 127, 491 N.E.2d 1138 (1986).
7. Ohio Rev. Code § 2935.33(C).

Voluntary Admission and Involuntary Commitment of Drug Addicts

The law in several states, including Ohio, provides for the treatment and commitment of drug addicts. MHPs provide evaluative and therapeutic services, as well as court testimony.

(A) Definitions

Drug addiction refers to the use of a drug of abuse to the extent that the person becomes physically or psychologically dependent on the drug or endangers the health, safety, or welfare of self or others.[1]

(B) Admission and Treatment

At the time of sentencing and after sentencing, when a term of imprisonment is imposed for a misdemeanor violation, and when the court has reason to believe that the offender is a drug-dependent person or is in danger of becoming a drug-dependent person, the court may require the offender to serve a portion of the sentence and suspend the balance of the sentence and place the offender on probation (a substitute for imprisonment but with supervision by a probation officer) with one of the conditions being that the offender enter into an appropriate drug treatment program. MHPs may be asked to examine the person to determine

---

1. OHIO REV. CODE § 3793.01.

the extent of drug abuse. The fact that a person is a repeat offender does not necessarily bar the person from the option of probation.[2]

(C) Patient's Rights

Ohio law does not provide any additional rights to individuals who are committed under these provisions that are not afforded other patients who are subject to commitment (see chapter 8.4, Involuntary Commitment of Mentally Ill Adults).

---

2. OHIO REV. CODE § 2929.51.

8.7

Services for People With Developmental Disabilities

The law provides various residential and outreach services to people with developmental disabilities and mental retardation. These include inpatient, outpatient, partial hospitalization, day care, emergency, rehabilitative, and other appropriate treatments and services. MHPs aid in evaluation and treatment.

For purposes of voluntary and involuntary commitments, Ohio law makes little distinction between individuals who are mentally retarded and those who have a developmental disability.

(A) Definitions

Chief program director means a person with special training and experience with mentally retarded persons, who is licensed in medicine, psychology, or social work. *Comprehensive evaluation* means a study of a person leading to conclusions and recommendations formulated jointly by a group of individuals with special training and experience in diagnosing and managing individuals with mental retardation or a developmental disability. The group of people must include professionals in medicine, psychology, and social work, and may include specialists in other fields as the individual case may require. *Habilitation* refers to the process by which the facility assists the resident in acquiring and maintaining necessary life skills. *Managing officer* means a person who is appointed by the director of mental retardation and developmental disabilities to be in executive control of a facility. *Mentally retarded person* refers to a person who has significantly subaverage general intellectual functioning and deficiencies in adaptive behavior, manifested during the developmental period. *Mentally retarded person subject to institutionalization by court order* means a person 18 years of age or older who is at least moderately mentally retarded who either presents a very substantial risk of physical impairment or injury to self evidenced by inability to provide for the most basic physical needs that cannot be provided in the community or who needs and will likely benefit from significant habilitation in an institution. *Development disability* means a severe, chronic disability that is characterized by all of the following:

1. it is attributable to a mental or physical impairment, other than a mental or physical impairment solely caused by mental illness;
2. it is manifested before age 22;
3. it is likely to continue indefinitely;
4. it results in one of the following:
    a. in the case of a person under three years of age, at least one developmental delay or an established risk of a developmental delay;
    b. in the case of a person at least three years of age but under six, at least two developmental delays or an established risk; and
    c. in the case of a person six years or older, a substantial functional limitation in at least three areas of major life activity; and
5. it causes the person to need special services for an extended period of time that is individually planned and coordinated.[1]

(B) Voluntary Admission to Services

Any person who is of majority age (age 18) or older and who is, or believes him- or herself to be, mentally retarded may make written application to the managing officer of any institution (called a developmental center) for voluntary admission. In addition, a parent or guardian may make application on behalf of a minor or an adult adjudicated mentally incompetent. The person may be admitted only after a comprehensive evaluation has been made and only if the evaluation concludes that the person is mentally retarded and would benefit significantly from admission. On the basis of a petition by the Legal Rights Services (a state-sponsored advocacy program for individuals involuntarily detained) on behalf of a minor or incompetent person, the probate division (a court with jurisdiction over such matters as guardian-

---

1. Ohio Rev. Code § 5123.01, Ohio Admin. Code § 3301-51-01(N).

ship, adoption, and detainment in hospitals) of the court of common pleas (a state court located in each county) must determine whether the voluntary admission is in the patient's best interest. The patient may be discharged by the managing officer of the facility if, in the judgment of the chief program director, the results of a comprehensive examination indicate that institutionalization is no longer advisable.[2]

If a voluntarily admitted resident requests his or her own release, the facility must release the patient unless, within three days, the managing officer files an affidavit (a sworn declaration) with the court to hold a hearing pursuant to an involuntary commitment request. If the request is made, the court must hold the hearing to determine whether an involuntary commitment is in order. If the resident's release is requested by counsel, a legal guardian, parent, spouse, or adult next of kin, the resident must be released. However, if the resident was admitted on his or her own application, release may be made conditional on the agreement of the resident if a continued stay is supported by the most recent comprehensive evaluation.[3] All residents receive reevaluations of their habilitation plans at intervals not to exceed 90 days.[4]

The philosophy of providing care for people who are mentally retarded or developmentally disabled is to keep them in their homes and local communities and out of more restrictive settings such as developmental centers. As a consequence, the county boards of mental retardation and developmental disabilities set up a range of services, including in-home support services and local community respite care homes, to assist disabled individuals in remaining in the least restrictive setting. Even if a person or family requested a voluntary placement in a developmental center, the county board and the developmental center would work together to provide the needed services outside of the developmental center, if at all possible, even if the person met criteria for admission. Admission to a developmental center is viewed as the last-choice placement.

(B)(1) Short-Term Care

Ohio law also provides for a brief inpatient stay of mentally retarded persons. Short-term care refers to services provided to a person for no more than 14 consecutive days and for no more than 42 days in a fiscal year. The services are provided in a developmental center (any institution or facility designated by

---

2. OHIO REV. CODE § 5123.69.
3. OHIO REV. CODE § 5123.70(A).
4. OHIO REV. CODE § 5123.85(D).

the Department of Mental Retardation and Developmental Disabilities)[5] to meet the family's or caretaker's needs for separation from the patient.[6]

Individuals deemed eligible for short-term care are the same as those who are eligible for a voluntary admission (see previous section) and they must meet the same criteria. The managing officer may admit a person for short-term care only after a medical examination has been made of the person and only if the managing officer concludes that the person is mentally retarded.[7] If application is made by a parent or guardian for care of a minor or of a person adjudicated mentally incompetent, at the request of the Legal Rights Service, the court must determine whether the admission is in the best interest of the person.[8]

The 14-day period may be extended at the discretion of the managing officer[9] but, at the conclusion of each period of short-term care, the person must return to his or her family or caretaker.[10]

As noted in the previous section, the philosophy of care of state and county agencies for individuals who are mentally retarded or developmentally disabled is to care for these people in their homes and local communities. Most counties have adequate support services (called respite care services) that provide in-home care or care in an approved home in the community, such that admission to a developmental center is unlikely to occur.

(C) Involuntary Admission

Typically, the proceedings for the involuntary commitment of a mentally retarded or developmentally disabled person start with the filing of an affidavit (a sworn statement) with the court in the county in which the person resides or where the person is institutionalized, in a manner and form prescribed by the Department of Mental Retardation and Developmental Disabilities. The affidavit may only be filed by a person who has custody of the person as a parent, guardian, or service provider or by a person acting on behalf of the Department. The affidavit must describe the grounds for the request and should include a comprehensive evaluation report that supports the belief that the person is eligible for involuntary commitment.[11]

---

5. OHIO ADMIN. CODE § 5123:1-9-01.
6. OHIO REV. CODE § 5123.70(B).
7. OHIO REV. CODE § 5123.701(C).
8. OHIO REV. CODE § 5123.701(D).
9. OHIO REV. CODE § 5123.701(B).
10. OHIO REV. CODE § 5123.701(G).
11. OHIO REV. CODE § 5123.71(A).

Before filing an affidavit for the involuntary commitment of an individual, the person who is eligible to file the affidavit must request that the county Board of Mental Retardation and Developmental Disabilities conduct an assessment of the individual's needs. The evaluation must be completed within 30 days of the request. The evaluation must include a determination of the person's current needs, an appropriate plan for services, a determination of whether the community is the least restrictive environment in which the person may be served, and identification of available resources to meet the person's needs.[12]

The criteria for involuntarily commitment of a mentally retarded person include the following: (a) the person must be 18 years of age or older and at least moderately mentally retarded, and either represent a very substantial risk of physical impairment or injury to self as manifested by evidence that the person is unable to provide for his or her most basic needs; and (b) that provision for those needs is not available in the community, or the person needs, and is likely to benefit from, significant habilitation in an institution.[13]

A person who is involuntarily detained is afforded a probable cause hearing to determine if the person is subject to commitment. The hearing must be conducted within two court days from the time of the request for commitment. The person must be notified that he or she may have the assistance of counsel and have an independent expert evaluation. If the court does not find probable cause to believe the person meets criteria for involuntary commitment, it must immediately release the person and expunge all records of the proceedings. On the other hand, if the court does find probable cause to believe the person meets criteria for commitment, the court may issue an interim order of placement and may order a full hearing within 10 days. The person may waive the full hearing, but in any case the court will hold a mandatory hearing between the 90th and 100th day after detention began, unless the person has been discharged.[14]

A full hearing is conducted to provide for the submission of all relevant information regarding the resident and the commitment. At the full hearing, all relevant documents and evidence in the custody of the state or prosecutor and the institution or other facility where the person has been held are presented. The resident may present information and evidence from other parties as well. The court must obtain and consider a current comprehensive evaluation of the person.[15] The resident has a right to be

---

12. OHIO REV. CODE § 5123.711.
13. OHIO REV. CODE § 5123.01(P).
14. OHIO REV. CODE § 5123.75.
15. In re Elmore, 83 Ohio App.3d 348, 614 N.E.2d 1116 (1992).

represented by counsel. The hearing is closed to the public unless the resident requests that it be open to the public. The resident has a right to testify but cannot be required to do so. If the court does not find by clear and convincing evidence that the person meets the criteria for commitment, it must discharge the person immediately. If, on the other hand, it finds by clear and convincing evidence that the person is subject to commitment, the court may order the person to an appropriate facility for up to 90 days. Any such order, however, is conditional on the consent of the facility to receive the person. In making the placement decision, the court must consider the comprehensive evaluation, assessment, diagnosis, and projected habilitation plan for the person and select the placement that is the least restrictive alternative consistent with the plan.[16]

A person who has been involuntarily committed may at any time during the 90-day period apply to the managing officer of the institution for voluntary admission. The managing officer will evaluate whether the person meets the criteria for voluntary admission. If the criteria are met, the managing officer must immediately notify the court, the person's counsel, and the director of the facility, and on receipt of the notice, the court must dismiss the case.[17]

At the end of any commitment period, the director of the facility must discharge the person unless at least 10 days before the expiration of the period the director of mental retardation and developmental disabilities or the prosecutor files an application with the court requesting continued commitment. Such an application must include a written report containing current evaluation and assessment information and an account of the patient's progress. A hearing on the application for continued commitment must be held at the expiration of the first 90-day period. Subsequent periods of commitment not to exceed 180 days each may be ordered by the court. These periods may be continued without a hearing if no hearing is requested, although a mandatory hearing must be held at least every two years, and no mentally retarded or developmentally disabled person may be held under involuntary commitment for more than five years.[18]

The managing officer of an institution, with the concurrence of the chief program director, must discharge an involuntarily committed resident when a determination is made that institutionalization no longer is appropriate. On discharge, the managing officer must notify the court that made the commitment.[19]

---

16. OHIO REV. CODE § 5123.76.
17. OHIO REV. CODE § 5123.76(G).
18. OHIO REV. CODE § 5123.76(H),(I).
19. OHIO REV. CODE § 5123.79.

The managing officer of an institution has considerable discretion regarding the appropriateness of a commitment of a person to the facility, and an appellate court[20] has ruled that the court has no power to restrict the power vested in the managing officer of the facility to discharge an involuntarily committed resident.

The chief program director of the institution may permit residents to leave the institution on trial visits when it is in the best interest of the resident. The director sets the period of time for the visit. An involuntarily committed resident who successfully completes one year of continuous trial visits must be discharged.[21]

(C)(1) Emergency Commitment

The probate division of the court of common pleas may, on receipt of an affidavit, and with probable cause, implement an emergency commitment by issuing a temporary order to either move the person to an inpatient facility, require the county Board of Mental Retardation and Developmental Disabilities to provide services in the community if those are available, or conduct a probable cause hearing within two days.[22]

(D) Rights of the Mentally Retarded and Developmentally Disabled

When a person is involuntarily detained, he or she must be informed of the right to make a reasonable number of phone calls or use other means to contact an attorney or a physician, and to have a hearing to determine if there is probable cause for the person to be committed.[23]

Mentally retarded and developmentally disabled patients may not be compelled to perform labor that involves the operation or support of the institution. Residents who volunteer to perform such work must be compensated at prevailing wages. A resident may be compelled to perform habilitative tasks and tasks of a personal housekeeping nature.[24]

All residents must receive, within 30 days of their admission, a comprehensive evaluation, diagnosis, prognosis, and treatment plan or habilitation plan. Residents must receive appropriate care

---

20. In re Elmore, 83 Ohio App.3d 348, 614 N.E.2d 1116 (1992).
21. Ohio Rev. Code § 5123.80.
22. Ohio Rev. Code § 5123.74.
23. Ohio Rev. Code § 5123.71(B).
24. Ohio Rev. Code § 5123.87.

consistent with the habilitation plan and the plan must be reevaluated by the professional staff of the institution at least every 90 days. Prompt and adequate medical care must be available for any physical or mental disease or injury.[25]

Residents must be allowed to communicate freely with others, including receiving visitors at reasonable times, being visited by counsel and a personal physician, having access to a telephone to make and receive calls, and having access to letter writing materials and stamps.[26]

In addition to the patient rights noted in this section, Ohio law provides a Bill of Rights for individuals with mental retardation or a developmental disability. The Bill of Rights includes, for example, the right to be treated with courtesy and respect, the right to a safe and sanitary living environment, the right to practice a religion of choice, the right to access to appropriate medical and psychological care, and the right to participate in decisions that affect their lives.[27]

All records, other than court journal entries or docket entries, regarding the mental health care of a mentally retarded or developmentally disabled person are confidential except when release of information is explicitly ordered by statute, approved by the patient or guardian, or it is the judgment of the manager of records at the institution that disclosure to a mental health facility is in the best interest of the patient.[28]

---

25. OHIO REV. CODE § 5123.85.
26. OHIO REV. CODE § 5123.84.
27. OHIO REV. CODE § 5123.62.
28. OHIO REV. CODE § 5123.89(A).

8.8

Hospice Care

Hospice care is a program of psychological and physical support offered to terminally ill persons. The emphasis is on increasing the quality of a person's last days or months through, for example, active participation by the family in caring for the person and openly facing the meaning and importance of death. There is continued medical assistance in such matters as the control of pain and other symptoms, to allow the person to concentrate on other aspects of life. A complete program may consist of three phases: home care with nursing, emotional, and religious support; inpatient care with overnight facilities for the family; and bereavement services for the family after the patient has died. MHPs may be involved in all three phases as members of the support team.

(A) Definitions

Hospice care program means a coordinated program of home, outpatient, and inpatient care that provides an array of services to hospice patients and their families through a medically directed interdisciplinary team to meet the physical, psychological, social, spiritual, and other special needs that are experienced during the final stages of illness, dying, and bereavement. *Hospice patient* refers to a patient who has been diagnosed as terminally ill, has a life expectancy of six months or less, and has voluntarily requested care. *Interdisciplinary team* means a working group composed of professional and lay persons that includes at least a physician, a registered nurse, a social worker, a member of the clergy or a counselor, and a volunteer.[1]

(B) Services

Ohio law provides for several services through hospice. These include nursing care; physical, occupational, or speech or language therapy unless waived by the Department of Health; medical social services by a social worker under the direction of a physician; services of a home health aide; medical supplies and appliances; physician's services; short-term inpatient care; counseling for patients and their families; services of volunteers; and bereavement services.[2]

Hospice programs and programs that use the term *hospice* in any way, including nursing homes, hospitals, and county medical care facilities, must be licensed by the state.[3] Licensing of hospice programs is managed by the Department of Health.[4]

---

1. OHIO REV. CODE § 3712.01(A).
2. OHIO REV. CODE § 3712.01(A).
3. OHIO REV. CODE § 3712.05.
4. OHIO REV. CODE § 3712.04.

Appendix

Table of Cases

References are to page numbers in this book.

M

Mann v. Gray, 283
Mohan J. Durve, M.D., Inc. v. Oker, 101

N

Namrow v. Commissioner of Internal
  Revenue, 75
Nickell v. Gonzalez, 83
Niemes v. Niemes, 229, 230

O

Oglesby v. City of Columbus, 223

P

Paugh v. Hanks, 223
Poythress v. Clark, 230

R

Ragone v. Vitali & Beltrami, Jr., Inc., 252
Rainay v. Lorain Correctional Facility,
  224
Rossiter v. Ohio State Medical Bd., 11
Rousculp v. Rousculp, 143

S

Sayre v. Hoelzle-Sayre, 143
State v. Berry, 280
State v. Buell, 266
State v. Cooey, 281
State v. Curry, 272, 290
State v. Daws, 262
State v. Draughn, 279
State v. Economo, 126
State v. Edmonson, 301
State v. Edwards, 270
State v. Eley, 270
State v. Fears, 99

State v. Huber, Hamilton County Court
  of Common Pleas, 260
State v. Johnson, 344
State v. Marshall, 280
State v. Martin, 262
State v. McGriff, 100
State v. Mitts, 287
State v. Monk, 272
State v. Napier, 101
State v. Rhodes, 284
State v. Rowe, 263
State v. Scott, 313
State v. Sneed, 264
State v. Souel, 256
State v. Spencer, 99
State v. Stowers, 253, 254, 263
State v. Sullivan, 281
State v. Tibbetts, 270
State v. Weston, 265
State v. Wong, 290
State ex rel. Toledo Blade Co. v. Telb, 107
Steele v. Hamilton County Community
  Mental Health Bd., 108, 341
Stone v. Stone, 147

T

Testa, Exr. v. Roberts, 227, 228
Thompson v. Community Mental Health
  Centers of Warren County, Inc., 116

V

Van Fossen v. Babcock & Wilcox Co., 222
Vnerakraft, Inc. v. Arcaro, 227

W

West v. Henry, 230
Western Reserve Mutual Casualty Co. v.
  Eberhart, 226

Y

Yeager v. Local Union 20, 222

Table of Statutes

References are to page numbers in this book.

Table of Rules of Court

References are to page numbers in this book.

Table of Administrative Rules and Regulations

References are to page numbers in this book.

Table of References to Constitution

References are to page numbers in this book.

Index

References are to chapters.

PSYCHOLOGICAL AUTOPSY
  Admissibility of, 6.5
PSYCHOLOGISTS
  Confidentiality issues, 3.3(B)
  Licensure and regulation, 1.4
  Mental status, 5.1(A)(7)
  Privileged communications, 3.4(A)
  Records maintenance, 3.2
  School, 1.7
  Subdoctoral and unlicensed
    psychologists, 1.5
PUBLIC RECORDS
  Access, 3.6

Q

QUALITY ASSURANCE
  For hospital care, 3.9

R

RECORDS MAINTENANCE
  Access to public records, 3.6
  Generally, 3.2
  Search and seizure of records, 3.5
REFUSAL OF TREATMENT
  Generally, 3.7
REGULATION. *See* CERTIFICATION
  AND REGULATION; LICENSURE
  AND REGULATION
RULES OF EVIDENCE
  Competency to testify, 6.4
  Expert witnesses, 6.2

S

SCHOOL COUNSELORS
  Privileged communications, 3.4(B)
SCHOOL COUNSELORS AND SOCIAL
  WORKERS
  Certifications, 1.8
SCHOOL PSYCHOLOGISTS
  Certification and regulation, 1.7
SEARCH AND SEIZURE
  Of records, 3.5
SENTENCING
  Competency to be executed, 7.19
  Competency to be sentenced, 7.10
  Competency to serve sentence, 7.15
  Of dangerous offenders, 7.13
  Generally, 7.11
  Of habitual offenders, 7.14

SEXUAL ASSAULT
  Competency of rape victim to
    testify, 6.4(C)
  Professional liability, 3.12(A)
  Rape trauma syndrome, 6.7
  Treatment of offenders, 7.21
SEXUAL BATTERY
  Professional liability, 3.12(B)
SEXUAL IMPOSITION
  Professional liability, 3.12(B)
SEXUAL MISCONDUCT
  Professional liability, 3.12(A)
SEXUAL OFFENSES
  Professional liability, 3.12(C)
SOCIAL WORKERS
  Confidentiality issues, 3.3(C)
  Licensure and regulation, 1.6
  Privileged communications, 3.4(B)
  School, 1.8
SOLE PROPRIETORSHIPS
  Regulation, 2.1
SUBPOENA
  For search and seizure of records,
    3.5(B)
SUBSTANCE ABUSE
  Admission and commitment of drug
    addicts, 8.6
  Chemical dependency counselors,
    certification and regulation,
    1.10(A)
SUNSET LAWS
  Generally, 1.14

T

TAX LAW
  Deductions for mental health service
    payments, 2.11

U

UNFAIR COMPETITION
  Generally, 5.11

V

VICTIM'S SERVICES
  Generally, 7.22
VOCATIONAL DISABILITY
  Evaluation for, 5.3
VOCATIONAL REHABILITATION
  Evaluation for services, 5.3(D)

VOTING
Competency for, 5.8

W

WARRANTS
For search and seizure of records,
3.5

WILLS
Competency of testator, 5.7
WORKER'S COMPENSATION
Generally, 5.2

Z

ZONING
For community homes, 2.8

About the Authors

Leon VandeCreek received his PhD in clinical psychology from the University of South Dakota, Vermillion. He is a professor in the School of Professional Psychology at Wright State University, Dayton, Ohio, where he teaches courses in ethics and professional issues and psychological assessment. He has served as president of the Pennsylvania Psychological Association, chair of the American Psychological Association (APA) Insurance Trust, chair of the APA Board of Educational Affairs, and representative to the APA Council of Representatives. He has published widely in the areas of ethics and professional issues.

Marshall Kapp received his JD from George Washington University School of Law, Washington, DC, and his MPH from Harvard University School of Public Health, Boston, Massachusetts. During the writing of this book, he was a professor in the Departments of Community Health and Psychiatry at Wright State University (WSU) School of Medicine, Dayton, Ohio, and director of WSU's Office of Geriatric Medicine and Gerontology, as well as a member of the adjunct faculty at the University of Dayton School of Law.

About the Authors

Leon VandeCreek received his PhD in clinical psychology from the University of South Dakota, Vermillion. He is a professor in the School of Professional Psychology at Wright State University, Dayton, Ohio, where he teaches courses in ethics and professional issues and psychological assessment. He has served as president of the Pennsylvania Psychological Association, chair of the American Psychological Association (APA) Insurance Trust, chair of the APA Board of Educational Affairs, and representative to the APA Council of Representatives. He has published widely in the areas of ethics and professional issues.

Marshall Kapp received his JD from George Washington University School of Law, Washington, DC, and his MPH from Harvard University School of Public Health, Boston, Massachusetts. During the writing of this book, he was a professor in the Departments of Community Health and Psychiatry at Wright State University (WSU) School of Medicine, Dayton, Ohio, and director of WSU's Office of Geriatric Medicine and Gerontology, as well as a member of the adjunct faculty at the University of Dayton School of Law.